P9-DHA-420

Lee & Grant

Lee & Grant

Profiles in Leadership from the Battlefields of Virginia

Major Charles R. Bowery, Jr.

AMACOM

American Management Association

New York • Atlanta • Brussels • Chicago • Mexico City • San Francisco
Shanghai • Tokyo • Toronto • Washington, D.C.

Special discounts on bulk quantities of AMACOM books are
available to corporations, professional associations, and other
organizations. For details, contact Special Sales Department,
AMACOM, a division of American Management Association,
1601 Broadway, New York, NY 10019.
Tel.: 212-903-8316. Fax: 212-903-8083.
Web site: www.amacombooks.org

This publication is designed to provide accurate and authoritative
information in regard to the subject matter covered. It is sold with
the understanding that the publisher is not engaged in rendering
legal, accounting, or other professional service. If legal advice or
other expert assistance is required, the services of a competent
professional person should be sought.

Library of Congress Cataloging-in-Publication Data

Bowery, Charles R.
    Lee & Grant : profiles in leadership from the battlefields of
Virginia / Major Charles R. Bowery, Jr.—1st ed.
        p. cm.
    Includes bibliographical references and index.
    ISBN 0-8144-0819-2
    1. Virginia—History—Civil War, 1861-1865—Campaigns. 2. United
States—History—Civil War, 1861-1865—Campaigns. 3. Grant, Ulysses S.
(Ulysses Simpson), 1822-1885—Military leadership. 4. Lee, Robert E.
(Robert Edward), 1807-1870—Military leadership. 5. Command of
troops—History—19th century. I. Title: Lee and Grant. II. Title.

E470.2.B77 2004
973.7'3'0922—dc22   2004016035

Printing number

10 9 8 7 6 5 4 3 2 1

Contents

Acknowledgments

Before beginning this project, I never realized that writing a first book would be such a significant emotional experience. I certainly did not do it alone. So many people have helped me to reach this point that it is difficult to know where to begin in acknowledging those contributions.

Several professors and senior army officers have earned my thanks for the opportunities they have given me as an officer and a historian. At North Carolina State University and the University of North Carolina—Chapel Hill, Professors William C. Harris, John David Smith, Joseph W. Caddell, James Crisp, Holly Brewer, and Richard H. Kohn trained me in the historian's craft and fostered in me a further appreciation for the lessons of the past. To Colonel Robert A. Doughty go my thanks for selecting me for one of the greatest experiences in my life: a tour of duty as a West Point history instructor. Teaching at West Point was for me the fulfillment of a dream, and without that opportunity this book would not have been written.

Good friends make life a sweeter experience, and I owe a great deal to my circle of comrades and companions. My best friend from William and Mary days, Matt Ritchie, has been a role model for me in many ways. Michael Weisel of Raleigh, North Carolina, has served as a confidant and sounding board. At West Point, Dave Heath, Jeff French, Paul Reese, and Chuck Hallman kept a smile on my face and always prevented me from taking myself too seriously. To Professor Ethan Rafuse, my "intellectual godfather" as a Civil War historian and my companion on battlefield journeys without number, my eternal gratitude for the doors he opened to me in the community of Civil Warriors. God has blessed me with so many other friends that it would require a book-length manuscript to name them all, so for all of them, and you know who you are, thanks.

To my editor at AMACOM, Christina McLaughlin, go my respect and thanks. She guided this first-time author to the finish line with patience and skill. This book bears her imprint as surely as it does mine.

Without the love, support, and guidance of my parents, Charles and Emma Bowery, I would not be who I am today. Thanks, Mom and Dad.

My cats, Willie and Mary, have attended graduate school and have walked across the keyboard more than once while I wrote this book. Frederick, the ever-present Great Dane, demands the daily walk upon which I do some of my best thinking.

I save the best for last. One person has, more than any other I have listed, endured my obsessions with all things Civil War and military with humor and understanding. Along the way, she has helped me to keep perspective, and she has been my best friend for fifteen incredible years. Mary Ann, you are the love of my life, and I cannot imagine life without you. Thanks for everything. This book is for you.

To all of the above belongs much of the credit for the pages that follow. Any errors that remain are mine and mine alone.

Introduction

In the spring of 1864, the two greatest generals of the Civil War met on the battlegrounds of Virginia. Their leadership shone throughout the Overland Campaign and determined the outcome of the Civil War and the future of America.

"We never knew what war was till this spring," said Private Joseph Graham, a veteran of two years of combat in the 140th Pennsylvania Infantry Regiment, in a letter to his family in late May 1864, after the battles of the Wilderness and Spotsylvania.[1] For many Yankees and Rebels, these battles, and the rest of the fighting in the 1864 Overland Campaign, were a different kind of war from the already three-year-long death grapple between the Union and the Confederacy.

A conflict that for both sides had begun in 1861 as a glorious crusade had turned into something much more deadly three years later. Over half a million Americans lay dead by the spring of 1864, and there appeared to be no immediate end in sight. In Washington, Abraham Lincoln worried about his chances for reelection in the coming fall as his two main armies occupied positions in Tennessee and Virginia that differed little from their positions when the war began. After three bloody years, the heartland of the Confederacy—southern Virginia and the Shenandoah Valley, the Carolinas, and Georgia and the Deep South—remained inviolate and defiant.

In northern Georgia, Joseph E. Johnston had done much to repair the damage that had been done to the Confederate Army of

Tennessee in the 1863 campaigns, and he stood ready to use the mountainous terrain north of Atlanta to slow or defeat Federal armies there.

But for Lincoln, Virginia was the real problem. Robert E. Lee and his Army of Northern Virginia stood poised along the banks of the Rapidan River, ready to move in any direction to defeat the thrusts of the Union Army of the Potomac. For two years, Lee had stymied a succession of Yankee generals, whose names have entered the American lexicon as expressions of defeat and frustration— McClellan, Pope, Burnside, and Hooker. On the soil of Virginia, "Marse Robert" and his legions had never suffered a battlefield defeat.

Pennsylvania was a different matter, however. When Lee determined to invade Northern territory once again in the spring of 1863, he did so at the peak of his army's powers, in the hope that he could force a decisive battle on his enemy. What he got was a battle, but not on his terms and not in a place of his choosing. The battle at the small Pennsylvania town of Gettysburg, the largest battle ever fought on the North American continent, was disastrous for Lee's army—thousands of irreplaceable casualties, including many in the ranks of his precious officer corps. In defeating Lee, Major General George G. Meade did what no other Union general had done before, but his failure to pursue and destroy Lee during his retreat southward brought Meade almost as much criticism as praise. Thus, Lee's armies returned to Virginia, bloodied but still intact. As 1863 turned into 1864, Lee and Meade sparred in several inconclusive battles across north central Virginia, but the military situation in the east remained static.

Two Great Leaders Come to Battle

With the 1864 election looming, Lincoln needed victories, and for that he turned to his most successful general, Ulysses S. Grant. Already a living legend by the end of 1863, "Unconditional Surrender" Grant, as he had come to be known in the press, had a long series of victories in the western theater to his credit: Forts Henry and Donelson and Shiloh in 1862; Vicksburg and Chattanooga in 1863. Known for his plain-spoken manner and unwavering persistence, Grant was the logical choice in Lincoln's mind for the post of general in chief of all Union armies, a personnel decision that was calculated to give the Federal war effort two qualities that it had lacked for most of the war.

Lincoln believed that *unity of command*, which ensures that one person directs all of an organization's various parts, and *unity of effort*, which has all of those parts acting in concert, would allow the Union to capitalize on the advantages she had held over the Confederacy since 1861: vastly greater supplies of men, war materiel, and resources.

The newly promoted Lieutenant General Grant, the first American since George Washington to hold that rank, journeyed from Tennessee to Virginia in February 1864 and took command. As one part of his strategy to apply pressure to the Confederacy on five separate but related fronts, Grant planned to have Meade and the Army of the Potomac move south against Lee's army and, eventually, the Confederate capital at Richmond, locking Lee in place in the Old Dominion and preventing him from reinforcing other sectors.

Instead of remaining in Washington as his predecessor, General Henry W. Halleck, had done, Grant decided to locate himself with the Army of the Potomac. Grant's decision to remove himself from the political snares of Washington and place himself in the heat of battle was a tacit acknowledgment of two facts: first, that Lee and his army were the hope of the Confederacy and her best chance for winning independence; and second, that Meade's army needed his attention.

The 1864 campaign brought together, in the same theater of war, the conflict's greatest commanders. "Lee's Army will be your objective point. Wherever Lee goes there you will go also," Grant stated to Meade in no uncertain terms.[2]

The "Overland Campaign" began on May 4, 1864. For the next two months, Lee's and Meade's armies were locked in a whirlwind of continuous combat that left even veteran soldiers like Joseph Graham at a loss for words. In a war full of bloody battles, Wilderness, Spotsylvania, North Anna, Totopotomoy Creek, and Cold Harbor were unprecedented in their scale and ferocity, a titanic series of clashes that redefined the savagery of the Civil War. It was the largest, hardest-fought, and most destructive military campaign ever waged on the North American continent, and it involved the opposing armies in combat on virtually a daily basis for the entire period. While neither Lee nor Grant spoke or wrote directly of a *mano a mano* "face-off" against the other, the campaign came to be seen as a titanic struggle between the two generals.

Overcome Your Leadership Challenges, Win the War

On this stage, Virginia 1864, another compelling drama acted itself out as the two armies clashed. Lee and Grant, two of the greatest captains in American military history, faced challenges that stretched, and often exceeded, their leadership abilities. Grant's was a problem that will seem familiar to many leaders: He had inherited control of a new (to him) organization, the Army of the Potomac, and he struggled mightily to come to terms with it.

During the course of the Overland Campaign, he became the de facto commanding general of the army, a role he had not anticipated when he accepted overall command, and one that was certainly not welcomed by Meade and his subordinates. Grant's time with Meade's army was a clash of instinctive aggressiveness and ingrained caution, of fundamentally different philosophies of how to defeat the enemy, and at a human level of very different personalities. In order to lead this army to victory, Grant had to surmount these and other problems of leadership.

Robert E. Lee faced no such challenges to his authority; the Army of Northern Virginia was his and his alone. But his problems were no less pressing. Gettysburg had robbed his army of much of its leadership and offensive power, turning it into a wounded animal—unable to strike, but still immensely dangerous when backed into a corner. This state of affairs did not suit Lee, who to many observers was the very personification of audacity. Nevertheless he had to reconcile himself to this state of affairs. Many of his finest lieutenants were dead, wounded, or gone from the army, leaving him with a high command that was simply not as capable as it once was. And facing him across the Rapidan River was a large, well-equipped, and capably led army, at the head of which was a general whom Lee had never faced in combat.

A Study in Leadership

In a war filled with grist for leadership studies, the Overland Campaign offers a unique opportunity. It allows the study of two of history's greatest generals, playing for a straightforward but momentous prize: the survival or destruction of the United States of America. On the surface, Lee and Grant led in very different ways, but once this veneer is stripped away, a core of similarity remains. Both men were supremely self-confident, highly skilled, and unfailingly devoted to the cause for which they fought. Their achievements and mistakes make the 1864 Overland Campaign a perfect leadership study and a great source of education and inspiration for leaders in any arena.

As we grow more distant from this defining cataclysm in American history, many Americans seem to thirst more and more for echoes of our Civil War. A trip to any bookstore or a perusal of the World Wide Web will confirm this thirst. A Web search for "American Civil War" yields literally millions of matches, and Civil War books emerge from the presses at a staggering pace. And even though the events are now almost 150 years in the past, they still retain the capacity to move us and to instruct us. Leaders, managers, and executives should not overlook the battles, campaigns, and personalities of the Civil War as a source for leadership lessons. The danger in this search for lessons from the past is ever-present, however. Some authors have attempted to boil down the war's battles and leaders into sets of aphorisms, and many have attempted to shoehorn them into modern management theories. That is not the intent of this book.

Lee and Grant is intended to be a concise, readable, exciting account of the 1864 Overland Campaign. Throughout this amazing story, the reader will find a succession of leadership lessons that are as pertinent in the twenty-first century as they were in the nineteenth.

In addition to the personal leadership qualities that these two incredible men shared, they also shared a military education at West Point. West Point has always developed leaders and currently does so through a leadership training program. Many of the lessons from this program are distilled in the U.S. Army's manual on leadership. You will notice that I include some theory from this manual to help illuminate the leadership lessons in the text. This is an excellent lens to clarify the lessons and transfer them to the modern business world.

Leadership Lessons from the Army

The U.S. Army's manual on leadership delineates three broad categories of activity: *direct, organizational, and strategic* leadership. Those categories apply to the business world every bit as well as they do to the military.

- *Direct leaders* get things done in, well, a direct sense. They manage offices, run assembly lines, create advertising campaigns, supervise areas within a department store. Their brand of leadership is very personal and face-to-face.

- *Organizational leaders* are at an intermediate level between the CEO and the guy or gal on the shipping room floor. They translate strategic plans into workable courses of action and then see that those plans are carried out. Because organizational leadership skills affect so many different audiences, and because Lee and Grant operated primarily at this level, it is here that this book will focus.

■ *Strategic leadership* occurs in the rarefied air of the highest levels of business and government activity. Decisions made here affect thousands, even millions of people and millions of dollars. Ulysses S. Grant wore two hats in 1864. As the Union army's general in chief, he functioned as a strategic leader. In the field during the Overland Campaign, he moved inexorably into the realm of organizational leadership because he saw the pressing need to do so. Chapter 6 discusses Grant's experiences as a strategic leader.

Beneath the broad umbrella of organizational leadership lie four categories of skills to which we will return quite frequently: *interpersonal, conceptual, technical,* and *tactical* skills.

In whichever of the three realms a leader operates, he or she must consider what *leadership style* will best get things done. The army identifies five styles, all of which were used during the Overland Campaign:

Figure I-1 Organizational leadership skills.[3]

Interpersonal
- Understanding subordinates
- Communicating
- Supervising

Conceptual
- Establishing intent
- Filtering information
- Understanding intent

Technical
- Maintaining critical skills
- Resourcing
- Predicting second- and third-order effects

Tactical
- Synchronization
- Orchestration

- *Directing leaders* issue orders and instructions without regard to the thoughts or ideas of their subordinates, then supervise those subordinates very closely. Directive leadership may be best in stressful situations, when time is short, or when dealing with inexperienced subordinates.

- *Participating leaders* ask subordinates for input and ideas on how to get things done, then made the final decisions themselves. This style can work well with experienced subordinates and when the leader has the time available to consult and think about problems.

- *Delegating leaders* issue broad guidance and suggestions, then step out of the way and let subordinates get things done without direct supervision. Delegation works well with capable subordinates because it allows them to express initiative and skill.

- *Transactional leadership* involves prescribed, clearly outlined instructions and an award/punishment arrangement: "Get this task done, and I will promote you. Fail, and you'll never work here again." "Management by exception" often involves this type of leadership, with leaders focusing on subordinates' failures and showing up to dispense punishment.

- *Transformational leadership* focuses on improving both the organization and the subordinate leader in the long term. This style takes advantage of subordinates' innate desire to do well and involves a great deal of delegation and latitude. Subordinates work hard in this environment because they share the leader's objectives and believe in them, not because they are afraid of the consequences of failure.[4]

Both Lee and Grant reached transformational leadership by the end of the 1864 Overland Campaign, and this journey was what made them great leaders. By extension, you as a leader can learn from their successes and failures, apply the right leadership styles, and transform your team to become extraordinarily successful.

Warfare is the most consequential activity in which human beings can participate; should it not then be the ideal stage on which to show leadership? I hope through this book to give leaders two fascinating models for insights into their daily struggles, and also introduce the reader to an incredible slice of American history.

PART I

THE MAKING OF LEADERS

Lee and Grant's Early Years

CHAPTER ONE

Marse Robert

Lee is audacity personified. His name is audacity, and you need not be afraid of not seeing all of it that you will want to see.

—COLONEL JOSEPH C. IVES, 1862[1]

A good leader sees clearly the task confronting him. He considers the capabilities and limitations of those around him, devises a plan that takes those factors into account, and supervises the execution of that plan to the best of his ability. Robert E. Lee is an excellent subject for leadership study because of both his successes and his failures in these areas, but his story is useful in this regard only if one is able to peel back the layers of myth, emotion, and misunderstanding surrounding "perhaps the most beloved soldier in American history."[2]

Lee's iconic status is an obstacle to a true understanding of his leadership qualities. In the most recent biography of Lee, Emory Thomas stated the case quite succinctly. People, noted Thomas, "usually venerate as a hero someone who exemplifies (or whom they believe exemplifies) virtues which they admire [or] to which they aspire." Thus, the concept of heroism "reveals more about the society that admires than about the hero." Over time, "Lee has been a Christ figure, a symbol of national reconciliation, an exalted expression of bourgeois values, and much, much more."[3]

Leadership is a product of a number of factors, including upbringing, education, and life experiences. It is the sum total of three properties: personal character, knowledge, and application. The U.S. Army, a fairly effective producer of leaders, calls these three properties the "Be, Know, Do" attributes. A leader should Be a person of solid *character* and should embrace and exemplify the ideals of the organization he or she leads. A leader must Know the *interpersonal*, *conceptual*, and *technical* skills that allow him or her to manage and derive excellence from people, machines, or organizations, whatever the case may be. Finally, a good leader must Do what is necessary to *influence* subordinates and coworkers, *operate* in a manner that accomplishes tasks, and *improve* the organization's ability to accomplish tasks in the future.[4] Robert E. Lee embodied the attributes of Be, Know, Do as well as any general in American history.

Leadership and Personal Character: Lee's Upbringing

Robert Edward Lee was born January 19, 1807, in Westmoreland County, Virginia, into one of the state's most prestigious families. Robert's father, Richard Henry "Light Horse Harry" Lee, was a Revolutionary War cavalry general and one of George Washington's favorite subordinates. This famous lineage shaped the son's leadership abilities in both positive and negative ways. Light Horse Harry was a brave soldier, but he lived a dissolute life after the Revolution, falling inexorably into debt. At one point, he installed a chain across the front door of his home, Stratford Hall, to ward off creditors. This negative example cemented one of the qualities Lee valued most in himself and in his associates: absolute self-control in all areas of one's life.[5]

Self-control was the cornerstone of Robert E. Lee's leadership style. On numerous occasions during his military career, his calm demeanor masked any inner turmoil that he may have felt, allowing him to influence his subordinates in positive ways. If you have ever "gone ballistic" in front of your coworkers and then regretted it, you know the negative impact that displays of this kind can have on organizational climate. Self-control is just as important in the computer age as it was in Lee's time.

Throughout his military career, Lee demanded this level of control from his subordinates. The example of uprightness, high standards, and fairness that Lee offered to those around him improved his army immeasurably. Lee was a *good* man as well as a *great* man. Many historical figures have been one or the other, but Lee was both, the living embodiment of the Be component of leadership. With Enron providing a negative example in this regard, it should be apparent to all leaders that character and integrity are key to the success of any organization.

The common popular image of Robert E. Lee is that of a distinguished, gray-haired older man, a so-called marble man of implacable impressiveness. Lee the young army officer was quite different. Upon his graduation from West Point, he stood five feet eleven inches tall, which was very tall for his time. A portrait of Lee painted in Baltimore in 1838 showed the thirty-one-year-old officer to be extraordinarily handsome, with brown eyes and thick black hair. A fellow cadet remarked of him, "His limbs, beautiful and symmetrical, looked as though they had come from the turning lathe, his step was elastic as if he spurned the ground upon which he trod."[6]

We all know people like the young Robert E. Lee: beautiful people who draw others into their presence and impress those others with their quiet competence. Along with that staid public demeanor, however, came a rapier-like wit and a playful manner with friends.

> The example of uprightness, high standards, and fairness that Lee offered to those around him improved his army immeasurably.

Lee's relationship with the women in his life showed that he had the "common touch" that enabled him to relate to all people, not just soldiers. Lee had a lifelong preference for the company of ladies, and in their presence was a very different man from the oft-portrayed warrior. After his mother, Ann, died in July 1829, Lee struck up a romance with an old family friend, Mary Custis, who then lived at Arlington, the Custis family mansion in Alexandria,

Virginia. Mary's father, George Washington Parke Custis, was George Washington's stepgrandson; this pedigree enhanced Robert's standing in American society. He maintained a long-distance courtship with Mary during an engineering assignment in Savannah, Georgia, and returned to Alexandria to marry her on June 30, 1831. It was a solid, acceptable match, and it promised everything for the young officer that his father's life had not.[7]

Leadership and Knowledge: West Point's Legacy

After Lee's Virginia upbringing, his time at West Point served as the most formative influence on his leadership ability. Lee entered West Point in 1825 and prospered in its austere environment. The West Point of the nineteenth century in many ways resembled a monastery: Its cadets were cut off from the outside world, and it employed a rigorous European-style curriculum of science, mathematics, engineering, languages, drawing, and military studies.

West Point's academic departments operated then, and still do to this day, on the Thayer method of instruction, named for the man who is considered the father of the military academy, Colonel Sylvanus Thayer, superintendent from 1817 to 1833. Cadets normally received one furlough in four years, between their second and third years, and spent their summers encamped for military training on "the Plain," the academy's grassy parade and training field. They earned demerits for infractions of academy regulations and were required to take annual examinations in their subjects in order to pass from one class year to the next.

Lee's academic and military record was one of the finest in the academy's two-hundred-year history. In mathematics, a subject that claimed over 40 percent of academy failures, Lee did so well that he accepted a position as an acting assistant professor, earning him an extra ten dollars per month. He finished second overall in the class of 1829, and he was the only cadet in West Point history to graduate without a single demerit against his name.[8]

Lee's sterling performance at the academy earned him a second lieutenant's commission in the army's prestigious Corps of Engineers, an achievement reserved at that time for only a small percentage of academy graduates. His high standing marked him for great things, and many of his seniors noticed him, among them Jefferson Davis, a member of the class of 1828. As a result of his West Point education, Lee knew his job as an officer as well as anyone in America.

Leadership Applied: War in Mexico

After a series of other engineering assignments and a promotion, the veteran of seventeen years of peacetime service went to war. President James K. Polk's expansionist designs on Texas led to a dispute over that territory's boundary with Mexico. Polk maneuvered this crisis into a shooting war by late 1845 and dispatched troops under General Zachary Taylor into northern Mexico. In a letter to the army's chief engineer, Colonel Joseph G. Totten, Lee expressed his desire to get into the action and to apply the knowledge he had attained: "In the event of war with any foreign government I should desire to be brought into active service in the field with as high a rank in the regular army as I could obtain."[9] Lee and many other officers who would face each other on the bloody fields of the Civil War received their first taste of combat in the Mexican-American War.

Lee received orders for Mexico in August 1846. After an uneventful few months' service under General John E. Wool, he joined the staff of General Winfield Scott, the U.S. Army's commanding general. Scott planned to lead an expedition down the Gulf of Mexico to Vera Cruz, and thence overland to the capital, Mexico City. Lee's connections and his successful career paid dividends in this case, as Colonel Totten, at this point Scott's senior engineer, recommended Captain Lee for the expedition. Scott and his staff sailed on February 15, 1847, and the entire expedition arrived off Vera Cruz in early March. After virtually unopposed amphibious landings, Lee stepped ashore on March 10.

Lee did not lead troops in battle in Mexico, but he nonetheless

burnished an already solid reputation as a thoroughgoing professional. As an engineer on Scott's staff, Lee was responsible for scouting locations for artillery emplacements and routes of march for
infantry. Much of the campaign was uneventful for him, but he was
mentioned in dispatches for one particular incident on the road to
Mexico City. As the American army crossed rocky, mountainous terrain on the way to the capital city, a Mexican force blocked its progress. It appeared that the impassable terrain on either side of the
road would force Scott to make a costly frontal assault in order to
get through, but Lee gave him another option. In doing so, he personified, even as a "middle management" leader, the Know and Do
components of good leadership.

On a hazardous nighttime scouting mission, Lee charted a route
through terrain that Scott, and indeed his Mexican enemy, thought
was impossible to traverse. Scott took Lee's advice, and his army
outflanked the Mexican position, forcing the enemy to retreat without fighting a bloody battle. Lee's performance during Scott's campaign, one of the most famous in American military history, showed
the army's leadership, and the commanding general in particular,
that Robert E. Lee was an officer with the potential for higher command.

Making a Difference: Lee's Years as Superintendent at West Point

After his service in Mexico, West Point once again became a crucible
of leadership for Lee. Against his personal wishes, he was assigned
to the academy in 1854 as its superintendent. In this capacity, the
now middle-aged Lee again demonstrated many of the traits that
made him an effective general. Because of his unquestioned integrity and abilities, the faculty and cadets of West Point came to view
Lee as a positive influence in a variety of ways.

In the nineteenth century, the superintendent of West Point was
largely a caretaker of the academy's day-to-day existence. An Academic Board composed of the school's senior professors made all
critical decisions regarding academic and military instruction. The

army's chief engineer, Joseph Totten, and the secretary of war, at this time Jefferson Davis, exercised oversight of the entire institution. For example, Lee had to apply to Totten on a case-by-case basis to allow individual cadets to receive items of clothing or money from their families; even a decision this mundane was outside of his sphere of responsibility.[10]

The intelligent and conscientious Lee was little more than an executive secretary, but he applied himself to his job with gusto. Faced with an institutional culture of micromanagement, Lee made a positive impact when and where he could. He recommended and implemented improvements in the cadet disciplinary system, such as a revision of the academy's demerit system that prevented habitually troublesome cadets from manipulating the system and doing just enough to graduate. His legacy to his alma mater was also one of physical improvement: Lee recommended and supervised many building projects that improved the quality of life of the officers, soldiers, and cadets

Most important, Lee served as a model of self-control and decorum for his young charges, the Corps of Cadets. His official correspondence reveals a man who was intensely concerned with developing in others the Be characteristics that he himself had internalized as a youth, and his conscientious execution of his duties is a great example for a leader in any organization. When faced with an organizational climate that seems to stifle individual responsibility and advancement, find the place where you can made a difference and do it.

The Secession Crisis: A Decision of Loyalty

After completing his tour of duty at West Point in 1855, Lee accepted a transfer to the cavalry and a posting as second-in-command of the newly formed Second Cavalry Regiment. This would be the lieutenant colonel's first taste of troop command. As civil war loomed in 1861, the U.S. Army's aging commanding general, Winfield Scott, paid Lee the ultimate compliment when he personally offered him the command of all federal armies preparing to suppress the rebellion. For Lee the Virginian, this was a difficult decision.

From the perspective of the twenty-first century, the decision of hundreds of long-serving U.S. Army officers to resign their commissions in favor of their native states appears to be nothing less than treason. The America of 1860 was a very different place, however; it was more a loose conglomeration of semi-sovereign states than the unified republic of today. Many southerners in uniform felt the tug of state and family loyalty working against their national patriotism and army professionalism. Further, many of these educated men did indeed interpret their nation's recent history (for the American Revolution was still recent history) as an affirmation of the power of states to leave the Union.

Make no mistake: Slavery was certainly part of this equation for many southerners. Lee's family owned slaves, and the economic well-being of those he loved was tied to that evil institution. That being said, Lee still acted out of attachment to his family and his state when he declined Scott's offer in April 1861 and resigned from the U.S. Army. This was no doubt a difficult decision for the veteran of thirty-two years of federal service; he was saying good-bye to the institution that had educated and nurtured him and trained him in his life's work. Lee left his home at Arlington, just across the Potomac River from the capital; he never lived there again. He then went to Richmond to accept command of Virginia's military forces.

It is impossible to provide effective leadership to an organization that you do not fully support. A big part of what made Robert E. Lee a great leader was the thought and passion that went into his decision to follow his native state. Other officers from southern states made the opposite decision with the same intensity, believing that national allegiance trumped state loyalty.

Lee's decision to resign and follow the Confederacy reveals neither treasonous leanings nor a lack of personal integrity. Critics of his decision seem to forget that absolutely nothing in his personal background or military career indicated any such shortcomings, and they fail to consider how hard this decision must have been for him. In the end, Lee's actions show the inner strength of character that made him the great leader he was. The Be qualities that he developed throughout his life enabled him to make this difficult decision with firmness and conviction.

In order to be a good leader, you must have absolute faith and confidence in your own beliefs and standards, and others must see that confidence on display. In hindsight, we may agree or disagree with Lee's decision, and indeed many of his contemporaries had misgivings about it, but the student of leadership should not ignore the example that Lee set in trusting his own convictions.

One of the fundamentals of being a leader that is not often discussed is being on a side that you can support. If you feel inner conflict about your cause or your actions, as Lee would have done if he had been fighting against his family, you will not be a good leader. So before you step up to "lead your troops," make sure that you are fully behind your company and your actions, and that you feel that you can lead with a clear conscience. Only then will you be able to lead with clarity and inspire people to follow you.

Identifying the Crux of the Immediate Problem: Lee Takes Command

West Point–trained officers were at a premium on both sides once war broke out at Fort Sumter, South Carolina. The Confederate government established its new capital at Richmond, Virginia, and commissioned Lee and four other officers as the Confederate Army's first generals. Lee was detailed to western Virginia, where his first combat command of the war was a muddy failure. Transferred to coastal Georgia, Lee did a short stint as an inspector of fortifications in the Savannah area before Davis recalled him to Richmond in early 1862 to serve as his chief military adviser. The fifty-five-year-old general was now in a backwater desk job, with no active command.

This relative inactivity did not leave Lee blind to what was occurring around him. Just as he had as superintendent of West Point, Lee overcame his frustrations and made what he could of his position, observing the war from a detached perspective. In your personal career, you may encounter such temporary frustrations; take Lee's example and make the best of them. In this capacity Lee observed the beginning of the Peninsula Campaign, during which Union General George B. McClellan moved his Army of the Potomac by water from Washington to Fortress Monroe, Virginia, and from there over land up the Virginia Peninsula toward Richmond. Confederate General Joseph E. Johnston commanded the army blocking McClellan's advance. After a short siege at Yorktown and a small delaying action at Williamsburg, Johnston withdrew his forces into the Richmond defenses. It seemed only a matter of time before McClellan's superiority in troops and artillery would begin to tell.

Johnston launched an attack on McClellan at Seven Pines, a few miles east of Richmond, on May 31, and was seriously wounded while arranging reinforcements late in the day.[11] Both Lee and Jefferson Davis had ridden out from the capital to observe the fighting, and together they observed the wounded Johnston as he lay on the ground. On the ride back to Richmond, Davis gave Lee command of the army. Johnston's second-in-command, Gustavus W. Smith, was physically and temperamentally unsuited to the post, so Davis turned to his military adviser, a man with impeccable credentials but at best a mixed record in the war to date, to save the fledgling Confederacy. Lee set to work the next day and began his tenure as commander by taking his army back to the basics: digging trenches and constructing new defensive positions.[12]

"King of Spades." "Granny Lee." These terms of derision, meant to imply excessive caution and a defensive mentality, leapt from the pages of Richmond newspapers and the mouths of Confederate soldiers in June 1862. Muckraking editors used them to describe Lee, who made a point of inspecting and improving his army's fortifications. He also assembled his generals at his new headquarters within two days of taking command in an effort to begin sounding out their abilities, and also to read them into his defensive plans.

Lee was able to ignore these criticisms and focus on the problem. His initial actions—improving fortifications and preparing for war—speak to his ability to identify the short-term problem: the weak defenses of the Confederate capital in the face of a numerically superior enemy.

But what of the long-term problem? A leader must be able to

spot that as well, and to fashion a course of action that deals with both problems. Short-term and long-term problems may be related, but they are often different in nature and importance. In this case, Lee's (and by extension the Confederacy's) problem was *time*: The South's capacity to resist had a very short shelf life, and Jefferson Davis's armies needed a strategic approach that took the initiative away from an ever-growing enemy and won victories quickly. In a June 5 letter to Davis, Lee showed his sure grasp of the problem facing him:

> *McClellan will make this a battle of posts. He will take position from position, under cover of his heavy guns, & we cannot get at him without storming his works, which with our new troops is extremely hazardous. You witnessed the experiment Saturday. It will require 100,000 men to resist the regular siege of Richmond, which perhaps would only prolong not save it.* [13]

Focusing on a problem and finding a solution is vital. John was a newly appointed CEO. When he was brought on, people cheered because they wanted swift change. But John's first course of action was to review the state of the company and the marketplace, not to jump directly into change efforts. After a few months, people began to talk. Maybe John was not the right choice. Where was the immediate turnaround that people were expecting? Why didn't he *do* something? John ignored these criticisms because he knew that before he initiated any change, he had to have a grasp of what needed to be

His initial actions—improving fortifications and preparing for war—speak to his ability to identify the short-term problem: the weak defenses of the Confederate capital in the face of a numerically superior enemy.

changed. He stayed focused on finding the problem, and his diligence paid off. He discovered a weakness in the company's product that needed to be fixed before the company could remarket that product.

As a leader, you will be under scrutiny like you've never been before. Your every move will be analyzed, and you will undoubtedly have critics. You can't be in a position of power and not have at least one person who is unhappy with your decisions. In fact, don't be surprised if you hear criticism of everything you do. Keep an eye on these criticisms, especially if they come from above. But you have to have a thick skin and exceptional focus. It is up to you to find the problems, both short- and long-term, and then find solutions. If you listen too much to criticism, you will be tempted to try to make people happy, which is not your primary job. Your job is to make the organization or the initiative succeed. In addition to facing internal criticism, leaders must be willing and able to face the competition.

Facing Adversity: Lee Defines a New Strategy

One of Lee's preeminent leadership qualities began to take root in his early days as army commander: the willingness to make difficult decisions based upon military necessity. One of the great myths that has come to surround Lee is that he was "too nice" to be a truly effective leader, that he was a gentleman whose sense of decorum prevented him from confronting hard choices. The stakes were surely high here; any misstep at the gates of Richmond could spell doom for the young Confederacy. But as the events of the coming days would show, Lee manifested a timeless quality of a great leader: the moral courage to face adversity and to follow through on difficult decisions. It was in the swampy lowland east of Richmond that Lee began to forge the reputation and record that led him to his confrontation with Grant in 1864.

Lee continued the June 5 letter with a bold proposal: a reinforcement of the small Confederate army under General Thomas J. "Stonewall" Jackson in the Shenandoah Valley. Jackson could then attack into Maryland and Pennsylvania, a move that would "change the character of the war." Lee had witnessed the failure of the Confederacy's "perimeter defense" strategy, in which the armies tried to defend every inch of Southern soil. This proposal was the beginning of Lee's "offensive defensive" strategy, which would see the Confederacy remain in an overall defensive position, but use its armies to carry out offensive campaigns against individual Union armies whenever possible.[14]

Lee's plan continued to mature in his mind, and on June 10 he unveiled his final decision in another letter to Davis. Lee proposed to hold McClellan's attention in front of Richmond with a few troops and his newly improved fortifications,

> Any misstep at the gates of Richmond could spell doom for the young Confederacy.

swing to the north and east of the city with the bulk of his forces, join with Jackson's army, which would secretly march from the Shenandoah Valley, and sweep down upon the northern flank of the Union army. This proposal, fraught with risks, displayed the audacity that Colonel Ives noted in his comments to Porter Alexander and would become the model for practically all of Lee's battles. By doing this, Lee hoped to capitalize on what he saw as the strengths of his army—hard-marching infantry, often fighting on familiar territory—and avoid the strengths of his enemy.[15]

June 26, 1862, began one of the most remarkable ten-month periods in military history. In a series of clashes known collectively as the Seven Days Battles, Lee's army, now christened the Army of Northern Virginia, battered McClellan's Army of the Potomac in a series of bloody and poorly coordinated, but ultimately successful, assaults. McClellan evacuated his positions on the outskirts of Rich-

> This proposal, fraught with risks, displayed the audacity that Colonel Ives noted in his comments to Porter Alexander and would become the model for practically all of Lee's battles.

mond and withdrew southeast to the banks of the James River, where he encamped under the protection of U.S. Navy gunboats.

The Seven Days Battles showed the Army of Northern Virginia for what it was at that point: a raw, virtually untested force, commanded by generals who were unused to working with one another on a large scale.

Lee expected a great deal from his commanders and his men in these battles, but their capabilities did not yet match his vision—something that a new leader needs to consider. Is your organization ready for your vision of success? If it is not, that certainly does not mean that it will not be ready in the future, but this knowledge can let you help it to craft small victories in the meantime. Larger victories will follow, as they did for Lee. Be prepared to face your competition both by crafting a vision that matches it and by making sure your team or organization is prepared to handle that vision.

Aligning Your Subordinates to Support the Vision

The period 1862–1863 is important for our purposes because it saw all of the salient aspects of Lee's leadership style take root and grow. In the immediate aftermath of the Seven Days Battles, Lee carried out a ruthless reorganization of his high command. In a matter of weeks he had weeded out incompetent commanders and promoted those in whom he saw potential. Names like John B. Magruder, Gustavus W. Smith, and Theophilus H. Holmes are perhaps familiar to the well-read Civil War historian, but not to the generalist. These men failed Lee at one point or another during the Seven Days Battles and were quietly moved out of command positions. In their place rose men who have attained great fame: Stonewall Jackson, James Longstreet, Ambrose Powell Hill, and J. E. B. Stuart, to name just a few. In terms of personnel, Lee was able to match his vision of how his army would fight by surrounding himself with those who could best put that vision into action.

Similarly, you need to evaluate your staff and your vision. Who is best able to help you lead? Who will hinder your change efforts? Are you missing key team members—people with new or unique skills that are necessary to make your vision a success? Align your personnel so that they are ready to support you in your campaigns.

Managing Up: Following as an Integral Part of Leading

Lee's relationship with his boss, Jefferson Davis, provides a lesson in *followership*, a skill that is often of equal importance with *leadership*. Lee's retiring nature and his wish to avoid confrontation were not, as many observers have speculated, qualities that prevented Lee from being effective at both these skills. While he wished to avoid conflict, he had absolutely no trouble exerting his will over his subordinates and working with his superiors. An "in your face," confrontational nature does not always equal effective leadership; indeed, it is often counterproductive.

Lee *understood* Jefferson Davis and gave him what he craved most: information—on the state of the army, on current operations, on Lee's views of strategy. Lee was an effective leader in large measure because he was an effective follower. An August 1862 dispatch from Lee to Davis is an excellent case in point. In the letter, Lee states, "I will keep you informed of everything of importance that transpires. When you do not hear from me, you may feel sure that I do not think it necessary to trouble you. I shall feel obliged to you for any directions you may think proper to give." The solid relationship he cultivated with Davis allowed Lee virtually a free rein for his conduct of the war in the Eastern Theater.[16]

By contrast, many of Lee's less successful Union opponents created much of their own misfortune and unhappiness by failing to understand and adapt to the philosophies of their superior, Abraham Lincoln. General George B. McClellan offers the clearest example of

> Lee was an effective leader in large measure because he was an effective follower.

this failing. A West Point–educated engineer and an ardent Democrat, McClellan disliked the Republican Lincoln personally and disagreed with him on virtually every point of military strategy and politics. This disagreement turned into a petulant, complaining nature that frustrated Lincoln and prevented the very competent Mc-

Clellan from earning the credibility and freedom of action that he thought he deserved.[17]

Unless you are head honcho at your organization, you will need to get the support and buy-in of your superior if your vision is to succeed. To do that, you need to know what your superior wants or needs from you. In addition, you need to keep your superior apprised of the situation, your progress, and the return on investment. Otherwise your relationship with your boss will negatively affect the mission.

Consider, for example, Phyllis Grann, former CEO of Penguin Putnam, Inc. Grann is famous in the publishing industry for establishing best-selling authors such as Patricia Cornwell, Tom Clancy, Amy Tan, and Nora Roberts. Though she is considered something of a guru in publishing and editing, she ultimately left her leadership position at Penguin because she and other key members of Penguin had a "difference of business philosophies."[18] She left her next job, vice-chair of Random House, after only six months for similar reasons. Rapport with your bosses and your staff is fundamental to success.

The Right Place and the Right Time

During the year following the Seven Days Battles, Lee and the Army of Northern Virginia produced a winning streak of monumental proportions, defeating successive Union generals—Pope, Burnside, Hooker—at Second Bull Run, Fredericksburg, and Chancellorsville, and fighting McClellan to a bloody draw near Sharpsburg, Maryland, in the September 1862 Battle of Antietam. These victories forged the command style that Lee relied upon for most of the war, a style built upon calculated risk, use of separated detachments of his army, centralized planning, and decentralized execution by capable subordinates.

As Lee described it to an observer, he believed that it was his responsibility to bring his troops to the battlefield at the right place and time, and from that point to leave the conduct of battle to his generals and to "Providence." This is a method that, when executed by the right leader and the right subordinates, can produce great success in any endeavor. Likewise, this method in the wrong hands can produce disaster.

The August 1862 Second Battle of Bull Run, fought near Manassas, Virginia, offers the best example of these tenets. Many historians consider Second Bull Run the greatest of Lee's victories and the campaign that best encapsulates Lee's qualities. After the Seven Days Battles, Lee's position near Richmond became, if anything, even more precarious.

Abraham Lincoln created a second army, christened the Army of Virginia, and sent it into central Virginia to menace Lee's vital supply link with the Shenandoah Valley and the western Confederacy, the Virginia Central Railroad. In command of this new army was a westerner, Major General John Pope. Pope was a bombastic, aggressive character, given to grand pronouncements about his abilities. He issued a circular to his army in which he all but predicted victory over Lee in short order. Thus, Lee was now caught between two armies: Pope menaced him from central Virginia, and McClellan's still-dangerous Army of the Potomac was encamped on the James River a matter of miles from the capital.

Lee reacted with stunning audacity. Declaring that he must "suppress" that "miscreant Pope," he dispatched a force under Stonewall Jackson to deal with an advanced detachment of the Army of Virginia. Jackson fought and won a battle at Cedar Mountain, in Culpeper County, on August 9, securing the Virginia Central Railroad for the time being. Once he felt certain that McClellan had no intention of renewing the offensive against Richmond, Lee joined Jackson with the remainder of his army, leaving a small force to guard Richmond. In short order, McClellan began withdrawing from his James River position, with orders to move north and join with Pope's army in central Virginia.

After sparring with Pope along the Rappahannock River, Lee conceived a plan that was designed to change the face of the war in Virginia. At a meeting in the hamlet of Jeffersonton on August 24, Lee proposed to Jackson a rapid flank march around the right, or western, flank of the Union army. This flank march would put Jackson at the rear of Pope's army, between him and Washington, and threaten his supply links to his capital. Jackson, who had practiced such maneuvers to perfection in the Shenandoah Valley the previous spring, sketched out his proposed route in the dirt, and indicated his target: the Union supply depot at Manassas Junction. Thus, Lee matched perfectly a plan and a subordinate capable of executing it. This plan was fraught with danger. Lee's and Jackson's wings of the army would be separated by almost fifty miles, with Pope's army squarely between them and parts of McClellan's army approaching Jackson from the east. There seemed to be equal possibilities of success and disaster, but Lee weighed his opponent and his situation and decided that this calculated risk was in order.[19]

Early the next morning Jackson's force set off. In two days, his "foot cavalry" marched fifty miles, crossed rivers and mountains, and arrived at Manassas Junction, to the dismay of the small Union guard force there. As Jackson's men feasted on captured Yankee provisions, Lee marched with James Longstreet's wing of the army over the same route. He joined Jackson near the old Bull Run battlefield on the afternoon of August 28 as Pope approached with his army.

After heavy fighting on August 29 and 30, during which Lee's men withstood furious attacks by the Army of Virginia, aided by portions of the Army of the Potomac, Lee turned to his other chief subordinate, James Longstreet. Lee called on his "old war horse" to launch an attack on Pope's left flank, which Longstreet did with crushing force on the afternoon of August 30. Pope's disillusioned army retreated into the Washington fortifications, and yet another Union general's name was about to join the American lexicon as a synonym for failure and frustration.

> There seemed to be equal possibilities of success and disaster, but Lee weighed his opponent and his situation and decided that this calculated risk was in order.

Lee coordinated the attack at the most opportune moment (when his men were ready for it), picked the best person to implement the plan, and ordered the attack when the enemy was at its weakest. The campaign and battle of Second Bull Run showed Lee, his generals, and his armies acting with one shared vision. Lee's success was the result of his belief in audacity and risk taking and his ability to match subordinates to tasks. Assessing risks and determining when to initiate your plan is a part of strategic planning and is your responsibility as a leader.

Trust Your Adviser's Instincts

The next spring, following the bloody draw at Antietam and a Confederate victory at Fredericksburg, an aggressive Union commander got the drop on Lee for the first time as he sat in position defending the Rappahannock River town. General Joseph Hooker employed many of the tactics that Lee had continually used to advantage, holding the Virginian's attention with a small force while most of the army moved westward around Lee's flank.

Hooker had some of Lee's aggressive qualities, but moral courage was not one of them. Flushed with his early success, he halted his army on April 30 in an area of tangled woodland west of Fredericksburg known as the Wilderness and issued a bombastic proclamation that "the enemy must now ingloriously fly or come out from behind his works, where certain destruction awaits him." Faced with imminent disaster, Lee sent a small force westward to check Hooker's advance and divided the army yet again on the night of May 1, leaving part to guard Fredericksburg and marching with the rest to the crossroads at Chancellorsville.

The evening of May 1 saw one of the most remarkable command conferences in military history. In a thicket near Chancellorsville, Lee and Stonewall Jackson met around a campfire and pondered their next move. The army's other senior general, James Longstreet, was not with the army; he and his corps were in southeastern Virginia on a foraging expedition and would not return in time for this battle. When a cavalryman arrived with the intelligence that the right flank of Hooker's army was "in the air," or not anchored on any defensible terrain, Jackson made a remarkable proposal: to separate the army yet again, marching around the front of Hooker's army to strike its flank. "With what force do you propose to make this movement?" Lee was reported to have asked. "With my whole corps," was the reply.

Lee's approval of this incredibly risky maneuver showed his unbounded confidence in Jackson and represented his entire leadership style in microcosm. He left the planning and execution of the flank attack to Jackson, who carried it out the next day with his customary aggressiveness.

The attack of May 2 and the fighting the next day defeated Hooker and drove him back toward Washington in defeat. While the Battle of Chancellorsville cost Lee the life of Stonewall Jackson, who was wounded in the fighting on May 2, it was the best possible demonstration of the leader that Lee had become. As Lee rode into the now-vacated Union position on the evening of May 3, his men, many of whom had dubbed him "Granny" a year before, stood and cheered. It was reminiscent, one of Lee's officers remarked, of the arrival of a Roman emperor. One measure of leadership is a leader's ability to forge esprit through success, and by all accounts Lee passed that test at Chancellorsville.[20]

Accepting Jackson's proposal was risky, but Lee knew that he had an exceptional general with good instincts. You need to make sure you choose advisers, managers, and team members who have the knowledge and skills to do their job well. But just having them on your team is not enough. You sometimes have to trust them to take calculated risks. Your support team needs your support in order to apply its expertise and drive toward succeeding.

Overconfidence Is Deadly

Flushed with the successes of the past year, but ever mindful of the clock ticking against the Confederacy, Lee decided once again to invade Northern territory in the hopes of defeating the Army of the Potomac on its home soil. Such a campaign, Lee thought, would rob the Union of its strategic initiative and would damage Union will badly enough to force a political settlement. Beginning in early June, Lee and the Army of Northern Virginia moved northward

down the Shenandoah Valley, through Maryland, and into Pennsylvania. At the end of Lee's journey was the crossroads town of Gettysburg, thirty miles south of the state capital, Harrisburg. There the
battle on Northern soil that Lee had anticipated was joined, but not
under the circumstances that Lee had anticipated.

If Robert E. Lee is one of the most talked about and written
about figures in American history, then the Battle of Gettysburg is
by far the most talked about and written about three-day period of
Lee's life. In the largest and bloodiest battle ever fought on the
North American continent, the Union Army of the Potomac, led at
that time by Major General George G. Meade, bested Lee and his
army after three days of fighting. Moving into Pennsylvania with his
army separated into two elements, as was his custom, Lee encountered a situation in which his usual methods worked against him.

The Army of the Potomac pursued Lee with unaccustomed
speed, interposing itself between Lee and his chief cavalryman, Jeb
Stuart, whom Lee had dispatched northward by a different route.
Thus Lee was deprived of accurate and timely information about his
enemy. Not until June 28, when the Confederate army was spread
about south-central Pennsylvania, did Lee learn of Meade's close
pursuit and proximity to his forces.

Both generals determined on Gettysburg as a point of concentration because of the many roads that converged there, and the
result was a battle that began on July 1 as a "meeting engagement,"
one in which neither side expects to fight the other. Accidents of
terrain and the aggressiveness of Lee and his subordinate generals
gave the Army of Northern Virginia a smashing tactical victory on
July 1, but from that point onward the situation was reversed.

While Second Bull Run and Chancellorsville showcased elements of genius in Lee's leadership, Gettysburg showed the Virginian at his worst, revealing some flaws in the façade of the "marble
man." The Lee of Gettysburg acted with his customary aggressiveness, but during this battle a pervasive overconfidence turned that
aggressiveness into poor decisions. After the great victories of the
previous year, Lee held his enemy in utter contempt and believed
that his men could do literally anything he asked. This overconfi-

dence led Lee to attempt assaults when withdrawal would perhaps have been the prudent thing to do.

The result, on July 2 and 3, was a series of bloody and unsuccessful assaults over difficult ground against a stationary opponent. At several points during the fighting of July 2, Confederate units came tantalizingly close to ultimate victory, but Lee's overconfidence put his troops in extremely difficult positions. When James Longstreet, now, in Jackson's absence, Lee's only experienced corps commander, advocated moving the army to interpose it between Meade and Washington, D.C., Lee's response was peremptory: "The enemy is there, and I am going to strike him!" Strike him Lee did, with disastrous consequences for the Army of Northern Virginia. The battle culminated on July 3 with Pickett's Charge, perhaps the most famous infantry assault in American history, in which 13,000 Southerners threw themselves at the center of Meade's defensive line. Less than 5,000 returned.

Legions of historians have attempted to explain why Lee acted as he did at Gettysburg. By most accounts, this was his worst performance of the war. As a result of heavy losses in Lee's officer corps over the previous months, Gettysburg saw the debut in high command of several Confederate generals. It was the first major battle for two of Lee's three corps commanders and seven of his nine division commanders. In spite of this inexperience in his high command, however, Lee did little to alter his decentralized methods.

> "The enemy is there, and I am going to strike him!"

Even if they are talented, inexperienced subordinates may sometimes require more prescriptive or detailed supervision. Lee did not make this adjustment at Gettysburg. Part of overconfidence is overestimating the abilities and confidence of your team. You need to constantly evaluate your team members and adjust your leadership style to their needs.

After his defeat at Gettysburg, Lee and the Army of Northern Virginia returned to their native state, on whose soil they had never lost a battle. The army after Gettysburg could be likened to a wounded predator: incapable of striking as before, but still incredibly dangerous when cornered and attacked. During the fall of 1863,

Lee and Meade sparred with each other across northern Virginia, with neither able to gain an advantage over the other and both growing increasingly frustrated with their inability to move toward victory.

As springtime dried Virginia's roads and turned the landscape green once again, Lee was undoubtedly the Confederacy's finest and most successful field commander. Idolized by his men and by the Southern populace, he and his legions were quickly becoming the sole hope of the Confederacy. The Robert E. Lee of 1864 was the product of a distinguished background, a West Point education, and the crucible of combat. The coming weeks and months of 1864 would decide once and for all whether Lee's genius for command could produce Confederate victory in the east.

Leadership Lessons

Robert E. Lee's life and career up to 1864 offer numerous pertinent leadership lessons, best summarized in the Be, Know, Do format:

Be
- Personal character and integrity are important. These are the attributes that cause everyone around you to want to follow you.

- The courage of personal convictions allows the leader to make difficult personal decisions.

- Self-control in all situations can help leaders and organizations overcome difficulty and stress. Likewise, breakdowns in self-control can have negative effects far out of proportion to the immediate circumstances.

- Don't let overconfidence blind you to the right course of action. Continue to think critically, even when everything seems to be going well.

Know
- There are no shortcuts to unquestioned mastery of your profession, trade, or skill. Without this hard work and prepa-

ration, how can you expect the same efforts by your subordinates?

- Knowing your job extends to personnel decisions. Integrity and courage allow leaders to make the right calls regarding hiring and firing.

Do

- Craft plans that are appropriate to the abilities of your subordinates and their staffs, especially at the outset. This careful matching of leaders to tasks will help you to win small victories right away, putting you on the road to greater success.

- Separate short-term and long-term problems, and think creatively about how to deal with both.

- Prepare yourself, and those around you, for calculated risks.

CHAPTER TWO

Sam Grant

"Well Grant, we've had the devil's own day, haven't we?"
"Yes . . . Lick 'em tomorrow though."

—GENERAL WILLIAM TECUMSEH SHERMAN AND GENERAL ULYSSES S. GRANT,
PITTSBURG LANDING, TENNESSEE, APRIL 6, 1862.[1]

U.S. *Grant and son, Galena, Illinois.* A very unassuming way for America's foremost soldier to sign a hotel register, but this phrase captured perfectly the persona of the Union Army's ranking general. When Grant and his son Frederick arrived in Washington, D.C., in February 1864 to meet with President Abraham Lincoln, they first secured a room at Willard's Hotel, not far from the White House. The desk clerk, who did not know the general by sight and who was no doubt accustomed to seeing generals pass through the busiest hotel in the capital, assigned him a small room in the hotel's attic. He of course gave Grant a second-floor suite once he realized his mistake, but the incident illustrated well Grant's noncelebrity status, even at the height of his military prowess.[2] At this pinnacle of his military career, "Sam" Grant maintained the low-key persona that was a key part of his leadership style. In an age when many men equated leadership with posturing and ostentatiousness, Grant led by example, with quiet confidence.

The Man and the Myths

If misunderstandings and misinterpretations of Robert E. Lee's life shaped his legacy after his death, Grant had to deal with those same misunderstandings *while he was still alive.* Indeed, Brooks D. Simpson, one of Grant's most recent chroniclers, gave his biography the subtitle "Triumph Over Adversity," an apt statement if ever there was one. Most historical figures endure peaks and valleys of popular regard once they die, but until recently, Grant, as general and president, has endured a clouded legacy.

Two myths, in particular, continue to shape Grant's place in our collective memory even today. A few years ago, as I taught a military history course to a group of West Point cadets, I began a sequence of lessons on Grant by asking my students to blurt out the first thing that came to mind when I mentioned the name "Ulysses S. Grant." The first response was unanimously "a drunk." Close behind, in second place, was "a butcher of his men." Grant the Alcoholic and Grant the Butcher have obscured the man as he really was: Grant, the most uniformly successful of all Civil War generals and one of history's great captains. Just like Lee's, Grant's abilities and shortcomings, considered honestly, are an ideal leadership study.

Ulysses S. Grant spent most of his life in obscurity, and this state of affairs suited him quite well. Born Hiram Ulysses on April 27, 1822, in Point Pleasant, Ohio, twenty miles from Cincinnati, Grant's upbringing was in many respects the opposite of that of his patrician Virginia opponent. Jesse and Hannah Grant, Ulysses' parents, were ordinary folk, in contrast to Lee's upper-class pedigree. When Ulysses was a year old, Jesse moved the family to Georgetown, Ohio, and set up a tannery business. Jesse was a domineering father who made the young man's life difficult in many ways, but he nevertheless provided a decent life for the family, which eventually included three boys and three girls. Grant did not have to spend his life compensating for his father's indiscretions, as did Lee, but nevertheless he felt a lifelong compulsion to move beyond his father's influence.

Grant's father was a gregarious, politically adept businessman, character traits that were, to Jesse's lifelong disappointment, completely absent from his son, a shy boy with very little head for business. Other boys taunted him for his classical name with chants of "Useless" Grant. Public speaking of any kind seemed to cause the young Grant almost physical pain, and unscrupulous people took advantage of him from a very early age.

Whatever his shortcomings in his father's eyes, however, acquaintances knew Ulysses as a kind, very earnest person. Grant also made a name for himself as a fantastic horseman. Indeed, as a youth, he was often more comfortable in the company of horses than of people. He could not stand the sight or smell of blood, and he would have nothing to do with his father's tanning business. Indeed, Grant's sensitivity to blood and his love for living things puts the lie to one of the two great Grant myths, that he was an insensitive butcher who did not hesitate to sacrifice his soldiers' lives.[3]

> Grant the Alcoholic and Grant the Butcher have obscured the man as he really was: Grant, the most uniformly successful of all Civil War generals and one of history's great captains.

West Point: "Hiram" Becomes "Ulysses" the Leader

Grant's lack of inclination or aptitude to follow his father into business, combined with America's economic troubles in the wake of the Panic of 1837, led Jesse to consider West Point a viable option for his son's education. The Grant family had no military background whatsoever, but West Point was nevertheless the country's premier school for engineering and mathematics, skills that would serve one well in any occupation, military or civilian.

Jesse used his political connections to secure his son a place in the class of 1843. Ulysses was less than thrilled about attending West Point, which was infamous for its rigorous lifestyle; he later wrote in his memoirs that he would have been content if an accident or "temporary injury" while he was en route to the academy had forced him to return home. But, as he went on to write, "Nothing of the kind occurred, and I had to face the music."[4] Even then, a dogged inner determination pushed him ahead to the task at hand.

If Grant and Lee had different childhood experiences, West Point held a very special place in Grant's life, just as it did for the

Virginian. Indeed, attendance at West Point gave him the name by which he was known for the rest of his life. It will be remembered that Grant was born Hiram Ulysses. When his parents stamped the initials H.U.G. on a steamer trunk for the trip to West Point, Ulysses decided that he was not willing to endure more kidding about his name, so he switched the ordering to Ulysses Hiram.

When he signed in at West Point, the academy's adjutant informed him that no Ulysses Hiram was listed on the roll. Two Grants, Elihu from New York and Ulysses *S.* from Ohio, were expected. It seems that when Grant's congressman wrote his recommendation for the West Point nomination, he had forgotten Ulysses' full name and listed him as Ulysses Simpson, assuming that his mother's maiden name was the boy's middle name. Ever the realist, Ulysses saw that there was no fighting city hall, and from that day on he was known propitiously as U.S. Grant. In a play on the initials, senior cadet William Tecumseh Sherman gave the new plebe the nickname "Uncle Sam" Grant, or "Sam" for short. He passed his entrance examinations with no real trouble, and Ulysses was now Cadet Grant.[5]

Sam Grant was a decidedly middle-of-the-pack cadet, in contrast to Lee's superlative performance. Military life held no charms for him, at least initially, and he contemplated serving out his time in the army and finding a job teaching mathematics. Passing grades were no problem for him in any subject, so he never had to work very hard to get by. Indeed, he preferred to spend his free time ensconced in the academy library reading novels.

This seeming lack of application concealed the development of a military mind, however. Grant noted that when the army's commanding general, Winfield Scott, visited during the class of 1843's first summer encampment, the pomp surrounding the general made an impression, leading him to a premonition: "With his commanding figure, his quite colossal size and showy uniform, I thought him the finest specimen of manhood my eyes had ever beheld, and the most to be envied. . . . I believe I did have a presentiment for a moment that some day I should occupy his place on review."[6] Even though Grant went on to deny any real military ambition, West Point planted those seeds.

As Grant made friends and escaped the onerous duties of the West Point underclassman, he came more and more to enjoy his time as a cadet. When the time came to pick his branch of service, a choice based then, as it is now, on a cadet's class standing, Grant chose the dragoons, or mounted infantry. His love of horsemanship influenced this choice, as did his final class standing of twenty-first in a class of thirty-nine. Cadets of higher standing normally chose the engineers or the artillery; it will be remembered that Lee was commissioned an engineer. The dragoons apparently had no vacancies, however, leaving Grant with an infantry officer's commission and an assignment to the Fourth U.S. Infantry Regiment at Jefferson Barracks, outside of St. Louis, Missouri.

Marriage and Mexico: Grant's Early Leadership Experiences and Influences

After his unremarkable tenure at West Point, Brevet Second Lieutenant Grant embarked upon his army career. It did not begin auspiciously. When he traveled home in his new dress uniform, no doubt in an effort to impress his family and friends with his new-found status, a Cincinnati vagrant mocked him and a stable hand near his parents' house wore a homemade replica of Grant's blue officer's trousers. The joke "was a huge one in the mind of many of the people, and was much enjoyed by them." Grant never forgot the slight, and it no doubt contributed to his lifelong dislike of military pomp and circumstance.[7]

> The line officer of the nineteenth century was expected to occupy the line of battle with his men, to execute the commands of his superiors, and above all to set an example of unflinching bravery in the face of enemy fire.

Grant's initial assignment to Jefferson Barracks was fortunate for one big reason: It was here that the young lieutenant met and courted his future wife. During a visit to the boyhood home of his West Point roommate and friend Fred-

erick Dent, Grant first met Julia Dent. The pair got along well from
the beginning and soon fell in love. Julia's father opposed the
match, introducing another difficult father figure into Grant's life.
As a gentleman planter and lion of St. Louis society, "Colonel" Frederick Dent had no intention of seeing his daughter marry a lowly
army officer. Julia was as headstrong as Ulysses, however, and their
courtship persisted in spite of her father's opposition. In April 1844,
on the brink of Grant's reassignment to Louisiana, Julia agreed to
marry him. The engagement lasted, with some difficulties, through
Grant's assignments to Louisiana and Texas. In March 1846, Lieutenant Grant joined Lee and many other future Civil War notables
in Texas, as the U.S. Army prepared to go to war against Mexico.

The Mexican-American War was a training ground for the young
Grant as well as for Lee, but the Ohioan took very different lessons
away from the conflict. Grant's regiment, the Fourth Infantry, served
initially in Texas and northern Mexico under General Zachary Taylor, "Old Rough and Ready." The plain-spoken, aggressive Taylor
came to occupy a place alongside Winfield Scott in Grant's estimation. Grant's comments about Taylor's leadership style could apply
anywhere, anytime as a model for emulation. They highlight the
leader's responsibility to be a good follower, as well as to set the
"mood" or climate of an organization:

> *General Taylor was not an officer to trouble the [presiden-
> tial] administration much with his demands, but was in-
> clined to do the best he could with the means given him.
> He felt his responsibility as going no further. If he had
> thought that he was sent to perform an impossibility with
> the means given him, he would probably have informed
> the authorities of his opinion and left them to determine
> what should be done. If the judgment was against him he
> would have gone on and done the best with the means at
> hand without parading his grievance before the public. No
> soldier could face either danger or responsibility more
> calmly than he. These are qualities more rarely found than
> genius or physical courage. General Taylor never made any
> great show or parade, either of uniform or retinue . . . but*

*he was known to every soldier in his army, and was re-
spected by all.*[8]

It was no coincidence that years later, during the Civil War, many
observers noted the same qualities in Grant.

While Lee served in Mexico as a staff officer, with interaction at
the highest levels of army command, Grant's experience was that of
an infantry line officer. The line officer of the nineteenth century
was expected to occupy the line of battle with his men, to execute
the commands of his superiors, and above all to set an example of
unflinching bravery in the face of enemy fire. At the battle of Palo
Alto on May 8, 1846, Grant stood in the line of battle and watched
as a cannonball ripped through the American formation, decapitat-
ing a nearby soldier and showering Grant with blood and brains. In
a letter to Julia after the battle, Grant remarked that although this
near-death experience and the horrors of battle were "no great
sport," he felt less afraid once the fighting began than when he was
anticipating the battle.

Although Grant realized that, as a junior officer, he probably
wouldn't affect the outcome of a battle, these early seasoning experiences reinforced the young man's self-confidence. James Longstreet, a fellow West Point graduate and future Confederate general,
later remarked, "You could not keep Grant out of battle," a high
compliment from one career soldier to another and an indication
of the persistence with which Grant applied himself to a job once
he started it.[9]

Grant the Quartermaster: Building a
Toolbox of Critical Skills

In mid-August 1846, as Zachary Taylor prepared to move his army
further into the interior of Mexico, Grant earned a promotion of
sorts, to the positions of quartermaster and commissary officer of
the Fourth Infantry. He held these jobs for the remainder of the
war, serving first with Taylor and later with Winfield Scott's Vera
Cruz expedition. These jobs gave Grant the responsibility for arran-

ging and supervising the feeding, clothing, equipping, and transporting of a regiment of almost one thousand men.[10] Then as now, these logistical jobs are not glamorous, but without capable officers to perform them, no military unit would move an inch.

An old saying holds that in the military, "amateurs study tactics, while professionals study logistics." While a real professional studies both, it is undoubtedly true that an understanding of these nuts-and-bolts functions is a critical element of professional competence. The professional education that Grant gained from this duty position served him in good stead throughout his career; no unit that Grant commanded in the Civil War, from a thousand-man regiment to a hundred-thousand-man army, went without critical supplies if he could help it.

There are jobs or skills like this, unglamorous but important, in any organization. A recent television commercial for Federal Express shows a young manager who is asked to take charge of a critical shipping job. The manager says that he has an MBA, implying that he is above that kind of work. "Oh, you have an MBA," the other employee answers. "Well, then, let me show you." Don't let this happen to you. A well-rounded leader masters the small, mundane jobs and builds a toolbox of important skills for future reference.

Postwar Troubles

Upon returning home after the war, Grant journeyed back to Missouri and married Julia on August 22, 1848. He expected this phase of his life to be his happiest, but in many respects his life took a turn for the worse. After four years of service at remote posts, including Sackets Harbor in upstate New York and Detroit, Michigan, Grant's regiment was transferred to the Pacific coast. Julia, who was pregnant with her first child, could not make the journey, leaving Grant on his own once again.

Life on his own at Fort Vancouver, in present-day Washington state, and Fort Humboldt, in northern California, turned Grant's loneliness to melancholy. Failures in modest business ventures and health problems led to drinking. Heavy consumption of alcohol was a fact of life for the officers of the "Old Army," but it was not so much that Grant drank heavily as that he was simply unable to handle liquor. One of his fellow officers commented, "Liquor seemed a virulent poison to him, and yet he had a fierce desire for it. . . . One glass would show on him, and two or three would make him stupid."[11] Many of Grant's fellow Regular Army officers went on to serve in the Civil War, and those with an axe to grind turned Grant's inability to handle alcohol into a disease. Thus was born the second great Grant legend: that he was an alcoholic. Grant spent the rest of his career attempting to outrun the shadow of these supposed indiscretions.

> Grant exhibited the qualities that cause people in any organization to follow a leader: competence, high standards, and a clear vision of success.

Resignation and Return: The Civil War Begins

Even though Grant finally earned promotion to captain in late 1853, his continued loneliness and a festering dispute with an old commanding officer convinced him that he had had enough of army life. On April 11, 1854, he wrote to Washington resigning his commission effective July 31. Where Captain Ulysses Grant was a moderately successful army officer, however, Mr. Ulysses Grant the farmer and businessman was an utter failure. From 1854 through 1860, Grant in turn tried his hand at agriculture, real estate, and government customs, and failed at all of them. In March 1860, he finally accepted his father's continued offer to join the family business and moved the family, now consisting of Julia, sons Fred, Buck, and Jesse, and daughter Nellie, to Galena, Illinois. Here he took over a general store with his brother Simpson and was beginning to put his life back together when the Civil War broke out in April 1861.[12]

If Grant had learned anything of substance from his time as a civilian, it was that military life suited him. In the wave of patriotic fervor that accompanied Abraham Lincoln's call for volunteers to suppress the rebellion, Grant actively sought out a commission as a colonel of Illinois volunteers, a position to which he believed his West Point education and wartime service entitled him. After an initial stint as a recruiting and training officer, Grant caught the attention of Illinois Governor Richard Yates and in June got his wish.

The Seventh District Regiment, which Grant had mustered into service at Mattoon, Illinois, needed a new colonel to replace its drunken commander. Grant assumed command at Camp Yates, near the state capital, and went right to work. Even as a lowly regimental commander, Grant exhibited flashes of the qualities that would lead him to success at higher levels. An accepted maxim holds that upon taking charge, a leader should bide his time, learning the good and bad of his new organization before initiating wholesale changes. Grant did so, but his "honeymoon period" lasted only long enough for him to see that the regiment's behavior under its old colonel was simply unacceptable. Relying upon his education and his Mexican-American War service as a quartermaster, Grant instituted Regular Army–style discipline and training, and this method worked. On June 28, virtually the entire group reenlisted for a term of three years as the Twenty-first Illinois Volunteer Infantry. In his first wartime command, Grant exhibited the qualities that cause people in any organization to follow a leader: competence, high standards, and a clear vision of success.

Grant's success with the Twenty-first Illinois caused the Lincoln administration to sit up and take notice, and Lincoln promoted Grant to brigadier general in August. He whipped a group of troublesome regiments into fighting shape and led them in a series of small engagements along the Mississippi River in Missouri and Kentucky.[13] As a general, Grant combined fighting skill, administrative ability, and an innate ability to manage civil-military relations within the area of his command. These abilities convinced Lincoln that Grant, more than any other Union officer in the West, understood the responsibilities of high command.

Henry and Donelson: "Unconditional Surrender" Grant Is Born

The early 1862 campaign in western Tennessee set Grant on the road to high command. Here, in February of the war's second year, Grant began to display the one quality that would elevate him above all others in the Union Army high command: the ability not only to visualize the way to victory, but to inspire and energize organizations to follow that path. Many Civil War generals, and many leaders in other walks of life, possess either vision or energy, but the combination of both should be every leader's personal goal.

From his base at Cairo, Illinois, Grant visualized the Tennessee and Cumberland Rivers as a strategic highway into the Confederate interior. The Confederates realized this as well and constructed Forts Henry and Donelson to guard the two waterways. After fighting a small battle at Belmont, Missouri, in November 1861, Grant gained the approval of his new department commander, Henry W. Halleck, to forge a joint Army-Navy expeditionary force to capture the two forts and pierce the rebel interior. The expedition departed on February 3, 1862, with Flag Officer Andrew Foote in command of the naval force.

> Grant began to display the one quality that would elevate him above all others in the Union Army high command: the ability not only to visualize the way to victory, but to inspire and energize organizations to follow that path.

Confederate commanders quickly evacuated Fort Henry and moved their forces to the formidable Fort Donelson. After the fort's gunners defeated a naval attack on February 14, a disheartened Foote withdrew all but two of his gunboats. Grant refused to give up; he moved his divisions to surround the fort and pound it into submission. After a Confederate breakout attempt on February 15 failed, the fort's commander, a prewar friend of Grant's named

Simon Bolivar Buckner, sent Grant a dispatch proposing a meeting to discuss terms of surrender. Grant issued a reply that would add to his fame: "No terms except unconditional and immediate surrender can be accepted. I propose to move immediately upon your works." This response led Buckner to surrender the entire garrison on February 16. "Unconditional Surrender" Grant had given the Union its most important victory to date.[14]

Following on the heels of the triumphs at Henry and Donelson, Grant yearned to continue his strike deep into the Confederate heartland. However, other Union generals in the west did not agree. Because he felt threatened by Grant's rapid rise to prominence, Halleck perpetuated rumors that "since the taking of Fort Donelson Grant has resumed his former bad habits," specifically drinking. It did not matter that this accusation was utterly groundless. Even though Grant's doctor prescribed daily amounts of beer or ale to counteract persistent rheumatism, Grant's chief of staff, prewar friend and avowed teetotaler John Rawlins, threatened to resign should the general ever drink heavily. At this point, Grant used his father's political connections to overcome the accusations, but infighting would continue to mar the Union high command's efficiency.

Shiloh: The Pitfalls of Overconfidence

Grant began to recover his health and reputation when he took the field once again in mid-March 1862, rejoining his army in its campsites on the Tennessee River at a small stopping place called Pittsburg Landing. Nearby stood a remote country church called Shiloh, the Hebrew word for "place of rest." This heavily wooded section of Tennessee would be anything but a place of tranquility in April. Here, before, during, and after the Battle of Shiloh, Grant encountered a problem that would bedevil him for the rest of the war, one that he shared with Lee: an optimism, borne of success, that blinded him to problems and flaws in his plans. It would take until 1863 for this optimism to cause Lee grief at Gettysburg; it caught up with Grant much earlier.

March 1862 would see the reunion in Tennessee of Grant and William Tecumseh Sherman. Division Commander Sherman assured Grant that the army's campsites were secure from attack by a disorganized Confederate force ten miles away at Corinth, Mississippi. In his optimism, Grant chose to believe Sherman, feeling that after Henry and Donelson, the entire Confederacy was on the verge of collapse. In the weeks before Shiloh, Grant, "as well as thousands of other citizens, believed that the rebellion against the Government would collapse suddenly and soon, if a decisive victory could be gained over any of its armies. Donelson and Henry were such victories."[15] As a result, Grant failed to order even rudimentary security measures or reconnaissance against Confederate General Albert Sidney Johnston's Army of Tennessee.

No Union commander anticipated what befell early on the morning of April 6, 1862. Johnston's army surprised and routed much of Grant's army, driving it back to Pittsburg Landing. Only darkness, the death of Johnston, and the near-suicidal stand of part of the Union force saved the Union army from annihilation. Even in this darkest of hours, however, Grant showed yet again the qualities that destined him for greatness. He saw not failure, but a new opportunity for the following day; thus his promise to Sherman to "lick 'em tomorrow."

Reinforcements began arriving from upriver that night, giving Grant a numerical advantage over the Confederate army, now deprived of its commanding general. His forces did "lick 'em" on April 7, driving the Confederates back to Corinth. The Battle of Shiloh, the bloodiest battle in the war up to that point, with over 24,000 killed, wounded, or missing on both sides, was a triumph of will, of Grant's refusal to fail. It also demonstrated, however, that Grant had a good deal yet to learn about generalship. For the modern leader, Shiloh also demonstrates what can happen when overconfidence causes laxness.

It's interesting to note that both Lee and Grant, though they were exceptional leaders, fell into the trap of overconfidence. Beware that you do not fall into this trap yourself. Before beginning any initiative, make sure that you and your team have done due diligence—that you have evaluated your strengths and weaknesses, those of your competition, and your readiness to embark on the initiative.

> He saw not failure, but a new opportunity for the following day.

Often companies are in such a rush to get a product out or to get sales that they promote the product before it is ready. Consider, for example, a product by Microsoft called ".Net My Services." Long before the technology was fully developed and before Microsoft even had a business plan for it, the company advertised a product launch. Ultimately this led to confusion in the marketplace and embarrassment for the company. Resist pressure to throw your people or your products out there before they are ready. Readiness is necessary for success.

Facing Criticism: The Importance of Personal Loyalty

Even though Shiloh was an important Union victory, dark clouds of political infighting continued to gather around Grant. He earned justified criticism for allowing his army to be surprised at Shiloh, but his critics went further. Most of the politicians and newspaper reporters who visited the army at Pittsburg Landing had never seen a battlefield before, and the carnage shocked them; reports of ghastly casualties, combined with the initial repulsing of the Union forces, gave unscrupulous reporters the opportunity to initiate the legend of "Grant the Butcher." Halleck and other Union generals saw an opening to continue their attacks on Grant's generalship and proceeded to do so, almost securing his removal from command.

Among the senior Union commanders, Sherman alone remained faithful to Grant during this period. Their friendship was strengthened by the latter's support for Sherman earlier in the war, when he had endured similar slanderous criticism of his abilities. Another feature of Grant's leadership became apparent: his absolute loyalty to those colleagues who stood by him in the face of criticism. Throughout the war, those to whom Grant showed loyalty responded by performing well in difficult situations.

Vicksburg: A Triumph of Will

Promoted by Lincoln to overall command in the west after Halleck's transfer to War Department headquarters in Washington, Grant set out to capture perhaps the most strategically important place on the Mississippi River: Vicksburg. The heavily fortified Mississippi River town was one of the last Confederate bastions remaining on the river, and its position blocked Union movements between New Orleans, Louisiana (in Union hands since early 1862); Memphis, Tennessee (also a Union city by now); and points north. Vicksburg was defended by a sizable Confederate force under John C. Pemberton, and another small army under Joseph E. Johnston lurked nearby.

Grant's first attempt to take the city, by simply marching southward from western Tennessee into Mississippi along existing railroad lines, failed when Confederate cavalry destroyed his supply base at Holly Springs, Mississippi. Grant learned two things from this defeat. The first was that the overland method of capturing Vicksburg from the north would be difficult, if not impossible, to accomplish. The second, and perhaps more significant, lesson came from the destruction of his supply base. Grant found out that his army did not need to rely on the primary nineteenth-century means of supplying a large army: railroad transportation of supplies.

Previously, Grant and other generals had considered "as an axiom in war that large bodies of troops must operate from a base of supplies which they always covered and guarded in all forward movements." Now, in the absence of his supply stockpiles, his men "lived off the land" in northern Mississippi and, if anything, were better fed as a result. Grant was "amazed at the quantity of supplies the country afforded," a "lesson which was taken advantage of later in the campaign." Grant would use this lesson to great effect in 1863, and would approve of Sherman's famous "March to the Sea" in 1864 as a result.[16]

Faced with the problem of capturing Vicksburg, Grant applied vision, persistence, and imagination. After several attempts to attack the city from the north failed in late 1862, many Union generals would have succumbed to caution and withdrawn their forces for the winter. Grant was different. He kept his men in the field, in miserable conditions, in the belief that doing something productive was better than doing nothing.

The strategical way of solving this problem would have been to march his entire army back to Memphis and start all over again, but Grant noted, with typical perceptiveness, that by late 1862, "many Union men believed that the war must prove a failure," and that the midterm congressional elections foretold waning popular support for the war. In Grant's opinion, then, "to make a backward movement . . . to Memphis, would be interpreted . . . as a defeat." In this case, "there was nothing left to be done but to *go forward to a decisive victory*" [author's italics].[17] No statement could better encapsulate why Grant was such an immense success as a general.

With this resolve, Grant began in March 1863 to attack his problem anew, believing that "it would not do [for his army] to lie idle all this time." After several attempts to dig canals, reroute the Mississippi channel at Vicksburg, and travel via other bayous and lakes to the south and west of Vicksburg, Grant got the break he needed on April 16, when naval forces under Admiral David Dixon Porter forced their way past Vicksburg's batteries and continued south. Grant marched some of his army over land, put others on Porter's transports, and moved his army past Vicksburg, where it could occupy the east bank of the river below the city.

This movement, with its attendant severance of Union supply lines, paralyzed John C. Pemberton and Joseph Johnston, the Confederate commanders in Mississippi. In a lightning march that began on April 30, Grant's army moved inland and dispersed Johnston's force at Jackson on May 14. From there, Grant turned west toward Vicksburg, defeating part of Pemberton's army at Champion Hill on May 16 and besieging Vicksburg later in the month. By July 4, it was all over. Vicksburg, with over 30,000 irreplaceable Confederate troops, surrendered, and with the capture of Port Hudson farther south, the Mississippi River was back in Union hands.

In a campaign that has been studied to this day as a model of calculated risk, audacity, and brilliant planning, Grant cemented his reputation and hushed many of his critics.[18] Just as Second Manassas showed Robert E. Lee and his army at the peak of their abilities, the Vicksburg campaign best represented the qualities that Grant brought to bear as a general.

> "There was nothing left to be done but to *go forward to a decisive victory*."

If the Vicksburg campaign catapulted Grant to "rock star" status, the subsequent Tennessee campaign cemented his qualities in the mind of Abraham Lincoln. Lincoln had dealt with a succession of failed generals in the east, but Grant was something different. Instead of seeing reasons to delay or reasons to withdraw, Grant saw opportunities and sought to create them if he did not see them.

Opening the Gateway: Grant in Tennessee, 1863

Grant confronted just such a situation in eastern Tennessee in the fall of 1863. After moving his Army of the Cumberland through Tennessee and capturing the vital rail center of Chattanooga, Major General William S. Rosecrans struck out into northern Georgia after Braxton Bragg's Confederate Army of Tennessee. Rosecrans allowed his columns to become separated in the mountainous terrain, and Bragg pounced on him, winning a victory at Chickamauga in late September. Rosecrans fell back to Chattanooga and Bragg followed him, laying siege to the city. Soon the Union army was cut off and going hungry. As the newly named commander of the Military Division of the Mississippi, Grant acted decisively. He removed Rosecrans from command, replacing him with Major General George H. Thomas. He then set out for Chattanooga, arriving there on the evening of October 23.

In taking over a defeated or downtrodden organization, it may be necessary to do *something* right away, even if that does not really address the ultimate problem. Grant did this by opening the so-called Cracker Line, a mule train supply line into the beleaguered city. He then set about figuring out how to solve the long-term problem, the Confederate hold on the numerous intersecting rail lines that made Chattanooga the "gateway city" to the Deep South. This he accomplished in a stunning series of battles in November, culminating in the "Battle Above the Clouds," in which Union forces scaled Lookout Mountain and ejected its Confederate defenders, and the Confederate defeat at Missionary Ridge. Although Thomas was a very capable general, it is difficult to imagine the Union forces achieving such a stunning victory without the personal presence of Grant. This series of battles set the stage for the Union drive to capture Atlanta during the summer of 1864. Grant repaid Sherman's loyalty to him by giving him overall command of operations in Georgia.[19]

General in Chief: Grant on the Eve of the Overland Campaign

The Union cause, which had seemed so hopeful after the twin victories at Vicksburg and Gettysburg, returned to stalemate in both east and west as 1863 ended. In the east, Meade's Army of the Potomac occupied virtually the same positions as had all of its predecessors, no closer than any of them to Richmond. In the west, although Grant had won great victories at Chattanooga and retained his hold on that vital city, Joe Johnston was busy revitalizing the Army of Tennessee and preparing to defend positions in northern Georgia.

> Instead of seeing reasons to delay or reasons to withdraw, Grant saw opportunities and sought to create them if he did not see them.

The solution, to Abraham Lincoln's mind, was Ulysses S. Grant. So Grant traveled east to meet with the president and take command of the Union armies with the newly revived grade of lieutenant general; Grant was the first American to hold this rank since George Washington. It was an amazing journey from Galena, Illinois, to the halls of power in Washington. Grant survived and persevered because of his absolute and unwavering determination to see himself through. This determination enabled him to use other, sometimes unseen, qualities. It also allowed him, in effect, to transcend defeat. During the course of the war in the west, Grant consistently turned battlefield setbacks or defeats into strategic victories; witness his reactions to the naval failure at Fort Donelson, to the initial defeat at Shiloh, and to the defeat of Rosecrans at Chickamauga. No leader in any organization can claim an unblemished record of success; a saying holds that "10 percent of life is what happens to us and 90 percent is how we react to it." Grant made the most of that 90 percent, demonstrating that a leader who can see through temporary setbacks and maintain his vision for success will, more often than not, get there.

To put it simply, Grant had an ability to see through trouble and confusion and to figure out what needed to be done. Many other generals on both sides, trained professionals like Grant, knew on an intuitive or abstract level the right course of action in a given situation. But Grant was a different matter entirely. His single-minded pursuit of his objectives, regardless of political pressures or of the inadequacies of those around him, brought him success. From colonel to lieutenant general, Grant applied unquestioned technical competence and an absolute will to win in every situation. While he was every bit the opposite of Robert E. Lee in upbringing, the deeper similarities of the two men in this regard made them as much alike as different. Thus, the stage was set in early 1864 for the titanic clash between Ulysses S. Grant and Robert E. Lee.

> A leader who can see through temporary setbacks and maintain his vision for success will, more often than not, get there.

Leadership Lessons

Just as Robert E. Lee's upbringing and military career offer pertinent Be, Know, Do leadership examples, we can also cull Grant's leadership experiences down to a few key points.

Be

- Pay attention to your public image. As you may well know from your own experiences, perception can become reality. Even at the height of his military success, Grant still had to fight rumors of drunkenness.

- Self-control and positive energy in all situations can help leaders and organizations to overcome difficulty and stress. Likewise, breakdowns in self-control can have negative effects far out of proportion to the immediate circumstances.

- Be yourself. Subordinates usually pick up on a leader who tries to be someone he or she is not. You are where you are for a reason—use your personality and unique skills to succeed. Lieutenant General Grant was very much the same as Mr. Ulysses S. Grant, Esq.

- Overconfidence kills. It was almost as damaging for Grant in 1862 as it was for Lee in 1863.

Know

- Pay attention to *all* of the skills related to your profession, and maintain those skills as you rise in rank and stature. Grant's inglorious days as a quartermaster translated directly into the higher-level ability to feed and sustain armies of thousands of men. If you can maintain some of the skills of your subordinates as you move up, you will earn credibility with them and be able to guide them more effectively without micromanagement.

- Develop within yourself the ability to think *conceptually*. Grant displayed this skill during the Henry/Donelson campaign and again at Vicksburg. His skill in this regard allowed him not only to envision the right thing to do, but also to envision courses of action that other skilled and professional officers could not.

Do

- When in doubt, do *something*. In difficult situations, get your people moving in the right direction and give yourself time to work things out. Grant's multiple stabs at the thorny problem of Vicksburg offer a great example. Grant's constant activity kept critics at bay, giving him the time and latitude to come up with the right answer.

PART II

The Overland Campaign

Crucible of Leadership

CHAPTER THREE

Lee and Grant Prepare for the 1864 Campaign

Leadership and Organizational Planning

"The only evidence you have that he's in any place is that he makes things git! Wherever he is, things move."[1]

—PRESIDENT ABRAHAM LINCOLN, DESCRIBING GENERAL ULYSSES S. GRANT TO HIS PRIVATE SECRETARY

The key difference between direct leaders, who carry out higher-level decisions and do the "nuts and bolts" work in an organization (an office manager, perhaps, or a team chief), and organizational leaders is that the latter have the responsibility for *planning* as well as executing. Organizational leaders must walk a fine line in the planning process. They must consider the capabilities of their subordinates, relate to those subordinates, and often exercise direct leadership without micromanaging. Organizational leaders must also take into account the capabilities of their subordinates when crafting plans, and must seek to find the "center of gravity" in any situation, an idea or decision that will create the conditions for success.

Both Grant and Lee operated in this realm during the weeks leading up to the Overland Campaign. Grant had the added diffi-

---

Figure 3-1 Conceptual leadership skills.

Organizational Planning Factors
- The Center of Gravity
- Capabilities and Limitations of Subordinates
- The Big Picture—External Considerations

---

culty of inheriting control of a new organization, the Army of the Potomac. The challenges that Lee and Grant faced will resonate with any leader who has ever stepped into a new role or position. The operational plans that both developed speak highly of their abilities and offer lessons for you as you create the blueprints for the success of your organization.

Lee and His Generals, 1864: Strengths, Weaknesses, and Personnel Decisions

In the interval between Gettysburg and the start of the 1864 campaign, Lee faced a timeless leadership challenge: the reorganization of his chain of command. A modern business leader might face the same challenge as a result of downsizing, the arrival of a new CEO, or any number of other situations. How do you do it? Do you promote from within, or do you bring in new blood? Do you combine the old with the new, or do you create entirely new teams? One thing is certain: Leaders must make personnel changes with one eye on the challenges ahead and the other on the existing constraints.

In replacing the heavy officer losses of the 1863 battles, Lee had to fight against many of the problems that modern managers face in dealing with personnel turnover. In any army (or corporation), only a certain small percentage of officers will show aptitude for ever-increasing levels of responsibility. By 1864, many promising Confederate officers lay dead or wounded; just one battle, Gettysburg, had claimed the staggering total of 15 out of 45 brigade and division commanders dead or wounded. This was the population from which Lee could reasonably expect to select division and corps commanders. Many of the remaining officers were simply not up to high command, but clearly someone had to fill the higher positions. Lee made an honest assessment of the officers he had available and then went to work reorganizing his officer corps.[2]

Given the already small pool of capable leaders available to him, Lee simply did not have the option of wholesale changes. Many of his

> Lee's decentralized leadership style demanded generals who were comfortable acting independently.

mid-level and senior-grade officers were volunteer soldiers, nonprofessionals who owed their rise in rank to political connections or simple survival. Lee had to balance these men with trained soldiers. Other political constraints were involved as well, such as the necessity of banding together units from particular Confederate states under particular leaders. The result was the first of three top-to-bottom reorganizations of his senior officer corps during the course of the Overland Campaign.

After this post-Gettysburg reorganization, Lee met with his corps and division commanders on May 2, 1864, to ponder the coming campaign. For his meeting place, Lee chose Clark's Mountain, in Culpeper County, Virginia. If Lee and the Army of Northern Virginia had a "home field advantage" because they had fought most of their campaigns in Virginia, then the Confederate signal station atop Clark's Mountain was the physical embodiment of that advantage. Clark's Mountain sits just south of the Rapidan River, the dividing line between the opposing armies in the spring of 1864. From its 600-foot summit, an observer could look northward and view the entire Army of the Potomac as it sat in its campsites. Dust, smoke, and large formations of troops would give Confederate Signal Corps personnel a clear indication of any impending Union advance. Spring was just beginning to bring a tinge of green to the landscape, and the muddy Virginia roads were drying just in time for renewed hostilities.

The command group that gathered around Lee was very different from the one that had surrounded him at Gettysburg, just eight months before. Lee's decentralized leadership style demanded generals who were comfortable acting independently, and serious questions remained as to whether his three corps commanders could do this. James Longstreet had taken his corps to Georgia in September 1863, and later led it in an independent operation against Knoxville, Tennessee. In this role Longstreet had been a failure. His campaign dissolved in mismanagement and acrimony, including court-martial charges against one of his division commanders. But there was still no denying that Lee needed his "Old War Horse," and Longstreet's return to Virginia in early 1864 was the occasion for joy in the Army of Northern Virginia.

> "... each man seemed to feel the bond which held us all to Lee."

On April 29, 1864, Lee held a grand review of the returning First Corps. Throughout military history, leaders have conducted reviews of troops to determine their fitness for battle. This review was an occasion that confirmed the bond that existed between Lee and Longstreet and the almost mystical relationship between Lee and his army. Longstreet drew up his entire corps, about 8,000 men and several batteries of artillery, in an open field near his headquarters at Gordonsville, Virginia.

As Lee and his staff rode through a gate into the field, a cannon boomed and the shrill rebel yell rippled through the ranks of Longstreet's veterans, troops hailing largely from the Deep South states of Texas, Arkansas, Louisiana, Mississippi, and Alabama. Lee stopped and removed his hat, prompting further shouting and waving of battle flags. Porter Alexander, who by this time had risen to command of Longstreet's artillery, remembered that "each man seemed to feel the bond which held us all to Lee." He described the scene as "a military sacrament, in which we pledged anew our lives." A nearby chaplain asked one of Lee's aides if the general was proud to see how the army loved him; the aide, Colonel Charles Venable, responded, "not proud, it awes him."[3]

The review symbolized perfectly the bond that almost two years of fighting and campaigning had created between the Virginian and his soldiers. All leaders should be so lucky! Despite their disagreements in the past, Lee relied on Longstreet and his corps. Longstreet's division commanders, Joseph Kershaw of South Carolina and the amiable Charles Field, were also solid performers.

Problems in Lee's Second Corps began and ended with its commander, Richard S. Ewell. Known by many as the most eccentric character in the army, "Old Bald Head" had inherited the command of the corps after the death of Stonewall Jackson. Ewell was an excellent division commander, and in fact was virtually the only Confederate officer of any rank to function harmoniously under the prickly Stonewall. He worked well under strict supervision, and he could carry out detailed orders quite capably. When confronted with the wide latitude that Lee gave his generals, however, Ewell was not up to the task. He usually made correct decisions, but he could be excitable and unstable, refusing to act until he had sought counsel from his peers and subordinates.

In the aftermath of Gettysburg, Ewell was roundly criticized for his indecision on the evening of the first day of the battle, when he elected not to attempt an assault on the main Union position as night fell. This criticism stung, and his recent marriage to a headstrong woman, many observers speculated, had robbed him of the aggressiveness required of a commander in the Army of Northern Virginia. In the coming campaign, Ewell would have the benefit of three excellent division commanders: Jubal Early, Robert Rodes, and Edward "Allegheny" Johnson. It remained to be seen whether the trio could compensate for Ewell's deficiencies.

The biggest question mark surrounded Lee's Third Corps commander, Ambrose Powell Hill. Like Ewell, "Little Powell" was a West Point graduate who had compiled an enviable record as a division commander; in September 1862 his troops, famously styled the "Light Division," had made a dramatic eighteen-mile forced march to literally save the day for Lee at Antietam. And, again like Ewell, Hill was elevated to corps command when the Army of Northern Virginia reorganized its high command after Chancellorsville. Never one to bestow idle praise, Lee remarked of Hill when nominating him for corps command (and in the process offering his criteria for a good general), "Hill is the best officer of his grade with the army. He fights his troops well and takes good care of them."[4]

Unfortunately for Lee and the army, however, Hill was another officer who had been promoted past his level of ability. The heavy administrative burdens of corps command wore on Hill, and his continuing health problems made the burdens unbearable. Unlike the Second Corps, the Third Corps could not count on a strong stable of division commanders to make up for its leader's deficiencies. Cadmus Wilcox, Henry Heth, and Richard Heron Anderson were, at best, average commanders. Of the three corps, it would seem that this one was the least fit to prosper under Lee's audacious, decentralized command philosophy.

> ". . . that man will fight us every hour and every day."

The one area in which Lee had little cause for concern was his cavalry. Major General James Ewell Brown "Jeb" Stuart had served as the army's cavalry chief since early 1862 and had acquired a reputation as a superb raider and scout. Questions about Stuart's performance in the Gettysburg campaign, where he became separated from the main body of the army and did not rejoin it until midway through the battle, were in the past. Such questions aside, Stuart was a superb cavalry general. Lee depended on him to be his "eyes and ears" while on campaign, and the coming weeks would see Stuart's finest performance of the war in this regard. They would also be the cavalier's last on this earth; he would be dead before the end of May.

Defense vs. Offense: Conceptual Thinking, Assumptions, and Calculated Risk

With the issue of the army leadership resolved, at least for the moment, Lee stood atop Clark's Mountain on May 2 and pondered what his adversary planned to do. Lee looked to the past for clues to his adversary's actions, looked around at the environment and sought to use it to his advantage, and fashioned a plan that took into account the tools at hand. You may need to do the same things when you plan for your organization. Your adversaries could be competitors for a contract, the environment the arena in which you operate, and the tools at hand your subordinates and their strengths and weaknesses. Applying these factors in the proper balance can make the difference between success and failure. In planning for your organization, you must be able to think *conceptually*, establishing a clear intent for your subordinates, filtering information from numerous sources with analysis and synthesis, and understanding the systems at your disposal. Lee did all of these things in preparation for the Overland Campaign.

Under normal circumstances, with a strong army, Lee would have fashioned a plan that involved taking the offensive and forcing Grant to react to his moves. The condition of his army made that option out of the question. He would have to fight on the defensive, hoping to damage Meade's army and break up Grant's campaign plans for 1864. The Confederacy's strategic options were by this time reduced to one: Hold on in the eastern and western theaters, locking Union armies in costly battles calculated to encourage the growing Northern sentiment for peace.

Lee filtered the information at hand, both about his own forces and about the enemy, to arrive at a feasible course of action given these imperatives. He knew that ex-General George McClellan was considering a run for the U.S. presidency in 1864 on the Democratic ticket, and McClellan was widely thought to advocate a negotiated peace. Many in the Army of Northern Virginia, from its commander down to the soldiers in the ranks, understood that holding on was their only realistic hope for victory. With Grant now traveling with the Army of the Potomac, this would be even more difficult. James Longstreet, Grant's good friend since their West Point and Mexican-American War days, remarked at the time that "that man will fight

---

Figure 3-2 Conceptual leadership skills.

Establishing Intent

Filtering Information

Understanding Systems

us every hour and every day." With Meade's army under Grant's watchful eye, the Confederates could not count on the cautious maneuvers and breathing spells that had characterized previous incarnations of the Army of the Potomac.[5]

Lee's defensive plan for the coming campaign rested on maneuvering to catch pieces of Meade's army as it crossed the Rapidan River. Lee had to assume that Meade would not make a frontal assault on his strong fortifications fronting the river. That left a movement either to the west, upriver along the Orange and Alexandria Railroad, or to the east, crossing downriver of Lee. Meade had tried the latter movement in the abortive Mine Run campaign the previous November, and Lee had stymied him without fighting a battle. However, an upriver crossing would take Meade away from Richmond and force him to rely on the tenuous single-track Orange and Alexandria Railroad for his supplies.

Based upon these deliberations, Lee operated on two assumptions: first, that Meade would cross downriver, and second, that he, Lee, would be able to react in time. A few miles east of Lee's camps was an area of thick woods, underbrush, and few roads called the Wilderness. In May 1863, Lee had used this confined terrain to even the odds between his army and Hooker's Army of the Potomac, winning the battle of Chancellorsville. The Wilderness robbed Union forces of two of their biggest tactical advantages: huge numbers of artillery pieces and masses of soldiers. The Wilderness could narrow the scope of battle and even the score somewhat between Lee and Meade. It was here that Lee hoped to bring Meade to battle, before the latter could emerge from the Wilderness into clearer terrain to the south and west, terrain that favored Union forces.[6]

> "I feel certain that we will whip Mr. Grant well, and that he will be sorry enough to have been put in command where Genl. Lee can get hold of him."

A tinge of the overoptimism that had doomed Lee at Gettysburg remained, however, in the form of his second major assumption: that his forces could move from a standing start and reach the Wilderness in time to hold the Union army there. This turned out to be exactly the case, but only because of problems with Union planning; the assumption was a dangerous one that exposed Lee's army to disaster should Meade get a jump on him. There is always something more, some unintended eventuality, for which you can plan.

As May 2 came and went, Lee completed his dispositions for the coming fight. Longstreet's First Corps remained in its camps near Gordonsville, with the mission of guarding both the army's left and the Virginia Central Railroad, the eastern Confederacy's main rail link with its breadbasket, the Shenandoah Valley. Remaining near the railroad also left Longstreet's corps able to move quickly to Richmond in case of a direct attack on the capital from some other direction. Hill's Third Corps formed the army's center near Orange Courthouse, and Ewell occupied the right of the line, making his the force closest to the enemy's expected route of march.

As the 1864 campaign was about to begin, Lee faced combat on terms that were unfamiliar to him, but his intent was clear to his generals as they met on Clark's Mountain. Heavy losses in 1863 had robbed his army of its offensive striking power. Hereafter, he would have to hope that his enemy telegraphed its punches, and to presume that his hard-marching veterans would make Grant pay for any misstep. Although much of their early-war jauntiness was gone, Lee's men radiated confidence. Lieutenant Colonel William M. Parsley of the Third North Carolina Infantry spoke for much of the army when we wrote to his sister, "I feel certain that we will whip Mr. Grant well, and that he will be sorry enough to have been put in command where Genl. Lee can get hold of him."[7]

Grant's Preparations: Reframing to Solve Persistent Problems

Does your organization have a persistent problem, one that you cannot solve? If so, do you continue to batter away at it in the tried-and-true method, hoping that something will change? In trying to defeat the Confederacy, the Union faced such a problem. Instead of attacking the problem in a traditional way, Grant proposed a solution that reframed it. In doing so, he was able to focus the Union war effort on attacking the old problem in a new way.

Grant made his visit to Washington in February for the purpose of planning, with Lincoln, the Union strategy for 1864. For three years, the Union Army had been unable, because of poor leadership and political infighting, to mount concerted offensives that placed pressure on the entire Confederacy at one time, taking advantage of the clear Union advantages in men and materiel. Grant saw these frustrations and compared the Union war effort to a balky mule team, with the mules always pulling at different times, never in concert with one another. When these offensives did not meet with success, Union generals hewed to the traditional rules of warfare and backed off, observing the traditional spring-to-autumn campaign season. These pauses enabled the Confederate forces to shift back and forth between the theaters to meet the greatest threat at any one time.

The fall of 1863 was a good example of how the Rebel army was able to shift its forces. As the Union forces under Rosecrans swept through Tennessee and into northern Georgia, Lee deemed the situation in the east safe enough, in the wake of Gettysburg, to transfer an entire army corps to the west to reinforce Braxton Bragg. These reinforcements helped the Army of Tennessee win at Chickamauga, effectively stymieing Union movement there for the rest of the year. Lee never really missed Longstreet, as Meade could not mount a large-scale offensive in Virginia that fall.[8]

> "Probably no army on earth ever before was in better condition in every respect than was the Army of the Potomac."

In Grant, Lincoln had a general with both the legal authority and the force of will to make the Union forces work together toward a common goal. The plan, as Grant explained it to Lincoln when they met in February, was to mount an offensive in all theaters of war simultaneously, with the Confederate armies themselves, instead of cities, as the primary objectives. These offensives would also, it was hoped, destroy the Confederacy's ability to supply its troops. Thus pressed from multiple directions, the Confederate armies would be overwhelmed and destroyed.

The overall offensive would consist of five separate movements. In the Deep South, General Nathaniel P. Banks would attempt to move from Louisiana into southern Alabama and capture Mobile, the last remaining Gulf Coast port in Southern hands. In Georgia, an army group under Sherman would move southward toward Atlanta, in the process breaking up Johnston's Army of Tennessee and nullifying Georgia as a source of supplies and industry for the Confederate war effort.

In Virginia, three generals would cooperate in sealing off Lee and destroying him. Franz Sigel, a German-American political general of questionable ability but with critical Democratic connections, would operate in the Shenandoah Valley, cutting Lee off from his main source of supplies. Meade would hammer Lee's army directly from across the Rapidan River, and a third force under Benjamin Butler would follow McClellan's old 1862 route, moving up the James River and threatening Richmond and Petersburg.

At the time that he conceived of this plan, Grant expected to remain in Georgia with Sherman, perceiving that theater to be the most critical to victory. But, as Grant went on to explain to Lincoln, it really mattered little which offensives were successful, as long as they all continued forward and worked together. This synergy of simple attrition would grind the Confederacy to pieces even if specific maneuvers failed. "Oh! Yes, I see that," Lincoln is reported to have exclaimed, going on to use a frontier analogy. "As we say out West, if a man can't skin he must hold a leg while somebody else does."9 With the broad outlines of the campaign in place and approved by the commander in chief, Grant took a short train ride to the headquarters of the Army of the Potomac to meet one of his chief subordinates, George G. Meade.

The mood in the camps of the Army of the Potomac was complicated. It became even *more* complicated on the rainy morning of March 20, when Grant's train pulled into Brandy Station, Virginia, a few miles north of the Rapidan River. Brandy Station was the nerve center, logistically and otherwise, for the largest, best-equipped army ever seen on the North American continent. According to

Map 3-1. Ulysses S. Grant's strategic plan for the 1864 campaign. (United States Military Academy)

Rufus Ingalls, the army's efficient quartermaster, "probably no army on earth ever before was in better condition in every respect than was the Army of the Potomac."[10] But, as Grant found out as he introduced himself to the army's commanders and staff, beneath this well-supplied façade, the Army of the Potomac faced some of the same leadership challenges as its Confederate opponent.

The airline industry sees a lot of high-profile failures. In the battle for the skies, airlines have focused on advertising such things as better food, more high-tech planes, luxury items, and movies. Rollin King and Herb Kelleher reframed the problem and focused on other issues: getting the passengers where they wanted to go on time at the lowest fare possible while making the flight fun. They believed that creating an airline that could consistently do these things would attract and keep customers. The success of Southwest Airlines proved them right.

The Army of the Potomac: Grant Inherits a New Organization

Taking the reins of a new or different organization is a significant emotional event in the life of any leader, because the decisions made in the first hours of taking charge can have lasting effects. Should you as a new leader step in and make wholesale changes in an effort to shake up a lethargic staff? Or should you sit back and quietly observe, and run the risk of perpetuating existing bad habits? Once he had made the decision to colocate himself with George Meade's Army of the Potomac, Grant had to solve this thorny leadership dilemma.

Part of the reason that Grant and Lincoln had a pressing need to reframe the problem of defeating the Confederacy was that the Union armies in the east and west had had very differing levels of success. Lincoln's western armies had enjoyed victory after victory throughout the war. In contrast, until Gettysburg, his eastern armies had known little but defeat. While these experiences had a lot to do with the quality of the enemies and the vagaries of fortune, two factors were critical: leadership and politics.

In the West, Lincoln had the luxury of having Grant, Sherman, Foote, and Porter, along with a capable cast of more junior officers. Union leadership in the east was uniformly poor at the army and corps levels, with some exceptions. For this reason, Lincoln had promoted Grant in the hopes of bringing western success to his eastern forces, particularly Meade's. Grant had a clear mandate from his boss: Change the culture and outlook of the Army of the Potomac.

Eastern generals also operated under the considerable handicap of their close proximity to Washington, D.C. The volunteer character of Civil War armies made them especially susceptible to political pressure; witness the federal government's Congressional Joint Committee on the Conduct of the War, a kangaroo court that focused its attention on Union military failure in the east simply because the capital was within easy telegraph range of the fighting front. For better or worse, western generals derived a good deal of latitude from being out of easy contact with the Lincoln administration. Grant faced a difficult situation when he inherited the mantle of general in chief.

Team Building: Grant and the Union Army High Command

Organizational leaders often face the challenge of building teams of subordinates. In building these teams, they must juggle all the factors we have already examined: their own leadership styles, the leadership styles of their subordinates, and the requirements and challenges that face them. Ulysses S. Grant and George G. Meade had two very different worldviews and two very different approaches to making war. Grant was a westerner by birth, of modest means, taciturn in demeanor, and directive in his dealings with others. While not an out-and-out Republican or abolitionist, he had a good deal in common with his antislavery president. As we have seen, his upbringing and outlook shaped his leadership style.

George G. Meade personified the eastern America of the nineteenth century, and his upbringing, too, shaped the way he led his organization. A Philadelphian of wealthy and prestigious background, he was also a plain-spoken man, but one of profoundly conservative outlook. Lincoln had preferred him to all other candidates to head the Army of the Potomac in 1863 because he was thought of as less involved than many other generals in the political machinations and cliques that had rendered the army inflexible and impotent. The Union victory at Gettysburg seemed to vindicate Lincoln's judgment.

> ". . . the feeling or wishes of no one person should stand in the way of selecting the right men for all positions."

As 1863 went on, however, the hero of Gettysburg became less and less popular in the Northern halls of power. His slow, deliberate pursuit of Lee after Gettysburg had allowed the Confederate army to return to home soil virtually unmolested. The autumn 1863 fighting in Virginia was inconclusive, culminating at Mine Run, where Meade earned the undying support of his men, and the undying censure of Washington, for flatly refusing to attack entrenched Confederate positions. For these supposed failures, Meade was summoned to defend his conduct before the Joint Committee on the Conduct of the War. Indeed, he had just returned from Washington when Grant went out to meet him at Brandy Station.[11]

Most, if not all, of the contemporary criticism of Meade was unjustified. He was a careful, competent soldier, but in politics, as in other areas of human endeavor, perception can become reality. For Lincoln, and for many other Northerners, Meade personified the spirit of caution and defeatism that had marked the Army of the Potomac for most of its existence. This perception was bound to make Meade's job even more difficult than it already was. For this reason, and perhaps because he sensed that some of the criticism leveled at Meade might have been justified, Grant changed his mind and planned to colocate himself in the field with the Army of the Potomac.[12]

Despite the differences between the two men, their relationship got off to a good start. Grant took a cautious approach to his new position, and Meade responded favorably. Meade, who was already in a bad mood because of his critics in the North's major newspapers, offered to step down as army commander and "take command of a corps" if Grant saw fit to replace him with his friend Sherman. Meade urged, Grant noted later, "that the feeling or wishes of no one person should stand in the way of selecting the right men for all positions."

Grant was impressed by this display of followership and retained Meade in command of the army. The two went on to have a fruitful discussion of the state of the Army of the Potomac. Meade wrote to his wife that "the views [Grant] expressed to me showed much more capacity and character than I had expected." Grant explained his overall plan to Meade, and expressed a desire to let Meade run the Army of the Potomac as he saw fit. Grant initially saw his role as that of a buffer between Meade and Washington, not as an orchestrator of the army's operations.[13]

If Grant took a step in the right direction in giving Meade the benefit of the doubt, he made a critical mistake in ignoring a significant deficiency in the high-command structure of Meade's army. This mistake points to the crucial importance of issues of hierarchy in organizational planning. Poorly thought-out relationships among senior leaders can sabotage even the best-laid plans.

The wild card in the Meade/Grant working relationship was Ambrose E. Burnside, commander of the Ninth Army Corps. The amiable Ohioan had served as the Army of the Potomac's commander in late 1862, and had had the dubious honor of presiding over that army's most lopsided defeat, the battle of Fredericksburg. Burnside and Meade were both major generals, but Burnside outranked Meade in seniority. His Ninth Corps was ordered south to cooperate with Meade, but not to work *for* him in the field. Thus, Grant would have to exercise operational command of both while Burnside "cooperated" with Meade in battle. This relationship was to cause important, and completely avoidable, problems in the weeks to come.[14]

Meade's three corps commanders reinforced Meade's natural tendencies toward cautious behavior and a participating leadership style. As a result, Grant differed in outlook not just from Meade, but from Meade's chief subordinates as well. Heading the Second

Corps, the army's largest, was Meade's most trusted subordinate, Winfield Scott Hancock. Known throughout the army without a trace of sarcasm as "Hancock the Superb," the Lancaster, Pennsylvania, native had excelled at every level of command, culminating at Gettysburg, where his men bore the brunt of Pickett's Charge. Hancock had sustained a serious wound at Gettysburg and in early 1864 was only just returning to active duty, still in considerable pain.

For command of the Fifth Corps, Meade elevated his chief engineer, Gouverneur Kemble Warren, another officer who traced his rise in prominence to Gettysburg. No one could doubt Warren's professional competence, but it remained to be seen whether he could exercise the duties of corps command. The Sixth Army Corps had an experienced major general, John Sedgwick, at the helm. Known affectionately to his men as "Uncle John," Sedgwick was reliable but cautious.

The organization of the army's infantry was solely of Meade's doing, but big changes in the army's mounted arm came directly from Grant. It was in the cavalry that Grant chose to exercise his prerogative to introduce a different style of warfare to Virginia. The Army of the Potomac's cavalry had suffered defeat after defeat at the hands of Jeb Stuart for much of the war, and only since mid-1863 was it beginning to achieve parity with the gray-clad troopers. Hoping to instill a more aggressive spirit in the cavalry, Grant brought in two westerners. He placed infantry division commander Philip Sheridan in charge of the cavalry, and he put an infantry brigadier general, James Wilson, in charge of a cavalry division.

This move was certainly in keeping with Grant's desire to infuse the eastern army with some of the swagger of its western counterpart, but it was to have unintended consequences in the form of a running feud between Sheridan and Meade over the proper use of cavalry. Grant knew Sheridan well, and by the spring of 1864 he knew Meade well enough to have been able to predict the friction that would develop between the two of them. As in the case of Burnside, Grant failed to pay adequate attention to matters of hierarchy and team building. All in all, though, the Army of the Potomac was in good hands; it remained to be seen whether the hierarchy that

Grant had cobbled together would hold up under the strains of active combat.[15]

Meade and Grant had an additional manpower problem that Lee did not have to face. Although on paper the Army of the Potomac outnumbered the Army of Northern Virginia by a wide margin, a significant percentage of its soldiers were three-year enlistees, and these enlistments expired in May 1864. Impending discharge from service was likely to make many soldiers unwilling to fight hard in the upcoming battles, and any replacements that the army received would be inexperienced.

Taking into account all of these issues, Meade's operational problem still boiled down to the same group of options as did Lee's: where to cross the Rapidan River, and on what line to operate. It was here that differences of opinion between Grant and Meade began to appear.

Leadership Using Centers of Gravity: The Union Plan Takes Shape

When you are trying to solve whatever problem your organization faces, where do you start? Do flagging sales point to a faulty advertising campaign? Do declining profits mandate changes in production or quality control? As you put your feet up and think about whatever issues you face, take a page from the military and try to think in terms of a center of gravity. To a general, a center of gravity is that facility, resource, or entity without which the enemy will fail. To cite a modern example, in planning Operation Desert Storm, U.S. leaders identified Iraq's Republican Guard divisions as Saddam Hussein's military center of gravity, and carried out a sustained bombing campaign to degrade their capabilities.

"When my troops are there," he pronounced, "Richmond is mine. Lee must retreat or surrender."

Your problem is not a military one, but it probably has a center of gravity. In the case of a faulty advertising campaign, it may be a key demographic that you have failed to reach. If you think in terms of a center of gravity, you may be able to see through confusion to the right course of action.

A similar debate occurred between Grant and Meade in the spring of 1864 as they pondered how to attack Lee. Meade advocated moving around Lee's western, or left, flank, in the direction of the Virginia Central Railroad. Grant, who was uncomfortable with separating himself from Burnside's Ninth Corps and Butler's Army of the James, which was operating against Richmond, preferred to move to outflank Lee on his right, or east. This route would take the army through the Wilderness, the scene of Union misfortunes the previous May. Implicit in this plan was Grant's understanding that the army would need to clear the Wilderness quickly so that it could emerge into the more open ground to the south. A lightning movement of this type would both remove the Wilderness as a defensive position for Lee and put the Army of the Potomac well south of Lee's prepared entrenchments.

After a good deal of debate, Grant's plan won out. Hindsight has shown that it made the most sense for a variety of reasons, not the least of which being that it offered the best supply lines for Meade's massive army. With the issue decided, Meade's chief of staff, Andrew A. Humphreys, drew up the orders that would put the army in motion. Meade grumbled a bit about being overruled, but the relationship between Meade and Grant remained positive.

On the evening of May 3, Grant held a meeting with his staff that was equivalent to Lee's Clark's Mountain conference. As he and the staff gathered around a map, Grant sketched the broad outlines of the impending campaign, omnipresent cigar in hand. He speculated that defeat at the hands of Meade would cause Lee to fall back to the Richmond fortifications, leading to a decisive battle near the Confederate capital. As if to punctuate this point, Grant circled with his finger a line around the Richmond–Petersburg area. "When my troops are there," he pronounced, "Richmond is mine. Lee must retreat or surrender."[16] On both sides of the Rapidan, all was in readiness for the beginning of the Overland Campaign.

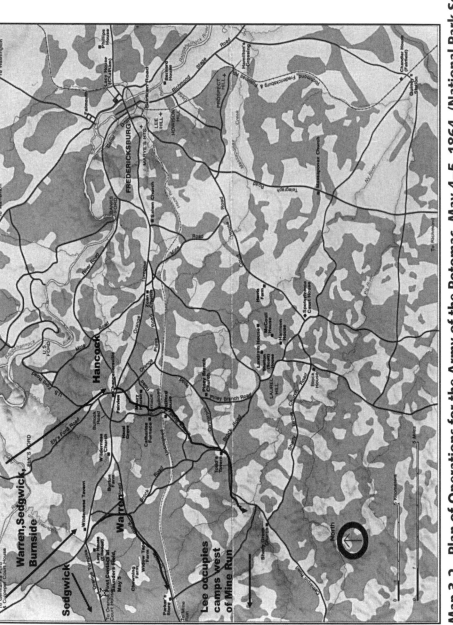

Map 3-2. Plan of Operations for the Army of the Potomac, May 4–5, 1864. (National Park Service)

Organizational Planning and You

Your organization has a center of gravity, too. Just as Lee and Grant did in the spring of 1864, you need to do your best to find it, organize your people to carry out your plan, apply good followership in supporting those above you, and move forward to success.

In their preparations for the Overland Campaign, Lee and Grant gave the modern leader both positive and negative examples of organizational planning. Just as Lee attempted to divine his enemy's center of gravity—the Northern public's will to continue the struggle—and attack it, Grant followed the same process. He saw the Confederate center of gravity as its interior lines and the relative safety of its hinterlands up to this point in the war. Both generals rightly crafted plans designed to target their foe's center of gravity, but they did so without completely reconciling their plans and objectives with the personnel available to carry them out.

Leadership Lessons

- *Try to match subordinates to your intent, and understand the systems that are at your disposal.* If your subordinates are not up to the challenges you present, they may fail to execute a great plan. Think carefully about what they can accomplish in the near term. Small initial successes may pave the way for your ultimate objectives. In Lee's case, only time would tell if his generals could apply his aggressive, decentralized leadership style against a new and more capable foe. Grant risked failure by asking Meade and his generals to throw caution to the winds and follow Lee to the death.

- *Analyze, synthesize, conceptualize.* Thinking in an ordered, comprehensive way allows you to filter the available information, make valid assumptions where necessary, and take calculated risks. Lee and Grant faced a myriad of military, political, and personal considerations as they set out to plan the Overland Campaign, and both came up with solid, workable plans because they tackled the problem in this way.

- *When in doubt, reframe.* Quit beating your team's collective head against a wall, and think about new and different ways to solve the same problems. Grant did this well; the approach he decided upon would give the Union victory a year after he instituted it.

- *Pay attention to hierarchy when building teams.* Grant ignored this key consideration at his peril. His relationship with Meade and the army's three corps commanders was initially productive, but he tolerated one really dysfunctional arrangement—Burnside and the Ninth Corps—and introduced another himself in the person of Sheridan.

- *Seek a center (or centers) of gravity.* Planning in this way can help you to avoid devoting unnecessary effort and expense to projects that may seem promising, but in the end detract from your long-term objectives. Lee and Grant were both especially good at this. They both thought hard about their enemy's weak points and designed operations to target them. Lee would certainly have preferred to go over to the offensive in the spring of 1864, but he knew that his army was simply incapable of this type of operation. A stout defense would bleed Grant's forces and drag out the contest until the 1864 presidential election.

Grant applied a similar logic in formulating his plans for the war in Virginia. A war of maneuver and sieges would lessen casualties and might lead to the capture of Richmond, but would also prolong the war, and might in the end fail to do anything to move the Union closer to victory. A strategy that targeted Lee and his army was the right approach. The next few weeks would determine whether Grant had in the Army of the Potomac the tools he needed to carry it out.

CHAPTER FOUR

The Wilderness

From Planning to Execution

"This region is an awful place to fight in. The utmost extent of vision is about one hundred yards. Artillery cannot be used effectively. The wounded are liable to be burned to death. I am willing to take my chances of getting killed, but I dread to have a leg broken and then to be burned slowly; and these woods will surely be burned if we fight here. I hope we will get through this chapparal without fighting."[1]

—A UNION SOLDIER'S DESCRIPTION OF THE WILDERNESS.

"If an opportunity presents itself for pitching into a part of Lee's army, do so without giving time for dispositions."[2]

—ULYSSES S. GRANT, DISPATCH TO GEORGE G. MEADE, MAY 5, 1864.

A frequently heard aphorism in military circles is, "No plan survives contact with the enemy." This certainly holds true in the business world as well. The best-laid, best-thought-out plans will often require significant alteration as circumstances change. Conceptual thinking and organizational planning will get your team to the starting line, but your ability to adjust your plan and help your subordinates to execute it will determine your success or failure. And if things really fall apart, how will you respond? Will you have the capability to lead by example and get things back on the right track? Robert E. Lee and Ulysses S. Grant faced these challenges in the first battle of the Overland Campaign, the Battle of the Wilderness.

Crossing the Rapidan: The Importance of Staffs in Organizational Leadership

At this point in your career, you have no doubt discovered that, more often than not, the capabilities of your subordinates determine your successes and your failures. This was no less true for Lee and Grant. As the Union army crossed the Rapidan River on May 4, Grant had the benefit of a large and capable staff, two staffs in fact—his and Meade's. Lee had to rely on a staff that was frequently not large enough to accomplish the tasks of army command, and this deficiency got the Confederate defense off to a rather rocky start.

> Grant felt that he might end up fighting his new army as much as he was fighting the rebels.

"I know the greatest anxiety is now felt in the North for the success of this move, and that the anxiety will increase when it is known that the Army is in motion. . . . I believe it has never been

---

Figure 4-1 Planning to execution.

Build a staff that can assist you.

Maintain initiative and momentum.

Allow the plan to work.

Steady, steady!

Lead by example.

Demonstrate moral courage.

my misfortune to be placed where I have lost my presence of mind, unless indeed it has been when thrown in strange company, particularly that of ladies. . . . Love and Kisses for you and Jess. Ulys." After writing this letter to his wife and snatching a few hours' sleep, General Ulysses S. Grant departed from his camp north of the Rapidan River and followed the Army of the Potomac as it crossed into enemy territory. Observers moving with the headquarters group noted that the normally plainly dressed general was resplendent in a new uniform.

Accompanying him, dressed all in black and looking conspicuously like an undertaker, was Grant's political mentor, Congressman Elihu Washburne of Illinois. Grant probably did not need this reminder of the immense political and military stakes for which he was playing, but there it was. As his letter to Julia hinted, Grant felt that he might end up fighting his new army as much as he was fighting the rebels.[3]

The initial stages of the Union Army's movement went almost exactly according to plan, though. Warren's Fifth Corps was to lead the march, stepping off just after midnight for the Rapidan crossing at Germanna Ford, the idea being to use the darkness to steal a few hours' lead on Bobby Lee. Once across, Warren was to move southwest, aiming at Lee's camps on the other side of Mine Run. Sedgwick's Sixth Corps would follow Warren and move westward on the Orange Turnpike, and a Union cavalry division would screen this movement of the right flank of Meade's army. Further to the east, Hancock's Second Corps would form the army's left, crossing the Rapidan and moving through the old Chancellorsville battlefield. Hancock would move a bit further south, then turn west to pull up alongside Warren.

This arrangement would put the Army of the Potomac across Lee's right flank, threatening his lines of supply and his communication southward. Once reunited, the three corps would let the army's supply trains catch up and use the Wilderness as a staging base for an attack on Lee's army. This tactical plan rested on the implicit assumption, shared by Grant and Meade, that the battle would occur not in the tangled Wilderness, but in the more open country to the west and south. This was a complex plan, with a lot of moving parts. Fortunately for Grant, his generals and his troops were up to it.

For several hours on May 4, it looked as if Grant's assumptions would turn out to be facts. A Union signal station on Pony Mountain reported no movement out of the Confederate camps until well after 9:30 that morning; the blue columns had been on the move for almost eight hours by that time. Union cavalrymen reported only isolated contact with Confederate pickets, and as the Federal infantrymen occupied their camps after a long, dusty day's march that afternoon, it seemed to many of them that the rebels were a long way off.

This seeming Confederate inactivity was deceiving, however. Lee's signal station on Clark's Mountain had begun reporting Federal movements before dawn, and by mid-morning Lee knew that Grant was in motion. Before he could respond, however, Lee had to determine upon which flank his enemy was moving. For this intelligence, he turned to Jeb Stuart. Confederate horsemen soon confirmed that Union forces were moving by Lee's right flank. This was enough for Lee to put his army in motion. Ewell's Second Corps and Hill's Third Corps vacated their camps around noon, and by nightfall they were facing eastward along Mine Run, ready to strike. Lee knew at this point that to remain in his old position was to invite disaster in the form of an encirclement, but to retreat south to the next natural defensive barrier, the North Anna River, was merely to postpone inevitable defeat.

The best remaining option, then, was to attack eastward and attempt to bottle up the Army of the Potomac inside the Wilderness. If Lee could hold Grant in position for May 4 and most of May 5, Longstreet's First Corps could arrive from Gordonsville to administer a killing flank attack. Grant's initial movement was adroitly executed, but Lee's response was intelligent and appropriate. The Union Army was across the river, but as long as it remained in the Wilderness, Lee was in no greater danger than he had been in the past.

This plan was certainly in keeping with Lee's audacious approach to battle, but given the wide disparity in troop strength—Lee initially had five divisions to Grant's ten—it left a great deal more to chance than usual. Given that Lee had predicted precisely this Union move, why had he not positioned Longstreet closer to the Wilderness? As it was, the First Corps had to endure a twenty-mile forced march on May 4, and almost the same on May 5, just to move within striking distance of the Union left flank. Even then, this plan allowed for no delays on Longstreet's part, and it exposed the rest of Lee's army to the possibility of defeat before he even arrived. Why leave so much to chance?

In his memoir, Confederate artillery officer Porter Alexander, who at the time of the Overland Campaign was serving with Longstreet, asserted that "lack of an abundance of trained & professional soldiers in the staff corps to make constant studies of all matters of detail" led to Lee's failure to position his troops to counter Grant's crossing of the Rapidan. By contrast, Alexander thought, the Union armies "owed their final success to the precision with which they combined some of their great movements, which are models of logistics—the science of moving armies."[4]

If Robert E. Lee had any great failing as an organizational leader, it was his reluctance to surround himself with a staff commensurate with his military duties. Throughout his time as an army commander, Lee was known to retain only a very small staff, and to use those officers only to conduct the regular business of the army headquarters. He was known never to consult his staff officers on questions of strategy or operations, but rather only on "matters of routine" around headquarters.

In May 1864, Lee's personal staff numbered only three men to accomplish the myriad of administrative responsibilities that Alexander alluded to.[5] Because his staff was so small, Lee had to do a great deal more work than he might have otherwise, leading to Alexander's comment that a larger, more professional staff might have pointed out to Lee the flaw in his dispositions against Grant. Ostensibly, Lee had left Longstreet at Gordonsville for easy access to the Virginia Central Railroad and Richmond, but a larger, more competent staff could have recommended troop positions that took both possibilities into account.

In contrast to Lee, Grant made the effort to surround himself with a large, professionally trained staff. Meade's Army of the Potomac staff contributed to this collective body of expertise, and the result was a solid plan for turning the tables on the Confederate foe. If you have the latitude to make such personnel moves in your own organization, do not let hubris or an overestimation of your own abilities blind you to the need for top-flight advisers. They can help you in the transition from planning to execution.

Lee and Grant in the Leadership Transition to Execution

The U.S. Army's modern leadership doctrine holds that an effective leader operates in two distinct realms. First, the leader makes plans and builds teams; it stands to reason that no organization will be successful without this groundwork. But once the planning is done, the leader *operates* and *executes*.[6]

We could certainly say that Lee fell short in the first of these realms by failing to plan his countermoves in depth. But he recovered and acted appropriately, and, most importantly, he did not panic when he was faced with an aggressive move by his opponent. Grant and Meade failed in both realms, first by planning on a highly suspect assumption, and second by letting initiative and momentum slip away in the glow and comfort of initial success. Plan to the best of your ability, but ensure that you execute in a spirit of pessimism. What could go wrong now? Have I accounted for that eventuality? If you can answer these questions, you can avoid unpleasant surprises.

For their part, Grant and Meade also came up short in the areas of being proactive and taking the initiative on May 4. Their assumption that Lee would stay behind Mine Run while the Union Army maneuvered at will was questionable at best, but as May 4 ended, the success of the first day's advance reinforced this mindset in the Union camp. Lee had acted in this uncharacteristic manner the previous November because he was without Longstreet's corps, but the defensive mindset had never been foremost in Lee's nature. Put simply, building what could have been the war's deciding campaign on this assumption flew in the face of the experience of the past two years.

Why think in this way? Again, one must presume that Grant, still an outsider here, approved this plan out of a lack of experience with Lee. It is true that constant worry about the "worst-case scenario" can sap an organization's drive and will, but here again we see Grant's inherent overconfidence asserting itself. Just as thoughts that his enemy was beaten led him to leave his guard down at Shiloh, the belief that Lee would not attack shaped Federal thinking on May 4.

Meade compounded this faulty thinking by ordering his two largest cavalry divisions to guard the army's supply trains from Confederate cavalry, leaving one understrength division to screen the entire army's front. The division commander was one of the stable of officers whom Grant had brought with him from his previous operations out west, and this would be his debut as a cavalryman. He would be responsible for a front of over three miles in width, and difficult terrain would compound his problems. As a result, Lee's troops moved virtually unopposed and undetected into their jump-off positions during the night of May 4. Caught initially in a difficult position, Lee recovered and was in a solid position as night fell over the Wilderness. One leader on this battlefield, Robert E. Lee, continued to seek the initiative, and this personal energy allowed him to salvage what was clearly a faulty plan.

The Armies Clash: Allowing the Plan to Work

Organizational leaders who successfully translate plans into action must react to unforeseen circumstances without scrapping the original plan. On May 5, the desire of Meade and his generals to overcome their reputation for caution led them to wreck the Union army's carefully laid plan. Grant was a willing accomplice; against their specific plans, the battle that developed that day occurred in the Wilderness, the worst possible place for the blue-clad army to fight Lee. What is more, Grant the organizational leader abandoned his carefully laid plans through a desire to come to grips with Lee. Had Grant paused for just a moment as the day developed to listen to his subordinates, he might not have been drawn into battle on ground of Lee's choosing. As it was, the Overland Campaign took a tragic turn on its second day.

As May 5 dawned, Meade planned to continue his movement through the Wilderness, while Lee planned to stop Meade precisely where he was. The first clash occurred west of Wilderness Tavern, where the Orange Turnpike split an open area known locally as Saunders' Field. This is one of those places where the modern visitor can really go back in time and feel the ghosts of the past. The field and its surrounding woods have changed little, if at all, in the intervening century and a half. Take away the pavement on the modern road and the few monuments that bear mute testimony to the battle, and a Union or Confederate soldier transported to the future would recognize the place immediately.

The soldiers of Warren's Fifth Corps division had the dubious honor of making the first contact with the enemy. Warren's two lead divisions broke camp at dawn and continued their movement to the southwest, taking an unimproved woods road that would eventually lead out of the Wilderness. This much of the morning's activity was according to plan. Warren's third division remained in reserve.

The Union high command assumed that the cavalry had all approaches from the west covered, but that assumption was about to go badly wrong. The inexperienced Grant protégé, James Wilson, left no horsemen to cover the Orange Turnpike. He disappeared into the woods to the south and would not be heard from for several hours. Meanwhile, some of Warren's men were preparing to leave their campsite at about nine a.m. when they were startled to see dust clouds looming above the turnpike. Gray-clad cavalry appeared, followed by long lines of infantry—Ewell's Confederate Second Corps, three divisions of troops.

At this point, the Union plan fell to pieces. Acting on their shared assumption that the Confederate force in front of them was only a scouting expedition and that the main rebel line remained at Mine Run, Warren and Meade planned to attack to "punish" the Confederates (and by implication show their new general-in-chief that they could fight). Warren's entire corps would stop its enveloping march around Lee's flank, form lines of battle facing to the west, and attack. Waiting several miles to the south, Hancock would have to turn his corps around and move northeast in order to support Warren's left flank. Hancock's initial objective would the intersection of the Plank Road and the Brock Road.

Out along the Orange Plank Road, Lee continued to seek the initiative in an effort to fight the coming battle on his own terms. He pushed his Third Corps to the east along the Orange Plank Road, and by mid-afternoon he had effectively split the Union army into pieces that were unable to support one another in the difficult terrain. Only hard fighting by Hancock's Second Corps saved the Plank Road/Brock Road intersection for the Union army. Thus, by midday on May 5, Meade's and Grant's faulty assumptions and erroneous dispositions were creating the conditions for a Union disaster. The battle was about to occur in precisely the place Grant least wanted to fight Lee; like two daggers, the Confederate Second and Third Corps were poised to slash into the disjointed Union position.[7]

> "Men disappeared as if the earth had swallowed them."

At Saunders' Field, minutes stretched into hours with no attack. This pause came at a critical time; Grant could have used it to think better of being sidetracked by Lee's aggressiveness, but he did not. Even as you move into execution and operations, do not miss the chance to take a moment to reevaluate before you continue with your plan. Aggressiveness and flexibility do not always equal solid execution; in this case, Grant the organizational leader could have stepped in and kept his generals "on task," but he did not, whether out of an aggressive instinct or through a complete misreading of his enemy. Grant could fairly easily have entrenched part of his army at the edge of the field and covered his movement to the southwest. Indeed, part of the army, the Second Corps, was already out in open country several miles to the south of the Wilderness.

At 7 a.m., conditions seemed to Warren to be ripe for an attack, and Meade assented, no doubt pleased to see a spark of aggressiveness in one of his corps commanders. Warren saw what was developing in front of him, though, and thought better of attacking. His line ended abruptly just north of Saunders' Field, and Sedgwick's Sixth Corps was still struggling through thick woods in an attempt to come in on Warren's right. In the meantime, the Confederate troops were extending their line to overlap his flank, and he could see them digging entrenchments in the woodline. Warren advised Meade to wait until Sedgwick was up, but Meade would have none of it. There was a sense throughout the army that its bravery was being called into question. Meade's response to Warren's entreaties was peremptory: "We are waiting for you."[8] Just after noon, Warren's men moved forward in a ragged line, and the Battle of the Wilderness was underway in deadly earnest.

The colonel of the 140th New York Infantry had called an attack across Saunders' Field "nonsense," and his prediction was right on the mark. A series of futile charges moved back and forth across the field and the thick woods to the south, and soon the four-hundred-yard stretch between the opposing lines was scattered with Union dead and wounded. A soldier of the 140th remembered that his "regiment melted away like snow. Men disappeared as if the earth had swallowed them." On the other side of the field, a Louisiana soldier in Colonel Leroy Stafford's brigade described the unequal contest: "The enemy's ranks were as thick as blackbirds," he wrote, "and the way we poured lead into them was a sin." Ewell's men occupied hastily dug trenches in the field's western woodline and would not be dislodged. Warren's attack was over in ninety minutes, and the Union plan lay in shambles, the victim of misplaced aggressiveness.

Sedgwick eventually came in along Warren's right, extending the Union line northward, and attacked at 3 p.m. Like Warren's troops south of Saunders' Field, Sedgwick's men became hopelessly tangled in the undergrowth, and got their lines straightened out only to run into Ewell's prepared defenses. This was an ideal position for Ewell, and the Union attack on Lee's Second Corps had ground to a halt by nightfall.[9] In an attempt to demonstrate that his army could act aggressively, Meade had abandoned a well-conceived operational plan and committed his army to the attack in a piecemeal fashion. The real fault, however, lay with the organizational leader: Ulysses S. Grant.

Another key to solid organizational leadership is the ability to delegate authority to capable subordinates and then stay out of their way, even if things don't go exactly as planned. The victim in this case was the Fifth Corps commander, Gouverneur K. Warren. At Saunders' Field, the army's newest corps commander also offered his own lesson in followership. Warren was a precise, often difficult, subordinate, with a tendency to question his orders to the point where he became a liability. He had gained a good reputation among his men the previous autumn at Mine Run by flatly refusing to attack entrenched Confederate positions; at Saunders' Field he began to exhibit the difficult nature that was his darker side. When Griffin's men first spotted rebels at Saunders' Field, Warren sent a dispatch to Meade that had the tone of a lecture: "Such demonstrations [by the Confederates] are to be expected, and show the necessity for keeping well closed and prepared to face toward Mine Run and meet an attack at a moment's notice."[10]

Warren went on to advocate an attack, but then revised his opinion when the size of the enemy in front of him became apparent. Warren's misgivings about the attack were well founded, but the atmosphere of mistrust, frustration, and unfamiliarity that surrounded the army's high command turned this disagreement, at least in Grant's mind, into yet another example of the Army of the Potomac's inability to close with and destroy the enemy. Warren did not work well with his superiors, and he made this situation worse as the morning went on. In this case, Warren's reputation for difficulty led Grant and Meade in effect to "shoot the messenger" instead of listening to a capable subordinate.

Effective organizational leadership is a two-way street. Warren could have served his case better by observing proper professional decorum, but his failures do not absolve Grant from guilt for not listening to him. Had Grant listened to Warren in this situation, he might have been able to get his plan back on track on May 6.

The dysfunctional state of Grant's high command on May 5 offers a distinct lesson in organizational communication. Leaders should strive to separate their feelings about subordinates from the information that those subordinates provide. Try to take information at face value, especially in stressful situations that may lead to miscommunication. On the other side of the coin, remember that the tone and manner with which you pass information up the chain has a great deal to do with how it is received. At Saunders' Field, Grant's aggressiveness and Warren's prickly personality inhibited the flow of information, with dire consequences for the soldiers of the Fifth Corps.

Steadiness in the Face of Frustration

The Wilderness was clearly the last place that Grant wanted to come to blows with Lee. Nevertheless, his frustration with the way the battle developed never leaked out to his subordinates. In pressure situations, the people around you will take their cues from how you behave, and Grant had a steadying influence on the army on May 5.

> "While the most critical movements were taking place, General Grant manifested no perceptible anxiety, but gave his orders, and sent and received communications, with a coolness which made a marked impression" on everyone around him.

His aide Horace Porter wrote that instead of rushing from place to place as events developed, Grant placed his headquarters in an easily accessible spot near the Rapidan River, sat on a stump, and commenced whittling a stick as reports on the battle came in.

Many historians and observers have latched onto this peculiar behavior. Porter and others seem to have found the whittling very soothing, as if nothing else worried the commanding general. At one point, when Confederate artillery shells began landing near the headquarters, a staff officer suggested that they move back across the river and out of danger. The reply he got was vintage Grant. As he smoked his cigar, Grant said in a calm voice, "It strikes me it would be better to order up some artillery and defend the present location." Porter noted that "While the most critical movements were taking place, General Grant manifested no perceptible anxiety, but gave his orders, and sent and received communications, with a coolness which made a marked impression" on everyone around him.[11] If Grant did nothing else during this battle, he inspired subordinates with his self-confidence and demeanor, no mean feat given the circumstances.

The nature of the Wilderness battlefield, with its two east-west roads, the Turnpike and the Plank Road, meant that the armies in effect were fighting two separate battles. In the south, on the Plank Road, Hancock's Union Second Corps and A. P. Hill's Confederate Third Corps faced off. Getty's Sixth Corps division held the critical Plank Road/Brock Road intersection, and the combative Getty even launched a counterattack against Heth's division, but he would need the support of the Second Corps to do any more.

After several frustrating countermarches in response to Meade's orders, the Second Corps reached the intersection and attacked shortly after 4:30. In the tangled woods on either side of the Plank Road, Hancock's men grappled with Hill's veterans. This was a brutal struggle, in which the opposing lines could not see each other until they were literally only a few feet apart. The bloody slugging match lasted until dark, with both lines of battle refusing to yield.

A concerted attack by either corps was impossible because of the dense woods and the noise and smoke of battle. As Lee sent Wilcox's division to assist Heth, Meade sensed an opportunity to unite the two wings of his army by having Crawford's Fifth Corps division attack southwest into Hill's left flank. Darkness, confusion, and an obstinate defense saved Heth and Wilcox; on this end of the field, blue outnumbered gray by a handy margin. The brutality of the fighting, which had mangled several Union brigades and killed one of Hancock's brigade commanders, also put the Federals in a defensive mindset. In the end, both sides were glad to see darkness call a halt to the fighting. Hancock's corps entrenched in the Brock Road, and Hill's men collapsed literally where they had fought. A short distance to their rear lay one of the few open spaces in the Wilderness, a field surrounding the cabin of the widow Catharine Tapp.[12]

In spite of what he deemed lost opportunities, Grant pronounced himself "pretty well satisfied with the results of the en-

gagement," a sure indicator that Grant was a "glass is half full" sort
of thinker. He believed that Lee had failed "to strike this army in
flank before it could be put into line of battle," and that since Burnside and Longstreet had not yet been engaged, the fighting of May
5 "has not been much of a test of strength."[13] These assessments
attest to Grant's combativeness; in these same woods a year earlier,
another Union army commander, "Fighting Joe" Hooker, had suffered a stinging blow from Lee's army and decided to end his campaign in a retreat. Grant planned to renew the attack, judging Hill's
corps (rightly) to be stretched to its breaking point. He issued orders for Burnside to come in on Hancock's right flank at dawn, and
for Hancock to launch a renewed attack at the same time. Caught in
this overwhelming vise, Hill would be destroyed.

Leadership Failure: Fatigue and Overconfidence Take Their Toll on Lee and Hill

William T. Pogue, an artillery commander in the Third Corps, was
emplacing his guns there at dawn the next morning, and "was surprised to see the unusual condition of things. Nearly all the men
were still asleep. One long row of muskets was stacked in the [Or-
ange Plank] road . . . and here and there could be seen bunches of
stacked guns." A nearby officer ex-

> "D— it , Heth, I don't want to hear any more about it; the men shall not be disturbed!"

plained to him that he "supposed
they [the enemy] were in the
woods in front." The officer struck
Pogue "as being very indifferent and not at all concerned about
the situation." During the night, Heth and Wilcox reported that the
fighting had left their lines "like a worm fence, at every angle," instead of aligned with one another and facing toward the enemy. A
soldier on the scene wrote that "none of the brigades seemed to be
in line—some regiments isolated entirely from brigades—in fact, no
line at all, but just as they had fought."[14]

Why did the Third Corps not entrench or straighten its lines? Who was to blame? The night of May 5–6 was destined to become one of the most controversial in the history of the Army of Northern Virginia, and it appears that there was blame enough for all concerned.

Robert E. Lee guarded his thoughts and memories of the Civil War very closely; as a result, he never explained his critical failure to demand that Hill fortify his lines on the night of May 5. Whether the unexpected ferocity of Grant's offensive took him by surprise, whether he was simply exhausted, or whether he still believed himself the master of his enemy, Lee remained in camp and did nothing. He learned at about 9 p.m. that Longstreet's corps would not arrive on the field until dawn, but nevertheless he told Hill after midnight to let the troops rest where they lay. Hill's chief of staff reported that Hill had repeatedly requested permission to adjust his lines, but that Lee refused. For that reason, and also because he continued to suffer from bouts of sickness, Hill did not direct Heth and Wilcox to adjust their lines of battle or to dig hasty entrenchments in case of enemy attack. When Heth visited Hill for a *third time* to question this decision, he received a response that would be familiar to any subordinate questioning a tired or overwrought boss: "D— it, Heth, I don't want to hear any more about it; the men shall not be disturbed!" Wilcox went directly to Lee, who repeated the contention that Longstreet would relieve him.[15]

In light of subsequent events, this episode touched off a firestorm of controversy, and various generals attempted to deflect the blame for what happened a few hours later. Perhaps the small size of Lee's staff prevented him from exercising control of his units; additional well-placed staff officers might have been more effective in communicating the state of Third Corps to the commanding general. For his part, Hill spent much of May 5 in an ambulance, unable to exercise command of his corps.

Hill's and Wilcox's actions highlight two critical points of leadership and followership: the impact of poor health on decision-making capability and the importance of empowering subordinates to make hard, necessary decisions, sometimes in contravention of a superior. Cadmus Wilcox was an experienced soldier, and no doubt had that sick feeling in the pit of his stomach that more needed to be done that night. He did not act on that feeling, however, and with this bizarre episode, the woods and lowlands fell silent, except for the cries of wounded soldiers.

"Lee to the Rear": Leadership by Example Redeems a Bad Decision

As May 6 dawned over the Wilderness, the men of A. P. Hill's Third Corps were due to feel the impact of their leaders' mistakes and Grant's persistence. Burnside was late getting into position, but at 5 a.m. Hancock's entire corps came screaming out of the woods surrounding the Tapp clearing, and Hill's line of battle dissolved like sand before an approaching tide. William T. Pogue, the artilleryman who had emplaced his guns in the Tapp field at dawn, described the scene: "Pop! Pop! Began the skirmishers and soon a terrific outbreak of musketry showed that the enemy were attacking in force . . . soon our men were seen to be falling back slowly on the right of the road." Pogue understated the disaster facing Lee; the Third Corps began to disintegrate before his eyes. For Union troops used to being on the receiving end of such attacks, this was an enjoyable experience; in the words of one Second Corps soldier, they "turned the Rebs right out of their blankets."[16]

Hancock's men had victory within their grasp, but Lee had one card left to play. Longstreet's men were in the last stages of a grueling forty-hour, thirty-five-mile forced march from Gordonsville, but they were not yet on the field. Lee needed to buy time for their arrival, and he turned to Pogue's gunners. They and some of Hill's men delayed the Unionists in the Tapp field, and soon Longstreet's veterans came running into view, two divisions abreast, on the Orange Plank Road. Men in the ranks reported that they covered the last part of the march at the "double quick," a jogging pace. Hill's chief of staff shook Longstreet's hand, no doubt with evident relief: "Ah, General, we have been looking for you since 12 o'clock last night." Joe Kershaw's and Charles Field's divisions deployed directly from the march into line of battle on either side of the Plank Road and checked the Federal advance. It was 6 a.m.

The next few minutes saw one of the war's most frequently re-told scenes, and it marked a watershed in Lee's command of the Army of Northern Virginia: the first situation, after two years of com-bat, in which Lee felt compelled to intervene personally on the battle-field in order to stave off disaster.

> "Go back men, you can beat those people."

Although Lee wrote later that day to Secretary of War James Seddon that "the enemy advanced and created some confusion," this bland description did not include his response.

Before Longstreet arrived, Lee steered his horse Traveller among the men of the Third Corps, who were now fleeing from the fighting. Lee attempted to jar his men back to their duty by calling upon subordinates he recognized. To a group of Georgians, Lee said "Go back men, you can beat those people." To a brigade commander, Samuel McGowan of South Caro-lina, he called out: "My God! Gen-

> "He was perfectly com-posed, but his face ex-pressed a kind of grim determination."

eral McGowan, is this splendid brigade of yours running like a flock of geese?" McGowan's protests to the contrary, these attempts were of no avail; it was up to Longstreet, now arriving literally in the nick of time.[17]

As Charles Field's First Corps division moved into the Tapp clearing and approached Pogue's line of guns, Lee fell in behind the famed Texas Brigade, commanded here by John Gregg. In a war full of famous units on both sides, perhaps none earned greater fame than "Lee's Grenadier Guard," the First, Fourth, and Fifth Texas and Third Arkansas Regiments, 850 strong on this day. Several ob-servers remarked that the usually taciturn Lee was unusually ex-cited, "moved to tears" in one man's estimation. Behind Pogue's guns, Lee asked the forming men to identify themselves. "Texas boys," they replied. "Hurrah for Texas!" Lee responded, along with an entreaty to drive the Unionists back, and offered to lead them in person. As they continued forward, Lee ignored scattered calls for him to move away from the firing, screaming "Texans always move them!" As Gregg formed the brigade for its attack, Lee walked Traveller behind the line of battle. After a few steps, some of the Texans noticed that Lee was still with them, and a growing chorus demanded, "Go back, General Lee, go back. We won't go forward until you go back."[18]

William T. Pogue, on the scene with his guns, noted that Lee had recovered his usual calm presence, and seemed energized by the moment: "He was perfectly composed, but his face expressed a kind of grim determination. I had not observed either at Sharpsburg or Gettysburg." It was clear that Lee intended to go forward with the Texans, but the troops would have none of it. One or more soldiers grabbed Traveller's reins and directed horse and rider away from the fight, and Gregg continued to plead with Lee to move away. A soldier in the Fourth Texas wrote that one of his comrades exclaimed, "Go back General Lee, go back! We have whipped them before, and damn 'em, we can whip 'em again!" A member of the Fifth Texas, with tears streaming down his cheeks, announced that he would "charge hell itself for that old man."

And charge it was. Lee moved to the rear, and with a bloodcurdling scream, the Texas Brigade launched itself into the Tapp field, slamming into Hancock's men and driving them back in one of the war's most furious charges. Gregg's men paid for their glory as they had on other fields, in blood. More than 550 of the 850 were killed or wounded in the charge; their brigadier's horse received five wounds, but Gregg himself miraculously survived. It was now the turn of Hancock's men to do the retreating; they fell back toward the critical Plank Road/Brock Road intersection almost a mile behind them.[19] This remarkable event cemented Lee's image in the minds of his men, but also underscored the desperation of the fighting in the Wilderness.

At this moment, Robert E. Lee also demonstrated the electric effect that a leader's presence can have on subordinates. Good leadership not only gets the job done but inspires *passion* along the way.

Map 4-1. The Battle of the Wilderness, position of the armies on May 7, 1864. (National Park Service)

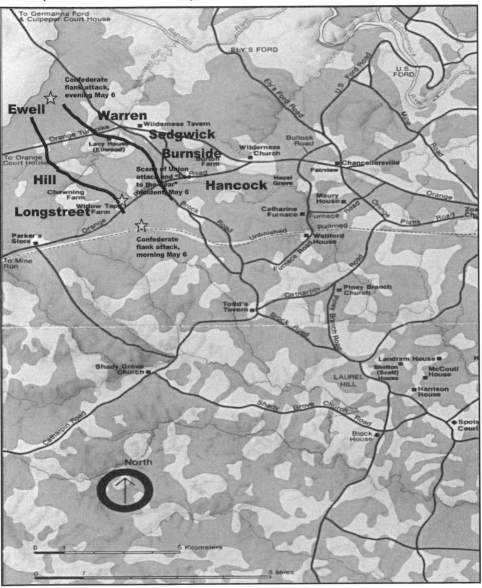

Steadiness in the Face of Adversity: The Leader's Hallmark

There may be times in the life of your organization that your calm, reassuring presence does more to restore the team's faith and confidence than any brilliant ideas or stirring words. Foremost among Grant's leadership qualities was this steadying presence. He demonstrated it time and time again, on numerous different battlefields. On the evening of May 6, Grant's army faced a situation it had faced before under different commanders. Those previous generals had backed down in the face of Lee's audacity even when their armies were still "full of fight" and ready to go on. This would not be the case with Grant.

Several miles to the north of the Tapp Field, the scene of Lee's famous episode with his Texans, elements of Lee's Second Corps launched a twilight attack that threatened the Union right flank, defeating two Sixth Corps brigades and capturing two generals. Like Sorrel's attack in the south, this effort was too small to achieve any real breakthrough, and the gathering darkness combined with the thick underbrush to sap it of all momentum, but the attack had a great psychological effect on Union headquarters. Veterans of Chancellorsville began to panic, thinking of Stonewall Jackson's flank attack.

At this moment, when many of his subordinates were taking counsel of their fears, Grant displayed the steadiness and ability to focus on the task at hand that marked him as a great captain. A general approached Grant, predicting doom: "General Grant, this is a crisis that cannot be looked upon too seriously. I know Lee's methods well by past experience; he will throw his whole army between us and the Rapidan, and cut us off completely from our communications." Aide Horace Porter wrote that Grant rose from his seat, took his ever-present cigar out of his mouth (he smoked twenty on May 6 alone!), and replied, "Oh, I am heartily tired of hearing about what Lee is going to do. Some of you always seem to think he is suddenly going to turn a double somersault, and land in our rear and on both of our flanks at the same time. Go back to your command, and try to think what we are going to do ourselves, instead of what Lee is going to do."[20]

This scene calls to mind the 1970 *Apollo 13* disaster, which threatened the lives of Jim Lovell and two other astronauts after their failed moon landing attempt. NASA mission director Gene Krantz kept the scientists and technicians at Johnson Space Center focused on their individual pieces of the solution, making it clear, as the title of his book later stated, that "failure is not an option." Krantz won the Presidential Medal of Freedom for his heroism and coolness in the face of an impending disaster. When your team faces adversity, the tendency may be to focus on all the bad things that could happen. Under your steadying hand, your team can refocus on solving the problem, not on the possible consequences.

Had Grant operated with a similar outlook from the very beginning, however, the Battle of the Wilderness might not have occurred in the first place. Steadiness in the face of adversity is often a leadership trait that is more prized than brilliance or innovation. Strive to cultivate that quality in those around you; plan for the unexpected, but do not let yourself be dominated by its possibilities.

As the Union veteran predicted, the woods caught fire and burned to death many of the wounded, lending an especially hellish quality to the battlefield. Horace Porter captured the scene quite accurately: "All circumstances seemed to combine to make the scene one of unutterable horror. . . . Forest fires raged; ammunition trains exploded . . . the wounded, roasted by its hot breath . . . and every bush seemed hung with the shreds of blood-stained clothing. It was as though Christian men had turned to fiends, and hell itself had usurped the place of the earth."[21]

Facing South: Lee and Grant Conclude the Battle of the Wilderness

As May 7 dawned, Lee and Grant eyed each other across the smoking expanse of the Wilderness. Grant had three options. He could withdraw across the Rapidan River, as Joe Hooker had done following Chancellorsville. He could remain in place and try again to grapple with the rebels. Or, he could attempt a maneuver around Lee and closer to Richmond. His decision spoke volumes about Grant the leader.

Just as Grant had promised to Lincoln and to the Northern populace, he refused to be deterred by tactical setbacks in the first few days of his campaign. Just as he had at Fort Donelson, Shiloh, and Vicksburg, he looked beyond immediate results and saw that his plan remained viable. He would try once more to use maneuvers to bring Lee to bay. As the armies remained in place and skirmished on May 7, Grant issued orders for the Army of the Potomac to disengage and shift to the south; the objective was the crossroads at Spotsylvania Courthouse, eleven miles to the south by the Brock Road. If he could grab this intersection of several roads, he would sit squarely astride Lee's supply lines to Richmond and limit Lee's freedom to maneuver. At around 11 p.m. on May 7, Grant's headquarters broke camp and rode south along the Brock Road, as the Army of the Potomac prepared to take the road to Spotsylvania.

> As May 7 dawned, Lee and Grant eyed each other across the smoking expanse of the Wilderness.

Grant's equivalent of the "Lee to the Rear" episode occurred about an hour later, as his entourage approached Hancock's trenches at the Brock Road/Plank Road intersection. Many soldiers of the Union army, veterans of several campaigns against Lee, expected to retreat after the bloody fighting of the previous three days. When they stood by the roadside, they observed Grant riding *south*, toward Richmond, not *north*, the direction of so many Union retreats! Many of the Union soldiers began cheering, and the cheers spread. *Huzzahs*, the Union soldier's version of the famous Rebel Yell, rang through the woods as Grant steered his horse along the lines of men and guns.

In a scene reminiscent of Napoleon's torchlight march among his troops the night before the Battle of Austerlitz, many Union soldiers lit pine torches and held them aloft as Grant passed. The general remarked that the cheering might alert the Confederates to the army's movement and sought to have it stopped, but it continued until he was out of sight.[22]

It had taken only a few days for the men in the ranks of the Army of the Potomac to become aware of the change in the army's leadership. As one of the army's most seasoned regiments, the 124th New York Volunteers of Orange County, north of New York City, marched along on the night of May 7, one of its soldiers commented on the change. "I say Joe, this little chap from out West—I don't believe he knows when he's whipped. If it hadn't been for his coming along with us we would have been back to our old camp again by this time." Joe replied, "I'll just bet you a plug of tobacco and a briarwood pipe, that this army never re-crosses the Rapidan until we go home to stay!"[23]

Once he learned from his cavalry of Grant's movement, Lee, too knew what needed to be done. His imperative was clear: Win the race to Spotsylvania Courthouse or else. With the First Corps in the lead, now under the command of Third Corps division commander Richard Heron Anderson, the Army of Northern Virginia took to several parallel roads in an attempt to beat Grant to the vital intersection. After a bloody beginning in the Wilderness, the Overland Campaign was about to enter an even more horrific phase.

The Hard Lessons of The Wilderness

The Battle of the Wilderness proved that several of Lee's and Grant's underlying assumptions about the coming campaign, and about each other, were wrong. Rightly or wrongly, Lee built his plans, as he always had, on his subordinates' ability to act in the absence of his specific presence and guidance, and on an inherent belief that his enemy would react by retreating after being dealt a severe blow. Grant invalidated the latter assumption with his move south. With Longstreet now out of action for an indeterminate period, May 4–6 showed conclusively that Lee's two remaining corps commanders, Ewell and Hill, would need much closer scrutiny.

After a good start in the defensive position along Saunders' Field on May 5, Ewell was again displaying the "want of decision" that Lee had seen in him since their days together in Mexico; his failure to act decisively on the evening of May 6, when he had substantial evidence of Union weakness opposite his position, was not in keeping with Lee's expectations of his generals. Whether a larger attack would have accomplished anything is beside the point; Ewell's behavior was the critical indicator of his growing unfitness for corps command.

Hill's behavior was even more problematic. His ongoing illness was now to have a direct and negative impact on his performance of his duties, and his failures on the night of May 5–6 exposed a third of Lee's army to destruction. Furthermore, once his men began retreating, he had no control over them whatsoever. Once the general whom Lee had deemed "the best of his grade with the army," Hill's star continued its post-Gettysburg decline.

What did the Battle of the Wilderness mean for Robert E. Lee? For his army, it meant 18,000 casualties that he could ill afford and definitely could not replace easily. For him as a leader, it showed that he had a new and more dangerous kind of opponent in Ulysses S. Grant. It would remain to be seen whether or not the techniques that had brought his army success on so many fields would work in these changed circumstances.

Second, conditions would now require a significant, and probably unforeseen, shift in the way Lee wielded the Army of Northern Virginia in battle. Instead of a command style that emphasized giving his subordinates wide latitude, the wounding of Longstreet and the shortcomings of Ewell and Hill might require more directive leadership, more hands-on tactical control of the army. These sorts of shifts are a definite challenge for a leader in any business or management environment. They demand both technical competence and mental flexibility.

For Grant, the Battle of the Wilderness showcased both the best and the worst of his leadership style. Overconfidence in his own army's abilities, a tendency that his aggressiveness exacerbated, again dogged him, as it did at Shiloh. He, too, reacted to the perceived overly cautious behavior of his subordinates, namely Meade and Warren, by stepping in and taking overt control of tactical movements instead of sticking to his plan. In hindsight, Grant acted too quickly in this regard, and this seizure of direct control of the army's movements was to have dire consequences in the days ahead. But the bottom line in the Battle of the Wilderness was that Grant's steadiness under pressure and his refusal to be sidetracked from his ultimate objective meant that he could turn a bloody tactical draw, for the battle was at best a draw for the Union forces, into an event that brought them closer to victory.

Leadership Lessons

The Battle of the Wilderness offers several pertinent lessons in the critical transition from planning to execution:

- *Build a capable staff and let them help you*. Lee's reluctance to employ a larger staff, and his general exclusion of his staff from questions of strategy, very nearly got the campaign off to a disastrous start for the Confederacy. Instead of limiting your staff to mundane duties, challenge them to help you visualize and plan. You may be surprised at the great ideas that emerge.

- *Once you get the ball rolling, seize and maintain the momentum*. If you put your organization on autopilot once your plan is in motion, you may be in for some unpleasant surprises. Grant and Meade did this in the glow of their success on May 4. The next twenty-four hours were a critical period, in which Lee wrested the initiative away from them. Stay involved, without micromanaging, as your subordinates execute your plan.

- *If you suffer an initial setback, take a deep breath and give your team some time to work it out*. Those situations that require your instantaneous correction will be relatively rare. By letting capable subordinates go to work and correct problems in crisis situations, you will gain credibility in their eyes and build competence throughout the organization.

- *Don't let faulty assumptions continue to dominate your thinking*. Thinking in an ordered, comprehensive way allows you to filter the available information, make valid assumptions where necessary, and take calculated risks. Lee and Grant faced a myriad of military, political, and personal considerations as they planned the Overland Campaign, and both came up with solid, workable plans because they tackled the problem in this way. Some of their key assumptions proved to be wrong, but that does not diminish the overall clarity of their thinking.

- *Lead by personal example in true crisis situations.* Lee galvanized a retreating army in the Tapp Field and turned what looked like a significant defeat into a stunning reversal of fortune. He did this by understanding what types of behavior motivated his men, and by applying just the right amount of personal example at just the right time.

- *"Think what you are going to do."* Take Grant's example when the chips are down. Display a calm demeanor, think for a moment, and keep at it.

CHAPTER FIVE

Spotsylvania

Adapting Your Leadership Style to Changing Situations

"I propose to fight it out on this line if it takes all summer."[1]

—LIEUTENANT GENERAL ULYSSES S. GRANT TO MAJOR GENERAL HENRY
HALLECK, CHIEF OF STAFF, MAY 11, 1864.

Have you given any thought to the style of leadership that works best for you? The position you occupy in an organization, or the work that you normally do, or the quality and levels of experience of your subordinates might seem to dictate a certain style of leadership, but beware of attempting to force a round peg, your personality, into the square hole of a particular style of leadership. If a leadership style is uncomfortable for you, you will have trouble being successful with it. Moreover, it is important that your subordinates know *how* you will lead them, and that your words and actions reinforce your message.

If you must change your leadership style, proceed with caution. Take a few minutes and consider the second- and third-order effects of this change, both upon you and upon those you lead. An ill-considered change can have lots of unintended consequences, while a smart and well-timed shift will demonstrate a great deal of sensitivity to the needs of your organization. No one leadership style will work all the time, especially at the organizational level,

Figure 5-1 Adapting Leadership Styles to Situations— Four Critical Questions

Is a change *really* necessary right now?

Which style will work best?

Am I personally capable of this change?

Will my subordinates respond positively to this change?

where you encounter an ever-changing set of requirements and varying levels of subordinate experience, skill, and motivation.

Army Leadership captures why leaders get paid big bucks to make such big decisions: "One of the many things that makes your job tough is that, in order to get their best performance, you must figure out what your subordinates need and what they're able to do—even when they don't know themselves."[2] This was the crux of the leadership challenge that both Lee and Grant faced as the Overland Campaign moved into its second week.

Lee: Is a Change *Really* Necessary Right Now?

If the Battle of the Wilderness exposed both Lee and Grant to a kind of fighting that was new in its ferocity, Spotsylvania forced both of them to make adjustments to their leadership styles that neither would have thought necessary a few weeks before. Both set out on the Overland Campaign with the intention of exercising *delegating leadership*, where leaders give subordinates the authority to solve problems and make decisions without the express approval or oversight of the leader. (See Figure 5-2.) More independent-minded subordinates will feel more comfortable in this environment; they will enjoy working without the boss breathing down their necks. Lee had had great success with delegation up to Gettysburg, but turbu-

---

Figure 5-2 Three Basic Leadership Styles[3]

Directive Leadership
- Leader-centric
- Little or no input from subordinates
- The "5 Ws": Who, What, Where, When, How; Detailed instructions
- Close supervision of execution
- Works best when: A leader is new to an organization; subordinates need detailed guidance; planning or execution time is short.

Delegating Leadership
- Subordinate-centric
- Some input from subordinates
- Broad guidance from the boss on What, leaving the other Ws up to subordinates
- Decentralized execution motivates capable subordinates to new levels of achievement
- Works best when: Leaders and subordinates know each other well; subordinates are mature, experienced, and enjoy working without close supervision.

Participating Leadership
- Team-centric
- Lots of input from subordinates on all 5 "Ws"
- Leader makes final decision and retains overall control
- Builds capable teams because subordinates take ownership in leadership decisions
- Works best when: Leaders feel that they can rely on advice from highly capable subordinates; planning time allows for consultation; leaders and subordinates are interested in long-term team building.

---

lence in his senior management—corps and division commanders—from the fall of 1863 on made it increasingly questionable whether he could continue in this vein.

The Battle of the Wilderness only exacerbated these concerns, given the wounding of Longstreet and the demonstrated difficulties of Ewell and Hill. With the exception of the episode in the Tapp Field on May 6, however, Lee stuck to his delegating style during the Battle of the Wilderness. From all indications, he planned to continue issuing broad guidance and allowing his subordinates latitude to execute his plans.

This was perhaps not a wise decision under the circumstances. Lee's decision to continue with a delegating style raises the issue of flexibility in leadership and offers an example of a situation in which a leader needs to change leadership styles. Two of Lee's three chief subordinates, Ewell and Hill, performed below the general's standards in the Wilderness, and Longstreet's replacement, Richard H. Anderson, would be exercising corps command for the very first time. As the next phase of the campaign opened, Lee decided to shift from a delegating leadership style to a directive style.

> "One of the many things that makes your job tough is that, in order to get their best performance, you must figure out what your subordinates need and what they're able to do—even when they don't know themselves."

In making this change in leadership style, Lee relied on the absolute faith and trust his subordinates had in him. Leaders are often hesitant to adopt a directive leadership style because they are convinced that it is autocratic and will be resisted. Lee didn't have this problem, because of the relationship he had with his men. If you develop a relationship of trust with your subordinates and respond appropriately to their needs, they will react well. If you are using a directive leadership style when your followers are capable of taking charge on their own, they will resent it and feel that you are being a micromanager. If they need you to give more direction and you don't, they will flounder and feel that you aren't leading well. So don't avoid using a directive leadership style; just be sure to use it only when it is appropriate.

Given lots of time and the battlefield conditions of 1862 and 1863, Lee would certainly have preferred to allow his corps commanders the time and space to get used to delegating leadership, giving them the opportunity to fail a little bit along the way. There is no doubt that once your key subordinates have some experience and confidence, they will benefit more from this type of working environment than from a directive, prescriptive approach, but it is equally apparent that certain situations may require you to be more directive, at least for short periods. An influx of new employees, an impending merger, or a period of downsizing might all require a bit more directive leadership on your part, at least until everyone gets used to new roles and functions. If your subordinates trust you, they will understand this necessity.

Grant: Which Leadership Style Will Work Best?

Before assuming command in Virginia, Grant had succeeded through the use of *directive leadership*. With this leadership style, a leader gives detailed instructions to subordinates without soliciting their input, and then supervises the execution of those instructions very closely. His forceful personality, his internal drive, and his clear understanding of what it would take to win battles and campaigns led Grant to choose this style, and it worked on numerous battlefields. When you are deciding which leadership style to use, you should also consider the experience of your subordinates. If they are very experienced, they will feel that they can take on the responsibility of leadership and will not respond well to a directive style. If they are new to a task or lack confidence, they may need more direction. Evaluate your staff to determine what kind of leadership style will be most effective.

At this point in the war, Grant had a new position as general in chief. As the commander of all Federal armies, Grant needed to be free from the daily business of the Army of the Potomac in order to control the five separate offensives he planned for 1864. Before he took the field with Meade's army, Grant asked himself question number one and arrived at a clear answer: Yes, a shift in leadership style was necessary. He could not follow through with his new responsibilities and still be closely involved in the battlefield.

This decision led naturally to the second question: Which of the other two styles of leadership would work best? Both would have been attractive options for Grant. Delegation would give Meade and his generals wide latitude to carry out Grant's intention, leaving Grant free to exercise the overall command of Union forces with which Lincoln had entrusted him. Participation would naturally create more "buy-in" of the plan on their part, because they would have significant influence on its formulation. The participating approach would also go a long way toward building a more cohesive command team.

Grant chose delegation for a number of reasons, not the least of which was his own personality and his relationship with Meade. You may encounter a similar dilemma when deciding between these two attractive options. Participating leadership requires a level of familiarity and rapport that delegation does not. When he moved east to Virginia, Grant could make an assumption, sight unseen, that Meade and his generals were capable professionals who could, at the very least, carry out his orders with minimum direction. Grant and Meade were very different men, from very different backgrounds, and before they gained a certain degree of familiarity and comfort with one another, it is difficult to envision a cooperative approach between them. Grant needed the freedom to run the affairs of the entire Union army, and given the track record of the Army of the Potomac against Lee, he felt that relying on the judgment of its generals in formulating his plan to beat Lee would lead to the repetition of past mistakes.

Over the three days of the Battle of the Wilderness, Grant had cause to ask himself this same question once more. His initial assumption, that Meade and his generals would carry out his intent wholeheartedly, proved to be mistaken. Grant could not seem to get Meade, Burnside, and the four corps commanders to act in concert and in keeping with his overall intent. In short order he was about to shift once more to directive leadership.

This was a conscious decision on Grant's part, born out of frustration with how the battle proceeded and entirely in keeping with Grant's personality and reading of the seriousness of the situation. With the fall presidential election approaching, he needed results, and in his mind the feelings of Meade and his generals would have to come second. Time would tell whether Grant would be able to balance the competing demands of strategic leadership, with its implications for national policy and hundreds of thousands of people, and organizational leadership of the Army of the Potomac.

The point here is not that a leader must adhere to one leadership style all the time; indeed, different situations and different subordinates can require a multitude of styles. Remember, though, to think about when, how, and why you change leadership styles. Make sure first that a shift is necessary, and then apply a healthy dose of introspection to ensure that you are capable of deriving maximum effectiveness from your organization with a different style. As intelligent and driven a leader as Ulysses S. Grant was, he may not have paid enough attention to the implications of setting out as a delegating leader and shifting back to a directive mode. That shift had a direct effect on the performance in battle of the Union Army and played out across the fields and woods of Spotsylvania County, Virginia.

Grant and the Meade/Sheridan Controversy: Will My Subordinates Respond Positively to My Changing Leadership Style?

Once you have decided that a change in leadership styles is necessary, you must consider how your subordinates will perform once this change is made. While you can never base this decision entirely on what your subordinates will think about it, thinking about their reactions may help you to communicate the decision in a more effective manner, and this in turn may enable them to perform more effectively.

> The general that controlled the crossroads at Spotsylvania Courthouse had the upper hand in the deadly game of chess that was developing.

The tiny hamlet of Spotsylvania Courthouse was an unlikely place to fight one of the most brutal battles in American military history. (The Civil War had a way of turning bucolic, isolated settlements into butchering grounds.) In 1864 the county seat of Spotsylvania County boasted a population of only a few hundred, a church, and a scant few businesses. Today it lies just a few miles from Interstate 95, just south of Fredericksburg, and seems the embodiment of small-town America.

In early May of 1864, however, Spotsylvania was a place of strategic importance. It lay at or near four roads that collectively meant life or death to the Army of the Potomac and the Army of Northern Virginia. The Brock Road, for which Hancock's Second Corps fought bitterly on May 6, led from the Wilderness through Todd's Tavern to Spotsylvania. At the courthouse, it intersected with the Fredericksburg Road, a vital line of supply and communications for the Army of the Potomac. For much of the campaign, the army transported the bulk of its supplies through Fredericksburg, ten miles to the north. Winding out of Spotsylvania Courthouse to the east, the Massaponax Church Road first crossed the Telegraph Road (the route of the modern Interstate 95) and then reached the Richmond, Fredericksburg, and Potomac Railroad at Hamilton's Crossing, a few miles below Fredericksburg. The general that controlled the crossroads at Spotsylvania Courthouse had the upper hand in the deadly game of chess that was developing.

By putting his army in motion shortly before midnight on May 8, Grant hoped once again to steal a march on Lee and reach the crossroads at Spotsylvania with at least part of his army. In his May 7 orders to Meade, Grant showed that he had now firmly made the transition to the role of army commander. He dictated to Meade the army's proposed disposition at the end of the march, and even specified that Warren's Fifth Corps would take the lead in the movement. The critical intersection lay a little over six miles south of the Union army's entrenchments.[4]

Grant's taking a more active role in the movement did not lead to its success, however. The night and early morning of May 8 was a time of great frustration as the immense Federal force became tangled on the small Brock Road. Sheridan's cavalry moved out ahead of the infantry in an attempt to secure the route and drive Stuart's horsemen away from Spotsylvania. They fought a sharp skir-

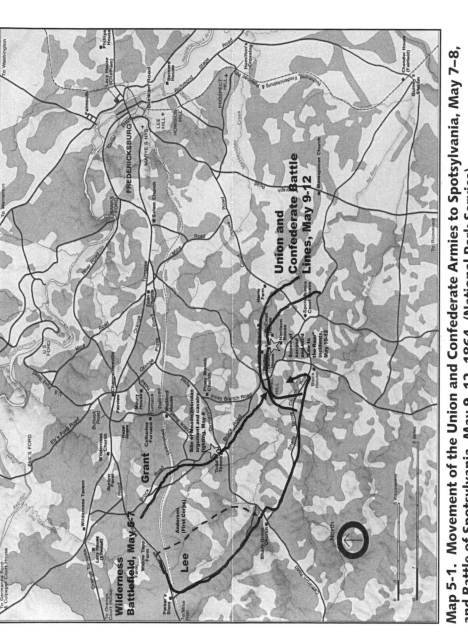

Map 5-1. Movement of the Union and Confederate Armies to Spotsylvania, May 7–8, and Battle of Spotsylvania, May 9–12, 1864. (National Park Service)

mish with the Confederate cavalry division of Fitzhugh Lee at Todd's Tavern and occupied Spotsylvania Courthouse for a brief time on May 7, but later withdrew. When Meade and Grant reached Todd's Tavern at about midnight, the trouble in the Federal high command began in earnest.

Meade was dismayed by the scene he found at Todd's Tavern. Bodies littered the ground from the cavalry fight of May 7, and he found the troopers of Gregg's and Merritt's divisions sound asleep around the tavern buildings, exhausted after battling Fitzhugh Lee's Confederates. Grant and Meade had expected Sheridan's cavalrymen to be firmly in possession of Spotsylvania Courthouse by dawn on May 8, as Warren's entire Fifth Corps was a short distance behind them and moving south. Instead, Sheridan's troopers were no further than Todd's Tavern, and in all likelihood the Confederates were continuing to move to the west unmolested.

Meade was already in a bad mood because of the delays in the army's movement, and this sent him over the edge. Sheridan was several miles away at his headquarters, so Meade jumped the chain of command and issued peremptory orders to Gregg and Merritt to get their men into the saddle and clear the Brock Road toward Spotsylvania Courthouse. The cavalrymen did so, and soon the sounds of gunfire echoed through the woods. The Confederate cavalry had used the few hours' respite to fell trees across the road to form roadblocks, and they remained on the defensive in force.

> ". . . concentrate all the cavalry, move out in force against Stuart's command, and whip it."

This misunderstanding brought to a head the conflict between George Meade and Philip Sheridan, and it symbolized the gulf that would come to separate Meade and Grant. In an early display of directive leadership, Grant had brought Sheridan, an infantry commander by trade, with him from the Army of the Tennessee. Sheridan was inexperienced, and Meade's cavalry suffered during the Battle of the Wilderness as a result. Meade continually gave him the tasks of providing security for both the infantry corps and the army's wagons, tasks Sheridan despised. The resulting shortcomings had contributed materially to Meade's lack of success in the Wilderness, and the situation at Todd's Tavern was the last straw.

The Meade-Sheridan conflict turned into open argument at about noon on May 8, when Sheridan made it to Meade's command post at Todd's Tavern. Sheridan felt that Meade had made a mess of his plans for the day; Meade blamed Sheridan for impeding the progress of the Fifth Corps and for ruining the army's chance to capture Spotsylvania Courthouse. Both men had short tempers, and they exploded in Meade's tent. Sheridan boasted that if given the proper latitude, he could "concentrate all the cavalry, move out in force against Stuart's command, and whip it."[5]

This disagreement put Grant in a very difficult position. He was duty-bound to support Meade as a subordinate army commander, but he himself had placed Sheridan in command of the army's cavalry. Meade immediately went to Grant and asked the latter to discipline Sheridan, relating the substance of the interview. Grant's only comment was, "Did Sheridan say that? Well, he generally knows what he is talking about. Let him start right out and do it." In one fell swoop, Grant sided with a subordinate over the wishes of the commander and, more significantly, deprived Meade of his entire cavalry force. By 1 p.m., Sheridan was on his way south with his entire force to battle Jeb Stuart. This decision had significant operational implications for the army's performance in the coming battle, and it went a long way toward souring the relationship between Grant and Meade.

This decision was typical of Grant. In order to solve a thorny interpersonal problem within his high command, he simply removed one of the irritants. Strategically, the move also made a lot of sense. Sheridan's expedition had the potential of hastening the defeat of Robert E. Lee by depriving him of his cavalry, upon whom Lee depended for the information he needed to craft his audacious plans.

Meade played the part of the good soldier and ordered Sheridan's expedition, but the damage was done. In this case, Grant's exercise of directive leadership was to have a decidedly negative impact on the Army of the Potomac. By not even listening to the argument of his chief subordinate, Grant demonstrated that he valued his western connections over the military chain of command, implicitly indicting the Army of the Potomac's conduct of the war to this point.[6]

For Grant, the Meade/Sheridan controversy was a case of directive leadership misapplied. In his desire to forge ahead toward victory, Grant worsened his relationship with the one man who, more than any other, could help him get there. This was a knee-jerk reaction on his part, not the type of clear-headed decision that organizational leaders need to make.

After this imbroglio, the Union army's bad day continued. South of Todd's Tavern, the Union cavalry and Warren's Fifth Corps first stalled in front of Fitz Lee's barricades, and then ran into Confederate infantry at a low rise called Laurel Hill. Owing to the confluence of good fortune and the mistakes of the Army of the Potomac, Lee's army won the race to Spotsylvania Courthouse. Early on May 7, Lee determined that Grant was moving toward either Fredericksburg or Spotsylvania; as the day wore on he determined that it was the latter and ordered Richard H. Anderson, the acting First Corps commander, to move his divisions to Spotsylvania Courthouse as quickly as possible.

Lee's original order called for Anderson to withdraw his men from the line of battle and let them rest until 3 a.m., but Anderson elected to begin his movement at 10 p.m. because the woods around the battlefield continued to burn, robbing his men of campsites. The First Corps continued to move throughout the night without stopping, again because they could find no suitable place to bed down in the tangled woods.

> Grant may have determined that a more directive leadership style was necessary, but he did not give a great deal of thought to carrying it out.

After moving all night, Anderson's troops emerged into the open ground around Spotsylvania Courthouse, literally in the nick of time to meet Warren's advance. Jeb Stuart, whose mounted troopers had contested the Union advance all day on May 8, met Anderson's men and guided them into position on Laurel Hill. At about the time that Meade and Sheridan were having their shouting match, Anderson's Georgians and South Carolinians delivered a stinging, unwelcome surprise to the Union Fifth Corps.[7]

Grant's experiment with directive leadership on May 7 and 8 was a failure. Because of the high stakes involved in beating Lee to Spotsylvania Courthouse, he assumed direct control of Meade's army and sided with a subordinate over Meade at a key moment. Grant may have determined that a more directive leadership style was necessary, but he did not give a great deal of thought to carrying it out. The result was another setback for the Union army. It is one thing to decide to change leadership styles, and quite another to carry out this change in a manner that leads to success. Grant would have been better served by allowing Meade some latitude and by forcing Meade and Sheridan to make peace, rather than simply allowing Sheridan to go away.

Lee: Am I Personally Capable of This Change?

In contrast to Grant, Lee was quite successful in the directive mode on May 7 to 9. He had to take a more directive role because of the high stakes for which he was playing; if he guessed wrong about Grant's intentions or allowed one of his less-capable subordinates too much latitude, the results might have been disastrous. Complicating Lee's thinking was the realization that Grant was going to be a different kind of adversary, one who would not admit defeat as his predecessors had done. As the armies watched each other on May 7, Lee issued very specific orders to Jeb Stuart to "thoroughly inform yourself about the roads on our right, which it would be advisable or necessary for us to follow should the enemy continue his movement toward Spotsylvania Court House, or should we desire to move on his flank in that direction." The next forty-eight hours would see the Lee-Grant chess game shift into high gear. In this environment, on his "home court," as it were, Lee was at his best.

After ordering this reconnaissance and finding out on May 7 that the Brock Road was still jammed with Federal troops, Lee ordered his chief of artillery, Brigadier General William Nelson Pendleton, to work with the army's engineers to construct a military road through the Wilderness to parallel the Brock Road. Anderson would use this road to reach Spotsylvania with his infantry.[8]

With James Longstreet recovering from his May 6 wound and numerous other generals wounded or out of action, Lee had to make a major reorganization of his officer corps in order to meet the current emergency. The masterful way in which Lee made this reorganization, while simultaneously fighting Grant to a standstill at Spotsylvania, is a model of organizational leadership and political skill. In making these changes, Lee demonstrated that he was capable of directive leadership, but was also capable of mixing this style with the participation of his subordinates at key moments.

Lee's first task was to put someone in Longstreet's place. Based purely on military skill, the natural choice for the job was Third Corps Division Commander Jubal Early. Early, a Virginia lawyer and West Point graduate to whom Lee jokingly referred as "my bad old man" because of his predilection for streams of profanity, was easily the most combative of Lee's division commanders—precisely the type of general that Lee could depend on to exercise initiative and conform to the spirit of his aggressive orders.

Early was a bad choice for the First Corps job, however, and Lee found this out by talking to the officers of the corps headquarters, most notably Colonel Moxley Sorrel, Longstreet's chief of staff. Early on the morning of May 7, as Lee waited for the return of the reconnaissance patrols he had ordered, he summoned Sorrel to headquarters, and the two sat under a shade tree, out of earshot of everyone else, to discuss the situation. Sorrel agreed with Lee that Early was a good general, but he did not recommend him to replace Longstreet because he thought that Early would be "objectionable to both officers and men" of the corps.[9]

The Army of Northern Virginia was a collection of citizen-soldiers from the various Confederate states, not a professional army of career soldiers. Southerners of the nineteenth century, and indeed most Americans at that time, held intensely local sympathies; loyalties to community and state were usually more important than conceptions of American patriotism. The men of the First

Corps hailed mainly from South Carolina and the Deep South states—Georgia, Florida, Alabama, Mississippi, Texas, Louisiana, and Arkansas. To put the Virginia-born Early, not the most politic of officers in any case, in charge of this corps would cause a great deal of bad feeling. Sorrel made another recommendation: Richard H. Anderson, who hailed from South Carolina.

Anderson was not the best choice from a military point of view. He had built a reputation as a solid and reliable, but entirely average, leader. Unlike Stonewall Jackson, he would require more close supervision, at least at the outset. But other factors besides simple military efficiency played a part in this decision. Anderson's division had served in the First Corps before being moved to the Third after the Battle of Chancellorsville. Sorrel felt that Anderson was the logical choice in this regard: "We *know him* and shall be satisfied with him." In making this key decision, Lee retained the final approval, but he listened to the advice of a capable subordinate, and in so doing employed a strategically placed bit of participating leadership. As it turned out, Lee made the right choice; Anderson performed very capably until Longstreet returned to the army later in 1864.

"Whom Would You Put in His Place?": Robert E. Lee and the Politics of Promotion

Whether or not you can delegate to subordinates depends in part who those subordinates are and whether they are capable of taking on the responsibility. What are the constraints, political and otherwise, that you face in the realm of human resources? Territorial issues may force you to promote a candidate from one section or division over a candidate from another area, even when that person is not necessarily the most qualified. Certain candidates for promotion may have connections in high places, even if they are not as highly skilled as others. In any case, you probably do not have the luxury of firing everyone who you think is not performing up to par; you may have to get along as best you can with the staff at your disposal. These issues are nothing new; Robert E. Lee faced them as he attempted to reorganize his officer corps "on the fly" after the Wilderness. The "best" decisions you can make regarding personnel may not be as simple as one résumé over another.

> "When a man makes a mistake, I call him to my tent, talk to him, and use the authority of my position to make him do the right thing the next time."

With the matter of the First Corps settled to the satisfaction of all, Lee turned to other leadership needs. Hill had proved in the Wilderness that he was unable to exercise effective command of his corps. Putting Anderson in Longstreet's place kept Jubal Early available to assume the Third Corps post, and Lee made that move on May 8. This temporary posting gave Lee the chance to evaluate Early at a higher level of responsibility, confirming or denying his capacity for a full-time position as a corps commander. Early's promotion, in turn, cleared the way for another of Lee's promising young generals to step up.

John Brown Gordon, a Georgia native and a natural-born soldier with no military training, had shown at every level of command from company to brigade that he was an outstanding soldier. He, too, moved up, this time to command Early's division. Gordon's promotion created yet another sticky situation, as another of the brigadiers, Harry Hays of Louisiana, actually outranked Gordon. Modern leaders often have similar problems: A lower-level leader may not have the skills necessary to perform, but that leader may have seniority, political connections, or something else that makes it difficult to remove her or him from power. In this case, issues of rank were every bit as sensitive as issues of state, and Lee applied dexterity to this problem as well. He moved Hays and his brigade to the division of Edward Johnson and consolidated them with the Louisiana brigade of Leroy Stafford, who had been killed in the Wilderness. This move gave the Louisianans one of their own to command them and removed the issue of rank between Gordon and Hays. To complete this reshuffling, Lee ordered the transfer of one of Robert Rodes's five brigades to Gordon's new division to replace the departed Hays. This move satisfied all of the generals involved and left all of the Second Corps divisions with an equal number of brigades.

This level of political sensitivity set Lee apart from most other Civil War generals. As a rule, West Point–trained generals held citizen soldiers and officers in low regard. Not Lee; he understood those whom he led, appreciated their sacrifices for what they believed in, and adapted his leadership to suit them. A few days later, while Lee and Hill looked on, one of Hill's political generals, Ambrose R. Wright of Georgia, mishandled an attack. Hill railed against Wright, promising to convene a court-martial to punish the Georgian. "These men are not any Army," Lee explained as if lecturing a student. "They are citizens defending their country. I have to make the best of what I have and lose much time in making dispositions," he went on. Hill would only humiliate Wright and antagonize the people of Georgia by pressing charges. "Besides," Lee asked Hill, "whom would you put in his place? You'll have to do what I do: When a man makes a mistake, I call him to my tent, talk to him, and use the authority of my position to make him do the right thing the next time."[10] Lee's sensitivity to both the needs of his organization and the needs of his people is a great example for any manager or human resources director to emulate.

The Pitfalls of Directive Leadership Misapplied

In contrast to the Army of Northern Virginia's responsiveness to Lee's directive leadership, the Army of the Potomac was coming increasingly to resemble the balky mule team that Grant had complained of to Lincoln earlier that spring. After the Sheridan episode at Todd's Tavern, Meade chafed under Grant's increasingly active role in the army's operations. Grant's presence made it difficult, if not impossible, for Meade to manage the army, and Burnside's awkward presence made the entire arrangement even more dysfunctional. The entire force of almost 100,000 men, spread over heavily wooded and compartmentalized terrain, was simply too big and cumbersome for one man to orchestrate with directive leadership. Grant's shift to directive leadership, born out of frustration over the army's lack of success thus far, was a very typical reaction by Grant to a difficult situation, but it led him to made serious tactical errors on May 9 and 10, 1864.

Because he had the advantage of a more compact defensive position ("interior lines" in military parlance), and because he stood on the defensive, Lee could shift his troops around at will and was able to parry Union attacks with relative ease. A lack of hard information concerning Lee's dispositions, compounded by the fact that Grant had allowed Sheridan to take his entire cavalry corps on the expedition to chase down Jeb Stuart, meant that Grant really had no idea of what sectors of his line Lee was weakening to meet each attack.

Grant further compounded his problems by attacking piecemeal, first at one end of the line and then at the other. In a very general way, he intended the various attacks to be coordinated with one another, but at this point the Army of the Potomac combined with Burnside's corps simply was not up to that task. Hancock's aide-de-camp commented that "the characteristic fault of the campaign then opened was attacking at too many points," instead of finding a weak point in the Confederate line, massing a sizable force, and following the attack through with resolution. The Union attacks on May 10 were, in the aide's estimation, "weak affairs in almost every case, unsupported; and mere shoving forward of a brigade or two now here now there, like a chess player shoving out his pieces and then drawing them right back."[11]

> The entire force of almost 100,000 men, spread over heavily wooded and compartmentalized terrain, was simply too big and cumbersome for one man to orchestrate with directive leadership.

In spite of these shortcomings, Grant inspired many in the army with his aggressiveness and calmness. Never one to remain passively at his headquarters, Grant rode out on the afternoon of May 10 to observe the army's attacks in progress. At one point, while under enemy fire, he dismounted and sat on a fallen tree to write out a dispatch. As he wrote, a shell exploded perilously close to him and showered him with dirt. Grant "looked up from his paper an instant, and then, without the slightest change of countenance, went on writing the message." Out of a group of wounded soldiers being carried by, an infantryman exclaimed, "Ulysses don't scare worth a damn." There is no way of knowing exactly what Grant was writing. The *Official Records* contain only one dispatch from Grant written on the afternoon in question, a letter to Burnside containing advice on the attack Burnside was carrying out at that time. No matter, though; displays of calmness in the face of adversity can have this sort of galvanizing effect wherever subordinates see them.[12]

Equally, though, Grant was rapidly demoralizing an army of veterans who wished desperately to see some sign that their efforts were bringing them closer to victory. May 10, 1864 cost the Army of the Potomac over 4,000 killed, wounded, and missing, to little good that the men in the ranks could see.[13]

Throughout his Civil War career, Grant's responses to adversity conformed to a pattern, usually involving more direction to his subordinates, in an attempt to conquer problems with resolve and force of will. In many situations this was an admirable example, but leader beware! A more hands-on

> "Ulysses don't scare worth a damn."

approach that is not backed up by carefully thought-out responses and actions can be disastrous, and may be perceived by subordinates more as desperation than as decisiveness. If you must step in to avert disaster, by all means do so, but consider the unintended consequences that may result from your actions.

Upton and Rodes: To Listen or Not to Listen?

You can probably think back to several instances in your career in which a subordinate offered an idea or piece of advice that led to great success. Knowing when to take a subordinate's advice and when to ignore it can be a prized leadership skill. On May 10, both Lee and Grant had the opportunity to take a subordinate's advice.

In one, and only one, case, Grant's aggressive approach to warfare paid off on May 10. The success of one Union attack that day allowed Grant to continue to exercise directive leadership. That evening, after other attacks on the Confederate left and right flanks had failed, a Union attack by a single reinforced brigade under Colonel Emory Upton penetrated the center of the Confederate line. Upton, an up-and-coming Regular Army officer destined for high rank after the Civil War, proposed the attack, and Grant approved it. The breakthrough occurred at a spot in the fortifications nicknamed the "Mule Shoe" because it formed a U-shaped salient, or bulge, in the line. Alas for Upton and his men, the attack accomplished nothing; other Federal units were supposed to advance to Upton's support, but typical delays and miscommunication ensured that he was unsupported. The temporary success encouraged Grant, however. With an optimism reminiscent of Shiloh, he remarked that evening, "A brigade today—we'll try a corps tomorrow."[14] In the case of Upton, Grant listened to a subordinate and achieved the only bright spot for Union forces thus far in the battle.

On his side of the line, Lee responded to the breakthrough in the same way as he had in the Wilderness: by attempting to ride to the front to restore order. For the second time in a week, a corps commander, in this case Richard Ewell, had allowed his line to be broken. Just as they had at the Tapp field, Lee's veterans demanded that he move to the rear and out of danger. Lee did so, and his men restored the Confederate line.

Where Grant took a subordinate's advice on May 10 and had success, when Lee did so, it almost cost him the Battle of Spotsylvania. In a meeting that evening, Lee indicated his concern about the earlier breakthrough in a question to one of Ewell's division commanders, Robert Rodes. Leaning across to Rodes he asked, "General, what shall we do with General Doles [the brigade commander on the scene] for allowing those

> "A brigade today—we'll try a corps tomorrow."

people to break over his lines?" "We shall have to let Doles off this time, as he has suffered quite severely for it already," Rodes responded. Perhaps Lee agreed with that assessment, because he said no more about the matter.[15] However, Lee's reluctance to step in more directly was to have dire consequences two days later.

The difference in the two situations (the advice of Upton and the advice of Rodes) was that Rodes's suggestion masked a deeper problem that Lee already knew about: the weakness of his line at the Mule Shoe. On a tour of inspection with Ewell, Lee commented that he thought the line could not be held. Ewell disagreed, believing that the line was safe if it was supported by plenty of artillery. Rodes's suggestion to let the matter pass may have quieted that little voice in Lee's head that warned of trouble.

On the other hand, what did Grant have to lose in listening to Upton? A subordinate was showing the kind of aggressiveness that Grant prized. Upton's suggestion dovetailed nicely with what Grant thought was the right approach. So, take your subordinates' ideas with a grain of salt. Don't let the desire to value their opinions blind you to what needs to be done. If you have moved into the mode of directive leadership, you did so for a reason! Don't back off and let less experienced subordinates sidetrack you.

Lee to the Rear Redux

If Lee thought his problems with his generals had worked themselves out, he was sorely mistaken. In the rainy predawn darkness of May 12, Hancock's Union Second Corps used a patch of woods close to the Mule Shoe to array for a quick rush across the intervening open ground. Thinking the Federals were about to evacuate their positions and move around his right flank once again, Lee decided to remove his artillery from the Mule Shoe that night in order to get the jump on Grant. This fateful decision was an incorrect one; when the Second Corps rushed out of the woods and overwhelmed elements of Ewell's Second Corps, there was no artillery for the defense. The entire Confederate line was in danger of collapsing.

At this critical moment, Ewell had the worst day of his military career, forcing Lee to intervene directly once again. The Union attack quickly captured large portions of the Second Corps en masse, including the remnants of the famous Stonewall Brigade. Many of the troops who survived the initial onslaught streamed to the rear in confusion. Their officers tried to cajole or force them into stopping and making a stand, but to no avail.

> "Gen. Lee rode out in front of the line and taking off his hat waved it in the direction of the enemy, thereby indicating his intention to lead them in the fight."

Lee had been up since 3 a.m., as was his habit while on campaign, and he heard the shots that signaled the beginning of the attack. He walked outside and saw Confederates beginning to filter back from the front line; his headquarters was in a tree-covered piece of low ground, so that he could not see the action. Lee looked around for a general to help him restore order and found Division Commander John Gordon, to whom he had entrusted the job of reserve force commander. Gordon formed the men he had immediately at hand, two brigades of Virginians and Georgians, and started them toward the breakthrough point. Just as he had at the Wilderness, Lee attempted to ride ahead with the troops.

A Louisiana captain, William J. Seymour, was nearby and wrote in his memoirs that "Gen. Lee rode out in front of the line and taking off his hat waved it in the direction of the enemy, thereby indicating his intention to lead them in the fight." In contrast to Lee's visible excitement on May 6, on this morning he "sat there on his splendid horse, his form erect, his grey head uncovered and eyes flashing with excitement . . . imposing and grand." The soldiers around him would have none of this; they crowded around his horse and refused to advance until Lee went back.

Finally a sergeant led Traveller back to the Harrison House as Gordon reminded Lee that his presence in front of the men would indicate "a want of confidence on the part of the Commander in Chief." So that his men could hear, Gordon repeated to his men as

much as to Lee, "They will not fail you here . . . Will you boys?"
Unlike the troops at the Wilderness, the men in Gordon's unit actually chanted this time: "Lee, Lee, Lee to the rear. Lee to the rear." A
few hours later, Lee again tried to lead reinforcements into the fight,
this time a brigade of Mississippi regiments. For the third and fourth
times in less than a week, Lee felt it necessary to lead his troops
personally into battle. This sort of event had simply never happened
in the days of the command triumvirate of Lee, Longstreet, and Jackson, and while Lee would never have said so in so many words, it
spoke volumes about Lee's level of confidence in his army's leadership.[16]

Lee's actions that morning at the Mule Shoe raise an interesting
point about leadership by example. Sometimes your presence in
the midst of the troops may actually be an unneeded distraction
that prevents people from doing their jobs. It may also smack of
desperation on your part, conveying the impression that you do not
trust your team. In Lee's case, his men thought nothing of the sort;
his status in the eyes of his men lent a supernatural air to everything
he did. In the incredible hysteria and danger of combat at the Mule
Shoe, Lee's actions probably motivated his men to even greater
achievements than he might normally have expected. This does not
mean that you occupy the same position in the eyes of your subordinates, however. Choose your moments of personal intervention
very carefully; they are like silver bullets, to be saved for the most
dire circumstances. Before or after the Wilderness and Spotsylvania,
Lee again attempted to intervene on the field of battle.

"You Must Restrain Yourself:" Lee and Ewell in the Heat of Battle

Gordon's men stabilized the situation in the Mule Shoe somewhat,
but the Confederate line was still in danger of falling apart as the
morning wore on. Lee went forward on foot toward the point of the
breakthrough, and together with Ewell worked to funnel fresh
troops into the ugly hand-to-hand fight that had developed. The
behavior he saw in Ewell must have dismayed him. Ewell, now his

senior remaining corps commander, was losing control of both himself and his men. Captain Seymour saw this exchange as well. "In a towering passion," Ewell "hurled a terrible volley of oaths at the stragglers from the front, stigmatizing them as cowards, etc." As men passed, Ewell would scream at them, "Yes, G-d d—n you, run, run; the Yankees will catch you; that's right; go as fast as you can."

Lee could stand it no more, and publicly rebuked the corps commander. "General Ewell," Lee yelled over the gunfire and shouts of fighting men, "you must restrain yourself; how can you expect to control these men when you have lost control of yourself? If you cannot repress your excitement, you had better retire." For Lee, who valued self-control and grace under pressure above all other qualities, this kind of behavior was simply unacceptable in a leader of men. Lee proceeded to direct arriving units into the fray himself.

The Confederate brigades that arrived to seal the breach clearly responded to Lee's calm, collected example. A Georgian noted that "Gen. Lee, in the calmest and kindest manner, said: 'Boys, do not run away, go back, go back, your comrades need you in the trenches.'" Captain Seymour was struck by the contrast between the two men. Where Ewell screamed and lashed out at retreating men, Lee "quietly exhorted the men not to forget their manhood and their duty." While Ewell's display of profanity "caused a good deal of merriment after the battle," Seymour noted with beautiful irony that "it is hardly necessary to say that Gen. Lee's course was by far the more effective of the two."

> ". . . you must restrain yourself; how can you expect to control these men when you have lost control of yourself?"

As they passed Lee's location, a succession of Confederate brigades formed up and ripped into Union lines of battle as they emerged from the forward trench line, sealing the breakthrough. The next twenty-four hours would see continuous hand-to-hand combat across the Mule Shoe. As an indicator of the ferocity of the fighting, an oak tree twenty-two inches in diameter standing just to the rear of the salient was literally sawn in half by gunfire.[17]

While your organization probably will not face a life-or-death emergency like that of Lee's army, the example that Lee provided is certainly worth remembering. Often your positive demeanor in the face of trouble is the only thing standing between a healthy management climate and an atmosphere of panic. Never forget that subordinates see and take cues from how you carry yourself every bit as much as they listen to what you say. Grant had provided the same calm example a few days before in the Wilderness, smoking a cigar and calmly whittling a stick after demanding that his generals stick to the game plan; during the fighting for the Mule Shoe, Grant sat by a campfire at his headquarters, calmly receiving dispatches and issuing orders.

The Case of Ambrose Burnside: Whither Directive Leadership?

The Battle of Spotsylvania demonstrated beyond a shadow of a doubt that Grant had no problem with exercising directive leadership, but in one situation that simply cried out for it, Grant inexplicably stepped back. Where Lee demonstrated great dexterity in shuffling the pieces of his high command for optimum results, Grant failed to do so in the one case where a similar course of action might have benefited the Union cause: Ambrose Burnside, commander of the Ninth Corps.

Burnside owed his continuing service in the Union Army to one simple fact: seniority. He had been a Union Army commander from the very beginning, leading a regiment of Rhode Island troops at the First Battle of Bull Run in July 1861. Since that time, though, he had been a liability to the Union cause on a number of battlefields, culminating in his disastrous performance as Army of the Potomac commander at the Battle of Fredericksburg in December 1862. Following the debacle at Fredericksburg and the abortive "Mud March" that ensued, Burnside was transferred to minor commands in the west.

Burnside owed his return to the eastern theater to political connections (he was a prominent Republican) and to a simple shortage of general officers with any sort of aptitude for high military command. Grant simply accepted Burnside's presence in Virginia, and furthermore accepted a command arrangement that was bound to fail given Burnside's demonstrated lack of initiative as an independent commander. It is one of history's ironies that Lee is castigated for being unwilling to "make the hard choices" regarding personnel, while Grant left Burnside in command of a significant portion of Union manpower for the remainder of the war. Burnside's corps was larger than any of the other three and had the potential to be a decisive weapon in the battle against Lee.[18] It is simply puzzling that Grant did not use his prerogative to remove the Ohioan.

The inconclusive sparring around the Harris Farm only added to the casualty lists of both armies and left Grant even more frustrated with his army than ever before. Offensive hammer blows had not brought Lee to ground; the only remaining option that would allow Grant to retain the initiative in the campaign, and move it closer to victory, was another attempt to turn Lee out of his Spotsylvania position. The Union army got underway once again on May 21, and the Overland Campaign entered its third unrelenting week.

Summary: Lee, Grant, and Shifting Leadership Styles at Spotsylvania

Lee's and Grant's experiences at Spotsylvania demonstrate that directive, delegating, and participating leadership styles all have their places, and that all three entail certain risks. The risks of delegating significant latitude to subordinates seem pretty clear-cut. To use delegation, you need subordinates who are not only technically competent, but capable of exercising discretion and comfortable in the absence of supervision. It is a leader's imperative to exercise delegating leadership only when the entire team has demonstrated the ability to function in this environment.

The pitfalls of directive leadership often fall more into the realm of unintended consequences. From the exalted perspective of senior management, a leader may see more intensive direction as a good thing in many circumstances, a way to correct problems and infuse an organization with a particular spirit or ethos. Directive policies may have the opposite effect, however, alienating capable subordinates who derive great satisfaction from demonstrating their capabilities through independent action. Meade and Warren were classic examples of leaders who felt more comfortable in independent roles and who became somewhat less than their best under close supervision. Grant might have been better served by giving Meade more of an opportunity to demonstrate that he could execute Grant's intent before stepping in and taking greater control. Grant's siding with Sheridan on May 8 was especially damaging in this regard.

Because he had much greater experience in dealing with his particular set of subordinates, Lee managed shifts between delegation and direction much more effectively. When he made necessary movements toward a more directive style, his clear credibility with his officers and men, combined with his outstanding interpersonal skills, made the transition virtually seamless. An implicit lesson to the modern manager might be to try to avoid drastic changes of approach in the initial stages of taking charge. While it is certainly true that you were put in charge for a reason, immediate and wholesale changes may not be the best course of action. Remember that because you are organizational leader, your shifts in leadership styles affect many more people, and can have ripple effects that persist for a long time. Do not take lightly the decision to become more delegating or directive.

Leadership Lessons

Lee's and Grant's performances at Spotsylvania have a lot to tell us about this aspect of leadership:

- *Leader, know thyself!* Along with knowing your job and knowing your subordinates, a key part of the Know dimension of leadership is knowledge of your own abilities and shortcomings. What is your preferred leadership style? What is your default mode under pressure? Do you naturally revert to micromanagement when you are worried about failure? Or are you reluctant to take greater control even when you know you need to? A clear understanding of your own tendencies will lead you to make good decisions about how to lead others.

- *If you are considering a change in leadership styles, ask yourself four questions.* (1) Is a change *really* necessary right now? (2) If so, which style—directive, delegating, or participating—will work best? (3) Am I capable of carrying out this change? (4) Are my subordinates capable of operating in this new environment? Of our two generals, Lee did a better job at Spotsylvania of asking and answering these questions.

- *When used in the right situations, directive leadership is a powerful tool for getting the organization back on the right track.* If time is short or things are really going wrong, the judicious application of some directive leadership can be just what the doctor ordered. Lee's actions at the Mule Shoe on May 12 are a prime example. Lee intervened personally on only a handful of occasions, but when he did, success followed. This success extended to his reworking of the army's chain of command after the Wilderness.

- *Flexibility is a cornerstone of effective leadership.* Once you make the decision to change leadership styles, certain situations may require temporary deviations. At certain points, both Lee and Grant had success with a temporary shift to a participating style of leadership. Lee took the advice of Moxley Sorrel in making his decision on Longstreet's replacement, and Grant listened to Emory Upton and earned his only real tactical success of the battle.

CHAPTER SIX

The Greater War

Grant and Strategic Leadership

"I will take no backward step."

—LIEUTENANT GENERAL ULYSSES S. GRANT TO MAJOR GENERAL HENRY
HALLECK, CHIEF OF STAFF, May 11, 1864.

A s Ulysses S. Grant maneuvered the Army of the Potomac southward in May 1864, he did so with an eye to his larger responsibilities. The offensive against Lee's army was only one of five offensives (albeit the largest) that were occurring at the same time across the breadth of the Confederacy. William Tecumseh Sherman commanded two Union armies in Georgia and intended to capture Atlanta while breaking up the Confederate Army of Tennessee. In Louisiana, Nathaniel P. Banks had launched his Red River Expedition before Grant took command, and was then expected either to cooperate with Sherman or to attack Mobile, Alabama. Two other, smaller armies were operating in Virginia: Franz Sigel's forces in the western part of the state and Benjamin Butler's Army of the James, which was moving up the James River against Richmond and Petersburg while Grant approached the Confederate capital from the north. Because of his responsibility for all of these offensives, and because Abraham Lincoln looked to him alone to win the war, we can consider Grant a strategic leader.

137

Strategic Leadership and You

Strategic leaders are the world's movers and shakers. They are CEOs, CFOs, and managers at the very highest levels of business and industry. The modern U.S. military has strategic leaders, too, those general officers and senior civilians who are responsible for policies and decisions affecting large organizations and thousands, even millions, of people.

> Strategic leaders must "think in multiple domains and operate flexibly to manage change."

Leadership in the strategic arena is different from leadership in the world of organizations in important ways. According to *Army Leadership,* it involves "an environment of extreme uncertainty, complexity, ambiguity, and volatility." Strategic leaders must "think in multiple domains and operate flexibly to manage change."[1] Does this sound like your job? Because of his position as general in chief of the U.S. armies, Grant held a position of strategic leadership that demanded of him unique skills and methods. Ulysses S. Grant's experience with strategic leadership holds important lessons for those who operate at the highest levels of their chosen endeavors.

Strategic leadership requires interpersonal skills of a different sort from those employed at the organizational level. (See Figure 6-1.) Where Grant had the option of dealing with Meade and his corps commanders in a directive way because he chose to colocate with

---

Figure 6.1 Strategic Leadership—Interpersonal Skills.[2]

Communicating

Using dialogue

Negotiating

Achieving consensus

Building staffs

them, this method is not always available to the strategic leader. Leaders at this level often interact with people over whom they exercise little or no authority. Even if you are not a strategic leader, you may work for one. In this case, you should attempt to understand the world in which your boss works so that you can be a better follower.

> Consensus builders overcome disagreement at the highest levels by building support for their plans.

Because strategic leaders cannot order other senior officers or executives to do things, *negotiation*, *dialogue*, and *building consensus* become part and parcel of leadership at that level. Negotiation always involves some give and take, a willingness to give away a little of what you intend in order to accomplish a greater good. Good use of dialogue requires consideration of what peers and superiors say, and allows a leader to convey ideas and concepts. Consensus builders overcome disagreement at the highest levels by building support for their plans.

Grant the Strategic Negotiator

If you work in a senior leadership position, you probably employ negotiation almost every day to get your ideas across to others. In a given situation, perhaps in the formulation of a company strategic vision or in the development of a sales strategy, you may agree with other executives about the general approach but differ on important specific points. Using your authority in an autocratic way, a "my way or the highway" approach, might be within your prerogative but would do more harm than good in the long run. A great example of Grant the negotiator occurred even before he assumed command. When the Lincoln administration began considering Grant for the position of general-in-chief, they asked him his opinion of the best way to solve the problem of Lee's continual success in the eastern theater. Grant stated his opinion of the best course of action in a typically straightforward letter to Chief of Staff Henry Halleck, written in January 1864.

Instead of lunging directly at Lee along the same line of operations as in all previous Union offensives, Grant proposed a more indirect approach. He wanted to concentrate all available forces to make a newer, bigger Army of the Potomac, move that force via the Chesapeake Bay and southeastern Virginia to North Carolina, and slice into the Confederate interior, "an abandonment of all previously attempted lines to Richmond." His intermediate target would be Raleigh, North Carolina, and by capturing this he would deprive Lee of the area from which he received most of his supplies and much of his manpower. In Grant's thinking, this offensive "would virtually force an evacuation of Virginia and indirectly of East Tennessee" and "would throw our armies into new fields, where they could partially live upon the country and would reduce the stores of the enemy." George McClellan had attempted a less bold version of this maneuver with his 1862 Peninsula Campaign.[3]

> Grant used dialogue and negotiation to get his essential point across where his predecessors had failed.

This plan made tremendous sense given the futility of Union efforts in Virginia since 1861, but it was destined for disapproval on the desk of Abraham Lincoln. Grant perceived one strategic imperative: a focus on the enemy's *armies* through maneuver and offensive action. Lincoln agreed with Grant in this respect, but he also operated under a second strategic imperative. Right or wrong, Lincoln demanded the continued security of Washington, D.C., and he demanded that this be achieved by maintaining a large force between that city and Lee's army. Grant's proposal to strip the capital of its defenses in order to form a large expeditionary force was simply anathema to the Lincoln administration. It did not matter that by 1864 Washington was the most heavily fortified city on earth, and that Lee saw perfectly clearly the impossibility of capturing it.[4]

Faced with this opposition, Grant used dialogue and negotiation to get his essential point across where his predecessors had failed. Earlier eastern commanders such as McClellan, Pope, and Hooker were inflexible to a fault; as professional soldiers, they took a dim view of Lincoln, who in all fairness to them often meddled in military policy. But the strategic conferences they held with Lincoln usually ended in dissatisfaction for one or both parties. They went beyond disagreement with Lincoln into open and acrimonious arguments that were inappropriate for all concerned. Their negotiations usually took the form of distributive, or zero-sum bargaining—that is, one side was bound to win (by the Union's adopting his strategy) and one side was bound to lose (by having his approach rejected or his feelings hurt). Distributive bargaining may be necessary in some situations, such as a discussion of prices with a customer, but in Grant's case, it was important for him and for the Union cause that he and Lincoln come to an agreement that satisfied all concerned.

Grant did this by employing integrative, or collaborative, bargaining, an approach that uses shared interests and cooperation to arrive at a satisfactory outcome. (See Figure 6-2.) Grant and Lincoln agreed on the end result they desired, and they really did agree on the overall approach—just not on the specific question of a line of operation. Grant was able to convince Lincoln of the soundness of his overall plan, and as a result he got much of it implemented.

He began the integrative bargaining process in his January 1864 letter to Halleck; after proposing his North Carolina offensive, he concluded the letter by reminding the government that he had the country's best interests at heart: "From your better opportunities of studying the country and the armies that would be involved in this plan, you will be better able to judge of the practicability of it than I possibly can. I have written this in accordance with what I understand to be an invitation from you to express my views about military operations, and not to insist that any plan of mine should

---

Figure 6-2 Negotiation.

Decide on the appropriate approach:
- Distributive (winner-loser)
- Integrative (win-win)

Keep emotion from the equation.

Find the common ground.

be carried out." On the issue of defending Washington, he planned for Meade's offensive to follow the traditional route that covered Washington, thus satisfying one of the president's primary concerns. In the end, he even got permission to use Butler's Army of the James in much the same way as he had planned to use his entire force in his earlier proposal.[5]

Relationships and Communication: Foundations of Strategic Leadership

If you are a senior executive, you probably got where you are today because you formed positive relationships with those around you and communicated your ideas to others in ways that made them want to follow you. Ask any employee about a boss that he truly admires and enjoys working for, and he will probably mention these qualities: "She seems to have my interests at heart"; "I would follow him anywhere"; "It all makes sense when she explains how we are going to get it done." Grant reached the highest command position in the Union army because he was a capable general first and foremost, but once he reached that exalted height he employed these sorts of skills on a daily basis.

Grant was at his best as a strategic leader because he communicated a solid vision while exhibiting good followership and negotiation skills, as seen earlier. In contrast to his predecessors, Grant never criticized his boss in public, even though he must have chafed under the restrictions placed on him.[6] Even though strategic leaders exercise control at the highest levels, they cannot forget the vital importance of followership.[7]

Grant's relationships with three of his subordinate generals were a case in point. Nathaniel P. Banks in Louisiana and Franz Sigel and Benjamin Butler in Virginia were so-called political generals. They had gained their positions of authority early in the war, when the difficulty of raising a mass citizen army meant that Abraham Lincoln often had to rely on men with political clout but little military ability, because of their influence with large portions of the citizenry of their states. Like it or not, you probably have to work with senior executives who owe their positions to political clout, and there is nothing you can do about it. Just as Grant did, however, you can use even these subordinates to get where you need to go.

Political influence became more, not less, important as the war went on, and it came to a head in 1864 as the presidential election approached. Banks and Butler were prominent Republicans, and thus were viewed as politically acceptable by the administration and by Congress. Sigel was a German immigrant who was immensely popular with the northeast's large German-American population. Grant, and by extension Lincoln, did not have the option of replacing these men, and in any case generals of proven ability in commanding armies were scarce. As a strategic leader, Grant had to make the best of the generals provided to him.

> ". . . to hammer continuously against the armed force of the enemy and his resources, until by mere attrition, if in no other way, there should be nothing left to him."

You may be placed in the same situation with your senior staff. If you cannot remove those who are in positions of responsibility, you must figure out a way to maximize your team's performance in spite of them. Grant did this through the application of a coherent vision of victory and by "stacking the deck" with other proven generals when and where he could.

The ability to articulate vision through *communication* comes with the territory of strategic leadership. (See Figure 6-3.) Your vision will not be as simple as that of a supervisor or a midlevel manager. You will need to account for a multitude of agencies, divisions, eventualities, and possibilities, and along the way you will have to inspire everyone. Almost from the day he assumed overall command, Grant was able to convey his vision for the U.S. Army's operations very effectively.

The way he explained his vision in his July 1865 final report is a good example. Grant felt from early in the war that "active and continuous operations of all the troops that could be brought into the field, regardless of season and weather, were necessary to a

Figure 6-3 Turning a Vision Into Action.

Develop a vision. Is it . . .
- Appropriate for the boss?
- Inclusive of the whole team?
- Most applicable to the problem(s) at hand?

Determine how best to communicate your vision to the team.

Get your vision out there!
- Be positive.
- Be nested, top to bottom.
- Be as simple as possible!

speedy termination of the war." He proposed, then, "to use the greatest number of troops practicable against the armed force of the enemy; preventing him from using the same force at different seasons against first one and then another of our armies" and "to hammer continuously against the armed force of the enemy and his resources, until by mere attrition, if in no other way, there should be nothing left to him."[8] Although Grant wrote this passage years after the fact, he had this vision from the moment he assumed command.

This simple, solid, positive guidance worked its way into the orders he issued to all of his individual subordinates, so that each of them knew where his piece of the puzzle fit within the larger process. When Grant wrote to Sherman in April 1864 to explain his intention for what would become Sherman's famous March to the Sea, the language was quite similar to Grant's overall vision. Sherman, Grant wrote, was to "move against Johnston's army [the Confederate army in Georgia], to break it up and to get into the interior of the enemy's country as far as you can, inflicting all the damage you can against their war resources. I do not propose to lay down for you a plan of campaign, but simply lay down the work it is desirable to have done and leave you free to execute it in your own way." He concluded with a simple but profound vote of confidence in his trusted fellow general: "I believe you will accomplish it."[9]

Grant's vision "answered the mail" in every respect: It addressed the real problems at hand (the Confederate armies and their resources, instead of just cities), and it was politically feasible because it dovetailed quite neatly with Lincoln's view of things. Given the capabilities (or lack thereof) of some of his subordinate generals, the real beauty of this vision was that its continuous, comprehensive pressure on the enemy meant that failure by one or more subordinates to destroy enemy forces did not doom the entire grand offensive to failure. As we shall see, the wisdom of Grant's hedging his bets against failure was to become a key to ultimate Union victory. This is why strategic leaders truly earn the big bucks: because of the wide-ranging implications of the quality of their vision. Grant went a step further by informing each of his army commanders, in writing, of exactly what he expected of them in the coming campaign and of the wider implications of their campaigns in the overall plan.

Alternative Plans: Hedging Against Failure

Grant knew that Sigel and Butler were liabilities, so he sought to place proven soldiers in division command positions immediately below them, in the hope that the political generals would in some cases defer to the professionals—a long shot, yes, but better than nothing. Sigel's official position was commander of the Department of West Virginia; Grant's intention for the campaign was to have two trusted subordinates, Edward O. C. Ord and George Crook, use the department's 10,000 troops as one striking force, aimed at severing Virginia's rail link with eastern Tennessee and moving northward down the Shenandoah Valley.[10] It became clear to Ord that Sigel had no intention of letting him carry out Grant's plan, though, and so Ord resigned on April 19.

Ord was correct in his supposition. Sigel disregarded Grant's intent and divided his force into three smaller elements, two operating in southwestern Virginia under Crook and William W. Averell, and the largest (of course), under his personal command, moving southward up the valley to link up with them. Sigel's blatant insubordination should not obscure the leadership principles that Grant attempted to employ, however.

In the end, the Shenandoah Valley expedition made some small gains only because of the general in chief's personnel decisions. Sigel ensured that the offensive failed to coordinate with Grant's overall strategy. Crook's was the most successful of the three columns, defeating a small Confederate force at Cloyd's Mountain, Virginia, on May 9. Averell's force also had limited success, but it was too small to do any significant damage and was not able to move into a position to support Crook, and so by mid-May the two were back in West Virginia. Aside from a small amount of damage to the Virginia and Tennessee railroad, this phase of the offensive achieved nothing.

This withdrawal allowed the Confederate commander in the Shenandoah Valley, former U.S. Vice President John C. Breckinridge, now a Confederate major general, to concentrate his forces against Sigel at New Market, thirty miles north of Staunton on the Valley Turnpike (the present-day U.S. 11/ Interstate 81 corridor). On May 15, Breckenridge's 5,300 rebels squared off against Sigel's 9,000 Unionists and defeated them soundly. The most noteworthy moment in the battle occurred when 227 teenaged cadets of the Virginia Military Institute charged to plug a gap in the Confederate line, suffering ten killed and forty-five wounded but capturing a Union cannon and ensuring victory for Breckenridge's little army. Sigel tamely retreated northward, and by May 19, Breckenridge and 2,500 infantrymen were on board trains en route to reinforce Lee and the Army of Northern Virginia.[11]

The larger point to remember is that a well-thought out strategic plan will not bet everything on one or two events turning out perfectly. Grant's strategy made allowances for this type of failure because all of the offensives, whether successful or not by themselves, contributed to the overall intention of putting pressure on the Confederacy everywhere at once.

Your plans should likewise allow for the distinct possibility that human frailty will intervene somewhere along the line. This sort of flexibility is, if anything, most important the higher you go in an organization, again because strategic decisions have such wide-ranging impact. What if your company's primary advertising campaign does not appeal to the target audience for which you intend it? Will anyone else get it in the meantime?

Strategic Personnel Decisions: Avoiding the "Accordion Effect"

As a lifelong and diehard Washington Redskins fan, I have endured the last decade or so of NFL football with great difficulty. I have watched one of the most important strategic leaders in my personal world, Redskins owner Daniel Snyder, make a continuing series of high-level coaching and management changes. Regardless of the good intentions behind Snyder's efforts, the end result has been poor performance by the Redskins on the field of play. Coaches and assistant coaches come and go with dizzying regularity, causing an "accordion effect" within the organization. For example, each new offensive or defensive coordinator arrives with a brand new system in tow, and the players must learn that system on short notice. The learning process usually involves, at least in the near term, losing football games. Just when the players begin to learn their way around the playbook, a new coordinator brings in a new system, and the frustration begins again. The employees, football players in this example, suffer because of the lack of continuity at the strategic level.

In his role as the Union army's human resources director, Ulysses S. Grant avoided this accordion effect, and in so doing kept some continuity at the highest levels of his organization. When he took command, he could have completely removed some leaders who were not successful, but that would have led to the accordion effect. When he took overall command, Grant had the authority to name his successor as commander of the Military Division of the Mississippi, and he chose Sherman, a close friend and trusted fellow officer. In Virginia, Meade's lack of success since Gettysburg meant that Grant could have removed him had he seen fit; Meade was a professional soldier, not a political general. Grant chose instead to leave Meade in command, an important strategic decision regardless of his later moves to usurp Meade's authority. In a May 13 letter to Secretary of War Edwin M. Stanton, Grant affirmed his confidence in Sherman and Meade: "General Meade has more than met my most sanguine expectations. He and Sherman are the fittest officers for large commands I have come in contact with."

Sherman was not a tactical genius, but he was the one general whom Grant could entrust with a large task with the assurance that he would hew to the overall intention of the campaign. Even though he did not achieve immediate and stunning success, he eventually overcame stubborn opposition by Joe Johnston. By May 15, as Grant and Meade sat mired in the mud of Spotsylvania, Sherman reported that he had driven Johnston out of Dalton, a major northern Georgia rail junction. When he chose to remain with Meade in Virginia, Grant had left his forces in the west under a leader whom he could trust.[12]

Staffs and Strategic Leadership

Once Grant had made the decision to take the field with the Army of the Potomac, his job as a strategic leader became much more difficult. He was hampered by the communications difficulties of the nineteenth century and by the actions of his subordinates. A capable staff was vital to mitigating these difficulties. Strategic leaders need staff members who "know the environment, foresee consequences of various courses of action, and identify crucial information accordingly."[13] Good staffs can also compensate for a leader's weaknesses. The greater a leader's responsibilities in any business or domain, the more important it becomes that the leader put thought into the selection of those who surround him.

Grant built upon his existing staff when he assumed overall command. Charles A. Dana, an assistant secretary of war who spent a good deal of time around Grant's headquarters in both the western and eastern theaters, had labeled Grant's previous staff, centered around Illinois friends John Rawlins and Ely S. Parker, "a curious mixture of good, bad, & indifferent . . . a mosaic of accidental elements & family friends."

As general in chief, Grant needed a more professional staff. Toward that end, he added two young West Point graduates, Orville E. Babcock and Horace Porter, both capable engineers and staff officers, or, as Dana put it, "thoroughly competent men, disciplinarians, & workers." Babcock, Porter, and Cyrus B. Comstock, who joined Grant as his chief engineer at Vicksburg, were better able than Rawlins and Parker to offer Grant sound military advice and to act as sounding boards for his ideas. Rawlins was indispensable to Grant as a personal friend and reminder of the evils of alcohol, but the commander of all Federal armies needed a professional touch in his staff. To his credit, Grant realized these requirements and applied his influence to fill them.[14]

> ". . . know the environment, foresee consequences of various courses of action, and identify crucial information accordingly."

The Technical Side of Strategic Leadership

Strategic leaders use *technical skills* to produce the plans that emerge from negotiation and statements of vision. (See Figure 6-4.) *Strategic art* encompasses applying theory and ideas to the realm of action, and *leveraging technology* allows the leader to use the means at hand to get the job done. *Translating goals into objectives* must occur in any organization, not just in an army.

In Grant's case, leveraging technology came down to a matter

Figure 6-4 Strategic Leadership—Technical Skills.[15]

Strategic Art

Leveraging Technology

Translating Political Goals into Military Objectives

of battlefield calculus. Both armies were equipped with the same rifles, cannon, and communications equipment; neither side had any real advantage in this regard. The Union technological advantage lay in its massive war resources, but the problem was how to employ them to win in the near term. Grant leveraged technology and employed strategic art by envisioning a campaign that continued for months on end, relying on the Union's ability to sustain itself through multiple seasons.

Unlike many other Union generals, Grant internalized the Union's naval superiority and capitalized on it when formulating his campaign plan. Instead of thinking merely in terms of movement and supply over land and via road and railroad, he integrated naval support into his vision for success. Butler used the Union navy to slash right into the heart of the Confederacy; that he failed to capture Richmond does not diminish the boldness of Grant's vision. Army/navy integration gave the Army of the Potomac great agility during the course of the Overland Campaign, a fact that will become apparent in Chapters 8 and 9. Strategic leaders in the businesses of the twenty-first century clearly have a mandate to leverage technology, and the stakes for their organizations may be just as high as they were for Grant.[16]

The role of media and information technology in our everyday lives highlights the importance of this principle. When I purchase a new personal computer for my home office, it is usually obsolete as I remove it from the box for the first time. Your managers of information technology have become as important as any other leaders on your team because everyone, you included, relies on the decisions they make. You must therefore pick the right people for those jobs and ensure that they can help you to communicate your strategic vision.

Mark Cuban, the owner of the NBA's Dallas Mavericks basketball club, is an example of a strategic leader who has consistently leveraged technology to his organization's benefit. In the mid-1990s, Cuban saw the potential of the World Wide Web as a communications device, and he developed facilities for transmitting radio programs via the Internet. He continued to innovate even after he became a billionaire, and today he runs HDNet, the television industry's leader in the production of high-definition TV content.

Sam Grant the Strategist

Ulysses S. Grant was a successful strategic leader because he translated *interpersonal* and *technical* skills into strategic leadership actions. Through solid communication and decisive decision making, Grant *influenced* the officers and men of the Union armies to move forward in 1864. By creating a culture of relentless aggressiveness and rewarding those qualities in his subordinates, he kept his organization on track through a campaign of unbelievable adversity. According to *Army Leadership,* strategic leaders "model character by their actions." This personal example is not confined to the organizational realm. Subordinates "will hear" of an organization's core values and "then look to see if they are being lived around them." If subordinates see them in action, "institutional culture is strengthened." If they do not, that culture suffers weakness. Through his candor and his single-minded pursuit of what he knew to be the right course of action, Grant reinforced a winning culture in his organization.[17]

Grant's strategic vision dovetailed with that of his boss and penetrated to the heart of the Union's overall problem, and he executed that vision to the best of his ability in 1864, given the constraints of political reality and human leadership failures around him. By mid-May, Union armies were not much closer as the crow flies to ultimate victory, but they were light-years ahead of their predecessors in strategic terms. Grant the strategic leader made this leap possible.

Leadership Lessons

If anything, Grant was more successful as a strategic leader than as an organizational leader. His ability to translate vision into action has special application for the modern business environment:

- *Learn the strategic skill set.* The executive boardroom demands different skills from those needed to manage the assembly line or branch office. The ability to negotiate is a must, and never forget that even as a strategic leader, you probably work for someone. (Feel free to disregard that sentence, Mr. Gates.) For all of his rough-hewn appearance and quiet mannerisms, Grant moved just as effectively in strategic circles as he did on the battlefield. Without Grant's strategic skill set, Abraham Lincoln would probably have needed a lot more of his second term in office to win the war.

■ *Turn vision into action.* You didn't get where you are without being able to figure out exactly what needs to be done. But, can you communicate that vision to *everyone* who needs to know it? Will they understand it? Will that vision inspire them along the way? Grant's simple but effective expression of what he wanted to do got strategic and organizational leaders in the Union army on the same page and moving forward, more or less in concert, for the first time in the Civil War.

■ *Leverage staffs and technology to reinforce your vision.* You probably work harder today, as a senior executive, than you did at any other point in your life; that workload comes with the territory of strategic leadership. If you desire to achieve true success without killing yourself, this principle is a must. "Stack the deck" by putting capable people around you and empowering them to help you do your job. Give equal amounts of attention to the technical and technological facets of whatever it is that you do. Imaginative thought in these areas can save time and effort, and can provide huge dividends for your organization.

The adversaries: Robert E. Lee and Ulysses S. Grant as they appeared in 1864. (Library of Congress)

Union troops crossing the Rapidan River at Germanna Ford, May 1, 1864. (Library of Congress)

Grant and Meade at Massaponax Church, Virginia, May 21, 1864. In this photograph by Timothy O'Sullivan, taken from the church's upper window, Grant leans over Meade's shoulder to look at a map. (Library of Congress)

Confederate dead photographed near the Harris farm, Spotsylvania, May 19, 1864. (Library of Congress)

Union troops in captured Confederate positions near the North Anna River, May 25, 1864. The river is in the distance, with the Confederate position south of the river marked by the distant horizon line. (Library of Congress)

Grant's favorite cavalryman, Philip H. Sheridan. (Library of Congress)

Grant photographed at City Point during the Overland Campaign. (Library of Congress)

Union cavalrymen cross the North Anna River, May 1864. (Library of Congress)

Union soldiers stand on a pontoon bridge over the North Anna River, May 1864. (Library of Congress)

Destroyed bridge of the Richmond and Fredericksburg Railroad. (Library of Congress)

50th New York Engineers constructing road at Jericho Mills, Virginia. (Library of Congress)

Union wounded from the Wilderness recover at a Fredericksburg hospital.
(Library of Congress)

Lieutenant-General Ulysses S. Grant and staff at Cold Harbor, June 1864. Grant is standing by the tree, right center. (Library of Congress)

Union army pontoon bridge over the James River in June 1864.
(Library of Congress)

Harvest of death: Skeletons recovered from the Cold Harbor
Battlefield. (Library of Congress)

Winfield Scott Hancock, U.S.A. (Library of Congress)

G. K. Warren, Meade's Fifth Corps commander.
(Library of Congress)

James Longstreet, C.S.A. (Library of Congress)

John Sedgwick, U.S.A. (Library of Congress)

Richard S. Ewell, C.S.A. (Library of Congress)

A. P. Hill, C.S.A. (Library of Congress)

Matthew Brady captured this image of Robert E. Lee in Richmond, Virginia, just after Lee's surrender in April 1865. (Library of Congress)

The McLean House as Matthew Brady photographed it in 1865. (Library of Congress)

General U. S. Grant writing his memoirs, Mt. McGregor, New York, June 27, 1885. (Library of Congress)

Robert E. Lee in a postwar photograph, probably taken shortly before his death. (Library of Congress)

CHAPTER SEVEN

To the North Anna

Organizational Leadership Skills for Crisis Situations

"I shall continue to strike him whenever opportunity presents itself."

—GENERAL ROBERT E. LEE TO JEFFERSON DAVIS, MAY 18, 1864[1]

"I don't care how you get it done, just get it done!" "This is your baby, so *do something!*" The big boss makes these pronouncements and leaves the room. Despite your best efforts and intentions, your plan has gone off the track. Now what? A shift supervisor, junior salesperson, or shop foreman has to keep only a small team of employees focused on the task at hand. As a leader, you must sustain organizational effectiveness and get maximum productivity out of your subordinates. Your problem is much more complex. Let's use the various facets of effective organizational leadership to get out of this jam.

Leadership at different levels requires different sets of skills. Some of these skills may be common to direct, organizational, and strategic leadership, but as we saw in Chapter 6, each level has its unique pitfalls and challenges. Leaders and managers of organizations must orchestrate the efforts of groups as well as individuals, and must demonstrate *interpersonal, conceptual, technical,* and *tactical* skills.

Grant and Lee had to exercise adept organizational leadership during the period from May 19 to May 25 in order to keep their armies alive and on the move. During this period, they both faced a number of crisis situations that mirror the challenges that you may face from time to time. By thinking about and developing these unique sets of skills (see Figure 7-1), you can become a more effective organizational leader.

Leadership in Crisis

The inconclusive fighting at Spotsylvania made it clear to Grant that he had to come up with a new course of action. Butler's failure to move against Richmond or Petersburg meant that Lee would feel no pressure from the south; he could remain in place at Spotsylvania indefinitely unless Grant dislodged him. After May 12, then, the Overland Campaign became something different, something unique among Civil War campaigns. Prior to the spring of 1864, two

---

Figure 7-1 Organizational Leadership Skills.[2]

Interpersonal
- Understanding subordinates
- Communicating
- Supervising

Conceptual
- Establishing intent
- Filtering information
- Understanding intent

Technical
- Maintaining critical skills
- Resourcing
- Predicting second- and third-order effects

Tactical
- Synchronization
- Orchestration

weeks of continuous fighting would have been unheard of; grand battles like Second Bull Run, Chancellorsville, and Gettysburg lasted for two or three days, after which the combatants withdrew almost by mutual agreement to lick their wounds and plan the next movement. Grant's new approach was to change all of that, and in the process he would demand of his army a new level of performance.

> "The Army of the Potomac has always longed for a fighting general—one who would fight, and fight, and fight—and now it has got him."

Although the modern reader knows the ultimate outcome of this story already, the outcome was not nearly so certain in mid-May of 1864. After thousands of casualties and untold suffering on both sides, the position of the two armies was little different from what it had been at any time previously during the war. Although for the Union cause it was a step in the right direction to still be south of the Rapidan River instead of back in the Washington fortifications, discontent over Grant's methods was swelling across the North. His soldiers had cheered him in the Wilderness for turning south on May 7, but by May 19 they were worn out and discouraged.

After Spotsylvania, one Union soldier offered a commentary on the campaign thus far. "The Army of the Potomac has always longed for a fighting general—one who would fight, and fight, and fight—and now it has got him," the wounded man said. "But, he does not know that Lee's veteran infantry cannot be driven out of skillfully constructed earthworks by direct assault. . . . The enlisted men have been sacrificed." A soldier who heard the man's comments remembered that "this was the first complaint I heard about Grant. I heard plenty before the campaign closed."[3] Grant's challenge was interpersonal. He had to sustain whatever positive momentum he had gained since May 4 without running his workforce into the ground.

Lee's Tactical Challenge

For his part, Lee had to be somewhat satisfied that he had continually parried Grant's blows, but like a lightweight boxer facing a heavyweight, time and attrition were destined to take their toll. Simply put, Lee had only a short space in which to strike a blow that was devastating enough to make Grant withdraw. That space could be measured in the distance from Spotsylvania southward to the North Anna River, a distance of about twenty miles.

> "We must destroy this Army of Grant's before he gets to the James River. If he gets there it will become a siege, and then it will be a mere question of time."

The line of the North Anna offered the last strong natural barrier before the armies reached the fortifications on the outskirts of Richmond. Holding at the North Anna was also important because a defensive line there shielded the vital rail terminus at Hanover Junction, where the Virginia Central Railroad arrived from the Shenandoah Valley. The Virginia Central was literally a lifeline for Lee's army; supplies and reinforcements from western Virginia rode its rails. As Lee told one of his generals that month, "We must destroy this Army of Grant's before he gets to the James River. If he gets there it will become a siege, and then it will be a mere question of time."[4] The leadership challenge for Lee was to turn an increasingly disadvantageous position into something positive in a very short time.

Second- and Third-Order Effects—Orchestration in Action

One of the key facets of organizational leadership is the orchestration and synchronization of sometimes widely separated parts into a whole plan of action. As a regional manager, for example, you may be responsible for branch offices in several states, or even in several different countries. Keeping these parts moving in the same direction can be difficult. After Spotsylvania, Grant decided to replace attrition with maneuver, and he developed a plan designed to take advantage of the very aggressiveness that had made Lee so successful on so many other battlefields. This plan would require a great

Map 7-1. Movement of the armies from the Wilderness to the North Anna River, May 4–25, 1864. (United States Military Academy)

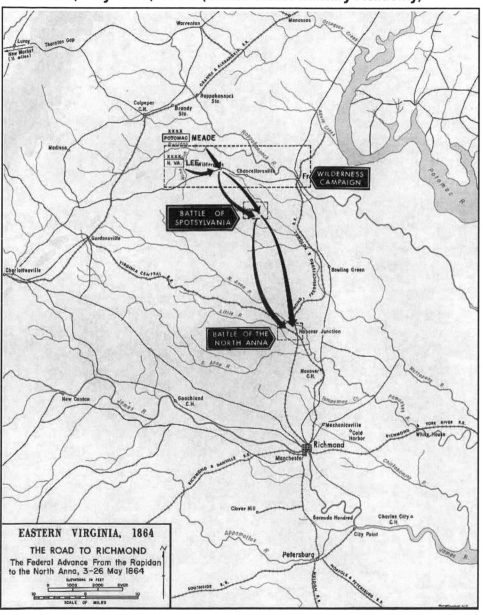

deal more synchronization than anything he had attempted thus far in the campaign.

After Lee's attacks on the Union right flank at Harris Farm on May 19, Grant told his aide Porter that "my anxiety now is to draw Lee out of his works and fight him in the open field, instead of assaulting him behind his entrenchments. The movement of Early [Ewell, at Harris Farm] yesterday gives me some hope that Lee may at times take the offensive, and thus give our troops the desired opportunity." From his position east of Spotsylvania Courthouse, he planned to send one corps, Hancock's Second, on a looping flank march to the south and east, ending up in the vicinity of Milford Station on the Richmond, Fredericksburg, and Potomac Railroad, south of the Mattoponi River and a few miles from Hanover Junction.

> "... there was no question in his [Grant's] mind as to whipping his opponent; the only problem was how to get at him."

This advanced position would give Grant a number of options for the movement of his other corps, and he operated on the assumption that he would be able to use the area's main north-south road, the Telegraph Road, to move the rest of his army directly to the North Anna River. Grant chose Hancock to make the march because of his consistently excellent performance over the previous two weeks. He was definitely earning his sobriquet "Hancock the Superb," but Hancock was also still recovering from the ghastly groin wound he had suffered at Gettysburg, and his corps had suffered very heavy losses in the Wilderness and at Spotsylvania.[5]

The Second Corps and its general was Grant's "go to" option, and this planned movement would dangle it in front of Lee, offering it as a tempting target for one of Lee's patented aggressive attacks. Once Lee emerged from his fortifications and lashed out at Hancock, Grant would respond by hurling his remaining three corps at the Confederate army while it was on the move. This was clearly the most ambitious, complex, and aggressive plan that Grant had conceived so far in this campaign.

Grant's risky plan reminds us that organizational leaders must consider the *second- and third-order effects* of any plans that they institute. Once those plans are in motion, it may be difficult to rein them in, and they may have unintended consequences unless they are very carefully designed. Grant deemed the risks of his plan worth the possible outcomes, and it was certainly characteristic of his thinking throughout the campaign. If Lee took the bait and attacked Hancock as he moved south, Grant could pitch into the outstretched Confederate forces as they moved south across his front. If Lee stayed in position near Spotsylvania, Grant could consolidate his position closer to Richmond, once again forcing Lee to give battle on the Union army's terms.

In the second case, possible second- and third-order effects were the destruction of the Second Corps and the Union army's vulnerability as it moved in widely separated wings. Porter dismissed these criticisms in his memoirs, calling Grant's plan "unquestionably wise generalship" because he "knew that Lee, from the distance over which he would have to move his troops, could not attack the isolated Hancock" with enough force to destroy him. Because Grant would be "in close communication with the several corps" of the army, he could bring up reinforcements as rapidly as could Lee. Ever the optimist, "there was no question in his [Grant's] mind as to whipping his opponent; the only problem was how to get at him."[6]

While an aggressive plan was certainly the right way for Grant to come to grips with Lee, the unfolding campaign once again demonstrated that aggressiveness and optimism frequently led Grant to underestimate the difficulties of his chosen course of action. This was especially true with regard to synchronization and orchestration. Seeking to be proactive is rarely a bad thing, but aggressiveness without due consideration can lead to disaster.

That disaster could easily have befallen Grant as he attempted to maneuver his army on May 21 to 23. The Union army was really in no shape, after the grueling combat that had taken place since May 4, to undertake a movement on this scale; even Grant and his senior generals were beginning to feel the strain. Hancock reached his objective at Milford Station, but as of mid-morning on May 21 he was effectively out of contact with Grant and Meade. The army headquarters chose to move along Hancock's route of march, positioning itself so that it could communicate neither with Hancock nor with Warren in any timely manner. Messages from corps commanders to Grant routinely took five or six hours in transit. Throughout the movement, Grant's four corps commanders moved without supervision—not a very good arrangement given Grant's distinct lack of confidence in any of them but Hancock.

This lag in communication left the scattered corps vulnerable, and also prevented Grant from doing precisely what he wished to do during the movement: Attack Lee's army while it was in motion. Lee figured out by late on May 20 that at least the Union Second Corps was in motion, but he could not move his entire force until he got confirmation that the other three were also evacuating the Spotsylvania position. In the meantime, however, he sent his own Second Corps, still under Ewell, eastward to seize a vital intersection on the Telegraph Road, making Lee essentially invulnerable to any flank attack and invalidating one of Grant's key assumptions (that he would be able to use the Telegraph Road to move quickly south to the North Anna).

As it became clear on May 21 that Grant's entire force was on the move, Lee considered his options and decided on Hanover Junction as his best point of concentration; it allowed him to both thwart Hancock and keep an eye on the rest of the Union army. Lee's First and Second Corps accordingly moved out on the Telegraph Road during the evening of May 21 and obligingly moved right across the front of the Union Fifth Corps. Grant was out of contact with Warren, however, and the latter general was in no mood to strike out at Lee's forces as night fell. Thus did a golden opportunity pass for Grant; this part of the plan was definitely a victim of unanticipated second- and third-order effects. As a result, Grant's aggressive plan fell to pieces from fatigue, stress, miscommunications, and Lee's sure-handed response. By midnight on May 21, the Army of Northern Virginia had won the race to the North Anna just as it had won the race to Spotsylvania.[7]

Lee also failed to anticipate the second- and third-order effects of a critical decision that he made once his army had reached the relative safety of the North Anna line. As his troops filed across bridges and fords and entrenched south of the river along the Virginia Central Railroad, Lee still did not have a firm grasp of Grant's intentions. Unlike previous opponents, Grant's persistence was making it more and more difficult for Lee to predict what he would do; Lee's adjutant Walter Taylor commented to his fiancée with grudging respect that Grant "certainly holds on longer than any of them. He alone would have remained this side of the Rappahannock" after the battles thus far."[8]

As always, though, Lee made troop dispositions based upon his educated guesses, and his guess on May 23 was that Grant would continue his movement southeast toward the Pamunkey River, where

> In this supposition Lee was terribly wrong, and it led to a tactical mistake; this miscalculation had the potential to destroy his army.

he could use the landing at White House to supply his army. This movement would avoid Lee's entrenched positions and put him in a position both to threaten Richmond and to cooperate with Butler at Bermuda Hundred. Walter Taylor reflected Lee's hunches in his May 23 letter when he wrote, "On the day before it was discovered that the enemy was leaving our front & making towards Bowling Green. He dared not, as we prayed he wd, attack us again at Spottsylvania. . . . I think it probably he will make still another move to the right."

In his May 23 update to Jefferson Davis (in general, Lee's updates to his boss were models of clarity and information), Lee offered that "all my information indicates that the movement of Grant's army is in the direction of Milford Station [to the east]," and that in his opinion the Union army was "very much shaken" by the events of the past week. He went on to state that he believed that the *entire enemy force* remained east of the Mattoponi River, reorganizing and receiving reinforcements.[9] Accordingly, Lee allowed his army to rest on May 23 without entrenching south of the North Anna River. He believed that he needed to hold his men in readiness to move rapidly to the east, and that Grant would not dare to attack him where he sat. Only small detachments of troops guarded the North Anna crossings.

In this supposition Lee was terribly wrong, and it led to a tactical mistake; this miscalculation had the potential to destroy his army. On the night of May 22, Grant issued orders putting the army in motion at 5 a.m.: the Fifth Corps toward Jericho Ford, the Second toward Chesterfield Bridge, and the Sixth and Ninth following behind. By midmorning on May 23, Grant had most of his army west of the Mattoponi River and well on its way toward the North Anna; he planned to retain the initiative by attacking Lee wherever he found him south of the North Anna, before he had time to prepare a strong defensive line.[10]

Interpersonal Skills and Organizational Leadership

You know your subordinates' names, you know their spouses' and their children's names, but do you really *know them*? How do they react under stress? Do they prefer more supervision in these cases? Or do they prefer to work out problems on their own? Do they need your constant guidance, or can you focus your attention elsewhere with the assurance that they will usually do the right thing? Whatever his shortcomings in visualizing the task before him, during the North Anna phase of the Overland Campaign Lee once again demonstrated his mastery of the *interpersonal* dimension of organizational

> "Unless we can drive these people [Union skirmishers] out, or find out whether they are all gone, we are detained here to our disadvantage."

leadership. He did so under the most trying circumstances possible. To deal with problems within his chain of command, Lee applied a sure hand in understanding his various subordinates, communicating with them, and supervising their actions to the extent he deemed necessary.

As he repositioned his army to the south in order to counter Grant's moves, Lee provided *supervision* and an *understanding* of the capabilities and limitations of his least experienced corps commander, Richard H. Anderson. A. P. Hill and Dick Ewell were capable corps commanders (even if both had disappointed Lee in the past two weeks). Anderson required a different sort of handling, however. He had performed reasonably well in the Wilderness and at Spotsylvania, where the Army of Northern Virginia maneuvered and fought in a fairly concentrated manner. The movement toward the North Anna was different, however; it was more akin to some of Lee's previous campaigns in northern Virginia, Maryland, and Pennsylvania, where he required his corps to move on dispersed routes.

As Ewell got underway with the Second Corps on May 21, Lee was quite specific in his guidance to Anderson, giving instructions in his dispatches that he would never have needed to give to more experienced generals. Lee reminded Anderson in one dispatch to "have pickets out on the road by which you marched, so as to avoid a surprise by the enemy." A second dispatch, written two hours later, shows the somewhat more directive touch of a concerned boss. In it, Lee informed Anderson that he had issued orders directly to one of Anderson's division commanders, Charles Field, "to sweep his front, and if he finds enemy gone, to prepare his troops to march and report result to you." The order continues, "I wish you, if he reports enemy gone, to put your troops in motion at once on the route which I have designated to you." A third note, transmitted one hour later, reminded Anderson rather gently that "Unless we can drive these people [Union skirmishers] out, or find out whether they are all gone, we are detained here to our disadvantage."

Lee himself wrote two of these notes; he left only the first of them to his aide-de-camp, Charles Venable, perhaps thinking that Anderson needed to hear his intention in a very direct manner. Under this close supervision, Anderson performed quite well on the movement to the North Anna. In this particular situation, directive leadership worked well, and Lee derived maximum performance from an inexperienced subordinate.[11]

The fighting on May 24 turned out precisely as Grant intended it. Lee's cavalry, now without the guiding hand of Jeb Stuart, misled Lee badly as to Union troop movements. Warren's corps crossed the North Anna and fell upon Hill's Third Corps while Lee was out inspecting the army's right flank. Hill responded badly, sending only one division to deal with Warren. Cadmus Wilcox's four brigades attacked Warren's men just south of Jericho Mills and temporarily drove them back, but the attack was poorly handled, and in any case was too small to do any damage. Wilcox retreated in the face of superior numbers, and by nightfall the entire Fifth Corps was astride the Virginia Central Railroad and poised to attack eastward. When he met with Hill the next day, Lee could barely contain his anger, no doubt exacerbated by the fact that he had not slept for more than two hours at a stretch since May 5. "General Hill, why did you let those people cross here?" Lee demanded. "Why didn't you throw your whole force on them and drive them back as Jackson would have done?" In fairness to Hill, there was plenty of blame to go around on this day.

Confederate misfortunes continued a few miles to the east when Hancock's Second Corps overran the small Confederate force guarding Chesterfield Bridge, where the Telegraph Road crossed the North Anna and entered the heart of the Confederate position. Jubilant Yankees put their own artillery into the Confederate fortifications and prepared to use the northern bank of the river, which was significantly higher than the southern bank, to bombard Lee's line. At nightfall, Grant had one corps across the river and the other four in possession of the major crossing sites. The mood at Grant's headquarters was equally jubilant that night. "Everything looks exceedingly favorable to us," Grant wired to Washington.[12]

Participating Leadership at Critical Moments

The mood in Lee's camp that evening was decidedly more circumspect; the Army of Northern Virginia was in a dangerous spot. At this critical juncture, Lee responded to a crisis situation in a way that demonstrated his *interpersonal* and *conceptual* skills. If you were faced with a similar crisis, would you tend to revert to directive leadership, making critical decisions by yourself? That might not be the best response, especially if you have a capable supporting cast.

Lee chose this moment to employ participating leadership, in which a leader solicits opinions and ideas from subordinates, deliberates on them with the group, and makes the final decision himself. He held what artilleryman Porter Alexander termed "a regular little council" under "a big, lone oak tree in a forty acre clearing." Instead of deciding on his own what to do next and making an immedi-

> Lee "sat on a root," his back against a large tree, and let his generals offer various proposals.

ate pronouncement, he opened a meeting of his staff and subordinate commanders by first receiving situation updates from them. Then he asked the opinions of the group as to what course of action to pursue. Porter Alexander wrote that Lee "sat on a root," his back against a large tree, and let his generals offer various proposals. Lee "heard the arguments, which were brief & to the point." In spite of some recent faltering performances by key subordinates, Lee resisted the leader's natural inclination, when facing dire circumstances, to grab hold of the reins and exercise direct control.[13]

The natural inclination for Lee's generals would have been to entrench along the elevated Virginia Central Railroad, but Warren's position meant that any straight line there would be automatically outflanked. Then one of the staff officers in the group spoke up with an idea. The officer was Martin L. Smith, Lee's chief engineer. An 1842 graduate of West Point, Smith had initially served in the western theater, where he designed the Vicksburg fortifications. Captured when Grant took the city in 1863, he was paroled and joined Lee's staff late that year.

Smith had demonstrated his capabilities to Lee on several occasions during the Overland Campaign. In the Wilderness on May 6, he located the unused railroad cut that Longstreet's men used as a concealed attack route in almost destroying the Second Corps. At Spotsylvania, Smith superintended the construction of Lee's formidable fortifications. As he wrote to his wife, he seemed to have "acquired the confidence of General Lee to the extent of his being willing to place the troops on the lines of my selection and stake the issue of a battle." This was no faint praise from Lee, himself a West Point–trained engineer.

Smith had spent May 23 riding the Confederate line and had found a series of ridgelines between the North Anna and a smaller stream to the south, the Little River. The ridgelines ran perpendicular to the railroad in the west, stretching from the Little River up to the North Anna. Smith's proposed line then fronted the North Anna for one-half mile, facing the river at the top of an impassable bluff. The line then bent back to the southeast, recrossing the Little River and cutting the Telegraph Road before ending to the northeast of Hanover Junction. As proposed, the line represented an inverted V, with its flanks anchored on impassable terrain.

Lee immediately saw the possibilities for this position. It gave him "interior lines," a military term for a situation that allows a general to move troops across the interior of a position more quickly than the opponent can move across the outside. The inverted V position had the Virginia Central Railroad running across its base, which would allow the quick movement of troops from one end of the line to the other.

This defensive position, combined with the locations of Grant's corps, gave Lee the greatest opportunity of the campaign to inflict damage on the Army of the Potomac. Warren's corps was separated from the rest of the army by the river, making reinforcement in great numbers by Wright's Sixth Corps almost impossible. Burnside's Ninth Corps faced an unassailable position; he would have to move either left or right and cross the river in order to attack. Once Hancock followed up his success of May 23 by crossing the river, he too would have his corps separated from the rest of the Union army. Any attempt by one of the corps to reinforce the others would involve crossing the river, moving through rough terrain, and crossing once again.

> "We must strike them a blow. We must never let them pass us again . . . we must strike them a blow."

Lee could leave a skeleton force guarding one side of the line and concentrate his forces against one or the other of the exposed

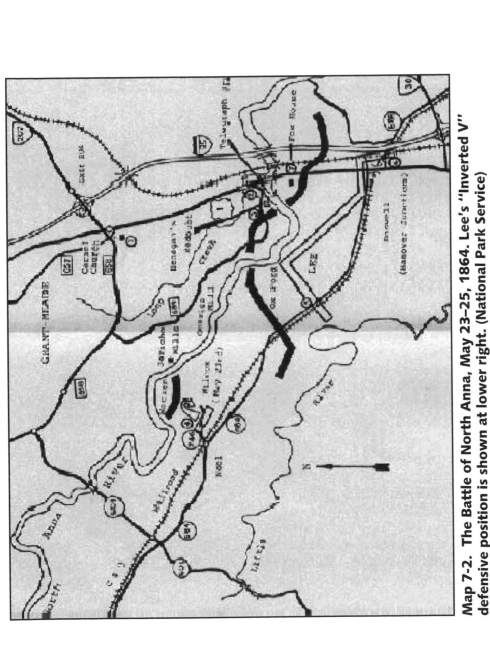

Map 7-2. The Battle of North Anna, May 23–25, 1864. Lee's "Inverted V" defensive position is shown at lower right. (National Park Service)

Federal corps; the lack of a stout defense all along the line of the river would also fool Grant into thinking that Lee was retreating once again. True, this defensive position was a salient, as had been the Mule Shoe, but this came as close as possible to being the perfect defensive position.[14] Lee had this golden opportunity because he consistently empowered capable subordinates to make hard decisions and come up with innovative solutions.

Once the Army of Northern Virginia left Spotsylvania, Lee did an excellent job of gaining *resources* in the form of troops from other areas of the Confederacy. Once Grant's other Virginia offensives had failed, Jefferson Davis and General Braxton Bragg, now Davis's adviser, felt comfortable in diverting troops to Lee's army. Ever the patient advocate for his own organization, Lee constantly reminded Davis in a tactful way that he needed reinforcements. As a result, several excellent brigades of Confederate troops, almost 30,000 men in all, joined Lee at the North Anna. As an organizational leader, you may have at your disposal additional assets from outside your area of responsibility. With planning and forethought, you can integrate them into your plan.

The day after Lee's council of war, May 24, Grant obliged Lee by moving straight into his trap, but at this critical moment Lee's health failed him, and his organization failed as a result. Hancock's Second Corps crossed in the direction of Hanover Junction, and Wright crossed behind Warren. Burnside attempted to cross at Ox Ford, facing the apex of the inverted V, and with that the trap was set. Six miles and a river separated the two wings of the Army of the Potomac, and Grant and his commanders still thought the Confederates were retreating. Hancock's corps, Grant's most trustworthy unit, was in by far the most dangerous position; it relied on two rickety pontoon bridges to get back across the North Anna if necessary, and it faced a Confederate force that outnumbered it considerably.

But Lee's masterstroke was not to be. Instead, he fell victim to a wave of dysentery that swept through the ill-fed and exhausted Confederate army; this condition was made worse by Lee's persistent health problems over the past year. In 1863, he suffered what may have been a mild stroke, and during the Gettysburg campaign exhibited signs of the heart disease that would help to bring about his death in 1870. On May 24, the accumulated strains of the Overland Campaign laid Marse Robert low; he spent the day confined to his sleeping tent, wracked with diarrhea. Unable to press an attack forward by the force of his will, as he had done so many times before, and without the services of Longstreet, Jackson, and Stuart, the command team that had stood him in such good stead for two years, Lee could "attend to nothing except what was absolutely necessary for him to know & act upon." At various times during the day, he was heard to mutter, "We must strike them a blow. We must never let them pass us again . . . we must strike them a blow."[15]

But no blow was to come. A. P. Hill's problems, physical and otherwise, continued, and his forces stayed where they were. Anderson was too new in command to make a bold attack out of his fortifications without Lee's supervision. Ewell also remained in place, apparently suffering from dysentery as well. At this moment of truth, the Army of Northern Virginia was unable to respond. Lee gave orders for his generals to attack, but another aide, C. S. Venable, put it aptly when he pointed out, "Lee confined to his tent was not Lee on the battlefield." Grant made some limited attacks on parts of the line, realized that Lee's position was rock-solid, and pulled away or entrenched his men in time to avert disaster. May 24 passed without any Confederate riposte.[16]

The Confederate army's failure sounds a note of caution for any leader. If you are sick or incapacitated, can your team carry on in your absence? A great litmus test for any organization is how it performs when the boss is not around. Lee found out in late May that his army was no longer in any sort of shape to function in the way he intended if he was not there to exercise direct authority.

Building redundancy into your chain of command is a vital task; we can use the National Football League as another case in point. The 1972 Miami Dolphins, the only team in NFL history to complete a perfect season, played much of their undefeated campaign with a backup, Earl Morrall, at quarterback. Unfortunately for Lee, attrition and poor health had robbed the Army of Northern Virginia of a similar redundancy. Don't let this happen to your team!

Organizational Leadership on the North Anna

The North Anna phase of the Overland Campaign ended on May 26, when Grant extricated his army from its bridgehead and attempted yet another move around Lee's right flank. Grant and Lee turned in mixed performances during this part of the campaign, in some cases offering as many negative leadership examples as they did positive ones. Because of overoptimism and slipshod planning and communications, Grant failed for the most part in the *tactical* skills of organizational leadership—the *synchronization* of the pieces of his army in accordance with his plan and the *orchestration* of their actions.

His relationship with Meade steadily deteriorated; the latter was effectively reduced to the role of staff officer by May 25, transmitting Grant's orders to corps commanders if he did anything at all. While certainly flexible in reacting to unanticipated turns of events, Grant consistently ignored the practical difficulties of implementing his increasingly ambitious plans. In the end, the Army of the Potomac was again on the move toward Richmond, but only because of Grant's dogged and absolute persistence and because of the mistakes of his opponent.

> Grant failed for the most part in the *tactical* skills of organizational leadership.

Lee once again displayed the model interpersonal and conceptual skills that had made him a winner. He applied differing levels of supervision to his subordinates in consonance with their capabilities, and he continued to monitor Ewell and Hill. Once he arrived at the North Anna, however, Lee displayed a troubling disregard for the aggressive tendencies of his opponent; he was indeed lucky that only a portion of his Third Corps suffered because of this laxity. At the end of the day, Lee's intermediate leadership was not able to respond when he was indisposed, a troubling development with deep implications for the rest of the campaign.

Leadership Lessons

- *Don't let optimism or a "can-do" spirit blind you to second- and third-order effects.* As Lee and Grant demonstrated for us after May 19, there is a very fine line between "can do" and "didn't." Grant's bold move worked out, but had it failed, history would probably have indicted him for asking the impossible from his men. In the end, you are in a critical position of leadership because you have demonstrated the ability to make the right choices. When the time comes to make critical decisions, put your feet up for a moment, think, and keep Grant's experience in mind. Neither was Lee at his best in this regard. Whether because he continued to downplay Grant's abilities, or because his health was failing him, or because he had simply *always* won on his home turf, Lee also failed to consider second- and third-order effects. He, too, left his army in some precarious positions as a result.

- *Pay constant attention to your interpersonal relationships.* An organizational leader must know not only herself, but also the tendencies, abilities, and shortcomings of each and every one of her subordinates. She must then be able to apply different leadership styles to them as different situations arise. Lee demonstrated this ability on the North Anna. As a result, his army performed at least at the level that he expected, with one notable exception: Hill consistently failed to live up to Lee's expectations. Lee had every reason to expect these problems, but he still did nothing.

- *Think about a participating leadership style in true crisis situations.* Sometimes crisis brings out the best in your people. If you deem your subordinates capable of this, go to them at crunch time, listen to them, and let them surprise you with their ingenuity. Your first reaction in a crisis may be to move more toward directive leadership—after all, you are responsible, and who can better make sure that things get done right? If you have trusted your people up to now, though, why stop?

Lee allowed a relatively junior subordinate to help him at the North Anna, and the result was a masterpiece of military science. This key moment came out of a participative conference, not a directive from the brain of Robert E. Lee.

■ *Build redundancy into your chain of command.* After his brilliant defensive dispositions, Lee fell ill at the moment of truth. As a result, his army was not able to take advantage of a great opportunity. We have demonstrated throughout this book that Lee's personnel moves were generally right on the mark, but his illness at the North Anna should remind you that you may not always be there to make key decisions for your organization. Because Lee did not have James Longstreet, his most capable general, at his side, there was no one to step in and attack the separated pieces of Grant's army at the North Anna.

CHAPTER EIGHT

Cold Harbor

Friction and Failure In Organizational Leadership

"Old U.S. Grant is very tired of us—at least it appears so. We are in excellent trim—and even in fine spirits—and ready for a renewal of the fight whenever the signal is given."

—COLONEL WALTER TAYLOR TO HIS FIANCÉE, JUNE 9, 1864[1]

Hubris, pettiness, exhaustion, political pressures, incompetence, or simple bad luck—all of these factors can combine to bring down even the best-laid plans. Carl von Clausewitz, the nineteenth-century German military theorist, summarized these negative factors in one simple word: *friction*. In his magnum opus *On War*, to this day one of the most studied works of theory in world history, Clausewitz describes this phenomenon. The business leader could easily substitute any other endeavor for the word *war*.

> *Friction is the only concept that more or less corresponds to the factors that distinguish real war from war on paper. The military machine . . . is basically very simple and therefore easy to manage. But we should bear in mind that none of its components is of one piece: each part is composed of individuals, every one of whom retains his poten-*

173

*tial of friction. . . . A battalion is made up of individuals,
the least important of whom may chance to delay things
or somehow make them go wrong. The . . . physical exer-
tions that war demands . . . aggravate the problem . . .*

*This tremendous friction . . . is everywhere in contact
with chance, and brings about effects that cannot be
measured. . . . Action in war is like movement in a resistant
element. Just as the simplest and most natural of movements, walking, cannot easily be performed in water, so in
war it is difficult for normal efforts to achieve even moder-
ate results.*

*Friction, as we choose to call it, is the force that makes
the apparently easy so difficult.*[2]

Cold Harbor. The words resonate with me because I was born
and raised only ten miles from the battlefield, one of the war's most
gruesome. I grew up a Civil War buff partly because of the stories
my parents told me, listening in morbid fascination to tales of the
thousands of Union soldiers who died in just a few minutes near
that obscure Virginia crossroads in 1864.

Even today, the Battle of Cold Harbor is enshrouded in myth
and mystery. But when one peels back these layers of misunderstanding, a fascinating leadership case study emerges. From the
leadership perspective, Cold Harbor is a story of missed opportunities, bungled decisions, and the tragic consequences of dysfunctional management relationships. At the end of the battle, Grant
remarked that he regretted the decision to fight at Cold Harbor
more than any other decision he made during the war. Likewise, at
the end of the Battle of Cold Harbor, Lee's back was truly against
the wall; from their trenches his men could hear the church bells of
Richmond, only seven miles away. Friction had a field day with both
Grant and Lee at Cold Harbor; modern business leaders can learn
from their mistakes in dealing with it.

Friction vs. Communication

For organizational leaders, one of the most dangerous effects of
friction is the negative effect that it can have on interpersonal rela-

tions, and particularly on communication. When things don't go well for a company, tempers can grow short and animosities can surface. Friction poisoned the relationship between Ulysses S. Grant and George G. Meade, with negative consequences for the organization they led, the Army of the Potomac. The army was still in fairly sound shape because of Grant's understanding of logistics, but the same could not be said for the Grant-Meade relationship.

After Grant's failed attacks at the North Anna on May 24, it once again became clear to him that maneuver, not frontal assault, would have to be the answer. As on the Rapidan, in the Wilderness, and at Spotsylvania, the options boiled down to two: east or west, Lee's right flank or left flank. Grant the gambler initially favored turning Lee's left flank because this would have been the more unexpected course of action.

But Grant had learned from the previous three weeks. The riskiest option was not necessarily the best in this theater of war, against this opponent. He chose instead to move again to Lee's right, in the direction of the Pamunkey River, a tributary of the York River, which in turn fed into Chesapeake Bay. This decision reflected Grant's growing prudence, but it also showed a good deal of operational sophistication. Grant was not merely a fighting general; he had, like great leaders in any field of endeavor, a deep understanding of *every* facet of his profession. For the "modern" general of the time, this meant a sound understanding of logistics.

One of the reasons that Grant was able to keep his army in the field, continuing to hammer away at Lee and causing the Virginian casualties he could not afford, was that he ensured that the Army of the Potomac was the best-supplied army the world had ever seen. When the Army of the Potomac occupied camps above the Rapidan River, it received its supplies via railroad and the Potomac River. As he moved south, Grant moved his supply depots first to Belle Plain, north of Fredericksburg, and then to Port Royal; both locations were accessible via the Rappahannock River. This logistical muscle gave Grant the flexibility to do what he thought best, but it also led him to make decisions that were grounded in common sense.

In this case, moving to the east and repositioning his base of supplies at White House Landing on the Pamunkey River was undoubtedly the right thing to do. It allowed Grant to rely on his increasingly close relationship with the Union navy, another fact that separated Grant from the pack of Civil War generals. By the next year, Grant was employing almost 400 vessels of all types to sustain his army in Virginia, at a cost to the U.S. government of $48,000 per day. This level of logistical support simply would not have been possible had Grant tried to rely on railroads and wagons for his supplies, and in any case not using sea power would have either limited or completely ruled out Grant's eventual movement south of the James River.[3]

This well-supplied façade masked deeper fault lines, however, and these fault lines were to exacerbate the growing friction within Grant's command structure. Grant's inability to create a healthy command climate within the Army of the Potomac was a powder keg that threatened to explode at any time.

The relationship between Grant and Meade was the spark that hovered over the powder keg. Grant set out on the Overland Campaign with the express intention of leaving the actions and movements of the Army of the Potomac to Meade's discretion so that he could remain free to focus on his duties as general in chief. Meade was satisfied with this arrangement, at least at first, but this division of effort was casualty number one of the friction that enveloped the Union army once it crossed the Rapidan.

The army did not move quickly enough for Grant's taste in the Wilderness, so he began taking upon himself some of the tactical decisions. On the road to Spotsylvania, Grant took Sheridan's side in his dispute with Meade over the mission of the army's cavalry, leaving Meade angry, disillusioned, and, more importantly, completely bereft of cavalry for two critical weeks. Although Sheridan took advantage of his newfound independence to do great damage to the Confederate cavalry, including mortally wounding Jeb Stuart at Yellow Tavern on May 11, Grant set a very bad precedent in siding with Sheridan.

> "Out here the enemy knows we can and will fight them like the devil."

At Spotsylvania, Grant made no attempt to leave Meade in

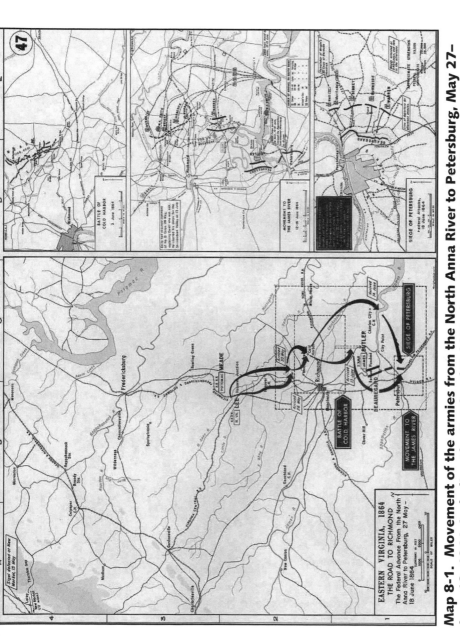

Map 8-1. Movement of the armies from the North Anna River to Petersburg, May 27–June 18, 1864, including the Battle of Cold Harbor. (United States Military Academy)

charge. The Pennsylvanian was in reality reduced to the role of staff officer, transmitting Grant's orders to the corps commanders. Although Meade played the good soldier, explaining to a correspondent that the description "the Army of the Potomac, directed by Grant, commanded by Meade, and led by Hancock, Sedgwick and Warren . . . about hits the nail on the head," this command arrangement did nothing to encourage Meade to buy into Grant's ideas about how to win. As any manager understands, there is frequently a wide gulf between a subordinate's decision to follow orders and that subordinate's true dedication to an idea.

Grant further damaged Meade's standing with the army by leaving Ambrose Burnside's corps outside of Meade's control. In effect, this required Grant to exercise direct control over no less than four separate army corps, spread across miles of tangled Virginia woodlands and labyrinthine Virginia back roads. Only on May 24 did Grant finally relent and place Burnside under Meade's command. Burnside pronounced himself satisfied with being placed under the command of an officer junior to him, but the damage caused by this unwieldy arrangement had already been done.[4]

Grant exacerbated this fault line in his high command by refusing to acknowledge the toll that this situation took on Meade and his staff. One incident during the North Anna fighting will illustrate this point. On May 24, Grant and Meade stopped and set up headquarters in a church. As they did so, a dispatch from Sherman arrived, giving Grant an update on the progress of Sherman's Georgia campaign. Assistant Secretary of War Charles Dana, a Radical Republican who deeply disliked Meade and his generals, read the dispatch aloud, including Sherman's caustic comments about the fighting prowess of the Army of the Potomac. Sherman predicted victory in Virginia if Grant could "sustain the confidence, the esprit, and the pluck of his army and impress the Virginians with the knowledge that the Yankees can and will fight them fair and square. . . . Out here the enemy knows we can and will fight them like the devil."

> "Can it be that this is the sum of our lieutenant general's abilities? Has he no other resource in tactics?"

Predictably, and quite understandably, Meade and his staff officers were enraged. "Sir!" Meade responded indignantly. "I consider that dispatch an insult to the army I command and to me personally. The Army of the Potomac does not require General Grant's inspiration or anybody else's inspiration to make it fight!"[5]

This attitude extended to the Army of the Potomac staff. Meade's aide Major James C. Biddle pronounced Grant "a rough, unpolished man" of "average ability, whom fortune has favored." Biddle found it disgusting to see Grant "lauded to the skies as being the greatest military man of the age." Not only did Grant allow these disagreements to fester, he encouraged them to do so by his refusal to smooth over his relationship with Meade, a general whom Grant had earlier pronounced one of the "fittest officers for large commands I have come in contact with."[6]

As a result of this conflict, even when Grant listened to Meade on questions of strategy, Meade and his staffers looked upon Grant's agreement with sarcasm and frustration. When Grant sided with Meade in deciding to move to Lee's east after the North Anna battles, Colonel Charles Wainwright of the Fifth Corps saw Grant's decision not as sound and sensible, but as plodding and unoriginal: "Can it be that this is the sum of our lieutenant general's abilities? Has he no other resource in tactics? Or is it sheer obstinacy? Three times he has tried this move, around Lee's right, and three times been foiled."[7] Grant succeeded in spite of the friction within his army, but friction can be very dangerous.

Another U.S. government agency, NASA, encountered similar communication breakdowns before the 1986 space shuttle *Challenger* disaster. A teleconference between officials from Morton Thiokol Industries (MTI), the manufacturers of the seal that malfunctioned and led to the explosion of the *Challenger*, and officials from NASA on the evening before the launch fell victim to such frictions. MTI engineers presented data that indicated that excessively cold temperatures on the morning of the launch would make the seals on the *Challenger*'s rocket boosters prone to failure. NASA's Larry Mulloy asked Joe Kilminster of MTI for his decision on the launch; Kilminster favored postponing it. Mulloy then asked NASA official George Hardy for his opinion. Hardy said that he was "appalled" at MTI's recommendation, but that he would not order the launch in spite of it. Mulloy then opined that MTI's data were inconclusive. Kilminster asked NASA for five minutes for an off-line caucus of senior MTI management.

Former MTI engineer Roger Boisjoly recalled that the source of this impending disaster was the friction between NASA's desire to get the *Challenger* into space as quickly as possible and increasingly persuasive MTI data that revealed problems in the shuttle's construction. Boisjoly remembered that "NASA's very nature since early space flight was to force contractors and themselves to prove that it was safe to fly," and that this desire forced MTI executives to make unethical decisions about the *Challenger*. During the off-line discussion, MTI General Manager Jerry Mason urged the group to "make a management decision"; the implication here was that they should cook the books in favor of a launch. As the discussion wrapped up, "Mason turned to Bob Lund, Vice President of Engineering at MTI, and told him to take off his engineering hat and to put on his management hat." MTI then recommended going ahead with the launch, and NASA concurred. On the next day, January 28, 1986, the *Challenger* exploded during takeoff, with the loss of all aboard. The *Challenger* and her crew were the victims of the same sort of organizational friction that Grant and Meade faced and were unable to deal with.[8]

The increasing desperation of the Northern political situation also weighed on Grant's mind. Lincoln was depending on his top general to bring him victories; instead, all he seemed to get was a never-ending stream of maimed and wounded soldiers. The ever-lengthening casualty lists were lowering morale throughout the North and encouraging the opposition Democratic Party. Indeed, both the Republican and Democratic parties were preparing to advance candidates to oppose Lincoln; the Democratic front runner was none other than George B. McClellan. Ruthless Northern speculators tied the price of gold to Union military fortunes, gouging investors by raising prices whenever bad news came in from the fighting fronts.[9]

In the western theater, Sherman was having just as much trouble. Johnston's Confederate army remained inviolate, falling back upon its own supply lines as Sherman's grew increasingly tenuous. Sherman's bloody assaults at Dug Gap, Rocky Face Ridge, and Resaca, Georgia, added to the discontent across the country. As the summer wore on, Lincoln began openly contemplating the possibility that he would lose the election. November was just around the corner, and without victories, his reelection bid was in trouble.[10]

Another important element of friction operating against Grant was the declining military efficiency of his army. Over a month of constant combat (some portion of the opposing armies were in direct contact every day from May 4 through the battle of Cold Harbor on June 3–4) was taking its toll on Union soldiers. Constant danger, disease, and poor food combined to produce what the modern military mind would understand as battle fatigue. Even seasoned veteran units had to be forced by their officers to move aggressively on the attack.

A growing flood of replacements did little to improve the situation. By mid-May, many of Grant's reinforcements had served in regiments known as "heavies": heavy artillery outfits that had spent the war manning the Washington fortifications. These "bandbox soldiers," as Army of the Potomac veterans derisively called them, were brave, but they were unused to the strains of field life, long marches, and bloody combat.

The balance of the army was composed of "bounty jumpers," men who had enlisted in Union regiments to earn local, state, or federal bounties. Many of these men signed up, reported to a regiment for a few days, then deserted and signed up somewhere else for another bounty. The volunteers of 1862 and 1863 looked upon these men as poison to their established units. Thus, the hard core of the Army of the Potomac was simply worn out, convinced that continuous attacks against an entrenched enemy were suicide, plain and simple. Although by late May replacements had brought the Army of the Potomac back up to its May 4 strength, this number was quite deceptive. There was a growing gap between what Grant expected of the Army of the Potomac and what it was truly capable of performing.[11]

From Direction to Delegation—
Overconfidence Strikes Again

The final ingredient in this poisonous mix was Grant's growing, but fundamentally incorrect, sense that Lee's Army of Northern Virginia was on its last legs, and that one big push would destroy it once and for all. This idea began germinating in Grant's mind after the withdrawal from Spotsylvania, when Grant interpreted Lee's failure to attack his exposed corps as a sign of growing weakness. The absence of a Confederate counterattack on May 24 at the North Anna, after Hill's weak attack the previous day, only reinforced Grant's belief. The final piece of the puzzle, to Grant's thinking, fell into place as the Union army crossed the Pamunkey River on May 28.

Aside from some inconclusive cavalry skirmishes at the river crossings, the Army of the Potomac had moved unmolested through the heart of the enemy's country. On May 26, Grant had assured Henry Halleck that "Lee's army is really whipped." He claimed that "our men feel that they have gained the morale over the enemy and attack with confidence," and that Union "success over Lee's army is already insured."[12]

With the possibility now existing, at least in Grant's mind, that one more big push would destroy Lee's army, Grant began to transfer back to Meade the responsibility for the tactical direction of the army. In other words, he began shifting back toward delegation, the leadership style with which he had begun the campaign. This decision had the potential to be a good personnel move, if it were properly carried out. Meade would most certainly have deemed it appropriate that he run his own army on a daily basis. But a lack of attention on Grant's part to the interpersonal dimension of his command was to have disastrous consequences for thousands of Union soldiers.

Grant's understanding was that Meade would take over not only the operational direction of the Army of the Potomac, but the tactical details of fighting its battles as well. Meade did not understand the situation in the same way. Disgruntled and disillusioned, he was not a willing participant in Grant's methods by the first week of

June, and therefore he was in no frame of mind to carry out Grant's intentions with absolute energy. A subordinate's attitude toward a plan can often be as important as that subordinate's skills or capabilities; if he does not believe in what the organization is doing, a plan may fail in any case.

After Grant pushed the Confederate army away from Totopotomoy Creek on May 30, Union cavalrymen attacked a combined rebel infantry/cavalry force at Old Cold Harbor on May 31, securing the vital crossroads. On June 1, the Confederates finally struck back. This Confederate attack by Anderson's First Corps, only a few miles from Richmond, confirmed to Grant that Lee was ripe for the picking.

Like Grant, Lee was moving back to more of a delegating style of command, and he too was doomed to have problems as a result. Anderson and one of his division commanders, Joe Kershaw, handled the battle poorly, squandering a golden opportunity to inflict serious damage. The inexperienced Anderson delegated control of the attack to Kershaw, who in turn misinterpreted Lee's intention of striking a massive blow and instead sent one brigade forward as a "reconnaissance in force." It just so happened that the brigade commander, a South Carolinian named Lawrence M. Kiett, was a regimental commander who had been with the army for *two days* and was in his first battle. Because Kiett was senior to the brigade's other colonels, Kershaw put him in charge, and the results were predictable. Kiett was killed almost instantly, and the attack fell apart.[13] With Anderson performing well only under direct supervision and Hill still suffering from his illness on a daily basis, Lee was reduced to one truly reliable corps commander, Jubal Early. Early was in charge of the Second Corps as of June 29 because Lee had finally decided to get rid of Richard S. Ewell.

Robert E. Lee and the Politics of Firing

When your personnel decisions do not work out, how do you fire someone? The way in which you remove someone can have a great deal to do with how your team functions after that person is gone.

In his treatment of Ewell, Lee offers the modern leader a great object lesson in the politics of hiring and firing, and in the communications skills that organizational leaders must possess.

At the end of the Battle of Spotsylvania, Lee continued to have trouble with his senior generals, a group that had given him such success on so many battlefields. Most worrisome of all was the behavior of Ewell. The man referred to affectionately by many in the army as "Old Bald Head" was exhibiting many of the bad characteristics that had made Lee hesitate to elevate him to corps command in the first place. At a critical point in the Battle of the Wilderness, he had shown indecision when faced with the opportunity to strike the Union line on an exposed flank. At Spotsylvania, he had been unable to control either his temper or his men when the Mule Shoe position collapsed, and he was unable to extricate his men from the Harris Farm engagement without assistance.

The last straw came at the North Anna River on May 24, as Lee lay in his tent, wracked with diarrhea and dysentery. Ewell apparently fell victim to the same malady, and as a result was unable to attack the exposed Union Second Corps. When the Army of Northern Virginia began its movement to react to Grant's crossing of the Pamunkey, Ewell again fell ill. He spent May 27 and 28 in an ambulance, trailing behind his corps as it tangled with the enemy. On May 27 Ewell relinquished command to Early, too sick to continue in command.

Lee sent Ewell a note on May 29 that encouraged the general to "proceed to some place where you can enjoy that repose and proper care of yourself which I trust will speedily repair the injury you have sustained from your late arduous services." Worried that Lee was maneuvering him out of command of his corps, Ewell responded with a letter claiming that he would be well enough in two days to resume command. He even enclosed a note from his surgeon, Dr. Hunter McGuire, attesting to this fact.

> "Everybody was uncomfortable . . . yet we all felt that his removal was inevitable & indeed was proper."

As time wore on, Ewell began to suspect that there was more at work than a medical issue. Lee wrote to him on May 31 and expressed gladness that Ewell was recovering, but refused to restore him to command. Lee explained that the Second Corps was "now in line of battle under Gen. Early & I do not think any change at the present time can be beneficial. . . . To report for duty now would be I fear to expose your life & health with out corresponding advantage."

Ewell refused to take the hint and reported for duty on May 31, stating that he was "unwilling to be idle at this crisis." Lee stated quite plainly his belief that Ewell was no longer up to the demands of corps command. He cited his continuing worries about Ewell's health, plus the difficulties of replacing leaders while they were in contact with the enemy. Furthermore, Ewell's best division commander, Robert Rodes, in Lee's recollection, "protested against Ewell's being again placed in command." There is no reason to doubt the sincerity of Lee's concern; he had a genuine regard for Ewell throughout their relationship and was "very reluctant to displace him." The second excuse held no water whatsoever, given Lee's constant shuffling of commanders during the campaign.[14]

Ewell was a dedicated and ambitious soldier, and he refused to yield to Lee. The two finally met face to face on June 8, after the fighting at Cold Harbor had concluded. Anyone who has ever been fired or has had to fire a subordinate will be able to imagine the scene. Ewell began by reassuring Lee of his physical fitness; he then asked if Lee preferred Early for other reasons. "It [corps command] is due Early," Lee replied, "and the Corps that he receive the appointment just as Anderson [the First Corps commander] has." Ewell replied that he would "go somewhere to be out of the way." "You are not in the way," Lee replied, no doubt growing exasperated by this time, "but you had better take care of yourself."[15]

In less pressing circumstances, Lee might have been able to rationalize retaining Ewell, thinking that his division commanders might be able to backstop the corps commander. Facing Grant's legions, however, changed Lee's leadership calculus. He called the meeting to an end and issued orders assigning Ewell to the command of the Richmond defenses and "Old Jubilee" to permanent command of the Second Corps. Second Corps ordnance officer William Allan wrote in his excellent memoir that "every body was un-comfortable . . . yet we all felt that his removal was inevitable & indeed was proper."[16]

Lee's handling of Ewell's removal points once again to his mas-tery of the human and political elements of leadership, and it for-ever puts to rest the myth that Lee was "too nice" to be an effective leader. Being a decisive manager of personnel does not mean that you run roughshod over people's feelings, making peremptory de-cisions about their lives. Lee initiated the process in the easiest way possible, by putting Ewell on a medical leave of absence. Ewell had suffered the aftereffects of having a leg amputated in 1862, and in-deed never really recovered fully. The harsh conditions of the Over-land Campaign took their toll on him, making the medical leave a sound idea in any case.[17]

Unfortunately for Lee and the Army of Northern Virginia, the Second Corps no longer had the combat power to accomplish any-thing significant on its own. Once Grant had shifted much of his army to Cold Harbor, Lee seized the opportunity to attack the Union right, or northern flank, with Early's corps. Early was to "get upon the enemy's right flank and drive down in front of our line." Old Jubilee even secured the assistance of Henry Heth, the com-mander of a division in the Third Corps, giving him four divisions. The resulting attack north of Cold Harbor on June 2 had initial suc-cess, but nowhere near the offensive punch to do anything other than inflict a few hundred casualties. Lee's other leadership project, Richard Anderson, had performed poorly once Lee stepped back and gave him the wide latitude that was standard operating proce-dure for the army's corps commanders. By nightfall on June 1, the crucial five-pointed intersection was firmly in Federal hands, and Lee had once again failed to wrest the initiative from his opponent.[18]

Radical Shifts in Leadership Style: Disaster at Cold Harbor

Like Lee's, Grant's decision to step back into the delegating role bore bitter fruit at Cold Harbor. He initially intended for the army to follow up its limited June 1 success with a general attack all along the line on June 2, but delays in troop dispositions caused him to postpone the attack until 4:30 a.m. on June 3. Whatever the reason, the offensive was poorly planned and coordinated; in fact, it was neither planned nor coordinated at all beyond the corps level. The five corps commanders involved (Major General William F. "Baldy" Smith and his Eighteenth Corps had transferred from Butler's Army of the James to Meade's command effective June 30) had made no arrangements between themselves to conduct simultaneous and co-operating attacks; each planned merely to drive straight ahead on his own accord.

The blame for this disastrous state of affairs lies squarely with Grant and Meade, Grant for peremptorily transferring authority back to Meade on the eve of a major battle without ensuring the latter's understanding of his expanded role, and Meade for failing to take even the most rudimentary measures to arrange his army's attack. In the largest sense, it was Grant's responsibility to ensure that Meade understood that this was his attack to execute, but when one considers Meade's state of mind since Spotsylvania, it is not surprising that he was not behind the idea heart and soul.

> The blame for this disastrous state of affairs lies squarely with Grant and Meade.

In any case, the June 3 attack was a bloody disaster. Modern estimates of Union casualties range between 3,500 and 5,000 wounded or killed within the first hour of the attack, not the traditional figure of "7,000 casualties in thirty minutes" that has often been quoted, but bad enough nonetheless. Units of Hancock's Second Corps punched a short-lived hole in the Confederate line on Lee's right flank, but they were not supported. On the Union right flank, Burnside's Ninth Corps stepped off ninety minutes late and accomplished nothing to assist their comrades. Perhaps because he sensed the pressure on him to accomplish something, anything, after all this marching and fighting, Meade continued the attacks even after it became apparent to the corps commanders that they were a total failure.

Confederate units across the line suffered around 1,500 casualties; this was the most lopsided battle in the history of either army. Rebel troops remembered with wonder the slaughter that ensued; many soldiers laughed and talked as they cut down Union attackers, while other units barely even knew that an attack was taking place. By nightfall, thousands of Union soldiers went to ground in the "no man's land" between the opposing trench lines, because to run back to friendly lines was to risk death. Over the next two days, the cries of the wounded and the stench of decomposing dead bodies grew more and more terrible.[19]

The next, and perhaps most famous, episode of the Battle of Cold Harbor did no credit either to Grant or to Lee. The Army of Northern Virginia had no reserves with which to mount a counterattack. Lee had to remain within his lines, his army stretched to its limit, and await the next Federal move. As he waited, the Tidewater Virginia summer exacted a terrible toll on the wounded lying between the lines, most of whom were Union soldiers.

Neither general did anything about this until the afternoon of June 5, when Grant sent a message to Lee proposing to allow stretcher bearers to move into no man's land to collect the wounded. Lee declined the offer, stating that these movements would cause confusion among his men and provoke more shooting. On June 6, Grant then suggested that his stretcher bearers could carry white flags, allowing them to be distinguished from skirmishers. Lee again declined, replying that Grant could send across a flag of truce, a formality of warfare at the time that would allow the collection of wounded.

> Over the next two days, the cries of the wounded and the stench of decomposing dead bodies grew more and more terrible.

Grant initially balked at doing this, because asking for a flag of truce was akin to admitting defeat, something that Grant was loath to do. The situation became so dire, however, that Grant finally relented on the evening of June 7 and sent out a flag of truce. By this time, though, most of the wounded had perished; their bloated bodies lay blackened in the sun, lending an especially hellish atmosphere to the battlefield. One Federal soldier sent out to recover bodies wrote, "Every corpse I saw was black as coal. . . . It was not possible to remove them. They were buried where they fell. . . . I saw no live man lying on this ground."[20]

Various postwar accounts of the battle have attempted to assign blame for this shameful episode either to Grant or to Lee. Truthfully, both were to blame. While there is no evidence to indicate that either general set out to inflict unnecessary suffering on the soldiers of either army, it seems likely that both were so frustrated and enraged by their inability to best the other that they turned this moment into a case of one-upmanship. Ever defiant, Lee held the upper hand and had won a stunning victory; his wounded and dead lay within his own lines, and his hospitals were only a few miles away in Richmond. Grant refused, until it was too late, to countenance the submission that a flag of truce would imply. In the end, Lee acceded to a version of Grant's first proposal that differed only in its wording, lending a tragic hue to the entire episode.

Hubris and arrogance have no place in organizational leadership, or at any other level, for that matter. The consequences of arrogance, a refusal to compromise, can ripple through a company and poison it. It is truly a commentary on the brutality of the Overland Campaign that two men such as Grant and Lee, both with an avowed aversion to death and suffering, could be reduced to such depths.

> The consequences of arrogance, a refusal to compromise, can ripple through a company and poison it.

Never let competition with another business or organization drive you to irrational or childish behavior, as happened to Lee and Grant at Cold Harbor. In the heat of battle to secure a critical contract or customer, never forget the core values to which your team subscribes. Subordinates will take their cues from you in these situations. If they see you rise above the fray and maintain a calm head, they will respond by doing the same thing. A rival may try and drag you down with such tactics, but resist the temptation to respond.

The Bitter Fruits of Friction

After the fighting died down at Cold Harbor on June 3, Grant and his staffers reviewed the day's events. Horace Porter recalled that Grant expressed remorse over the failure of the attack, stating that "I regret this assault more than any one I have ever ordered." In the interests of propriety and out of dedication to his boss, Porter probably understated Grant's reaction to what had been, in the words of one blue-clad soldier, "murder, not war." The man who had once refused to work in his father's tannery because he could not stand the sight of blood was surely demoralized by the outcome of the latest attack, but in a testament to his strength of character, he moved on quite quickly. Grant's brother Orvil had visited headquarters during the battle, and he left with the impression that "every thing looks favorable, the taking of Richmond is only a question of time."[21]

There was no denying, however, that Grant had not really taken the measure of his opponent. Meade commented that "Grant has had his eyes opened, and is willing to admit now that Virginia and Lee's army is not Tennessee and Bragg's army."[22] The Battle of Cold Harbor cemented Lee's reputation as a master of the tactical defensive, and it confirmed that the Army of Northern Virginia, when occupying solid positions and when capably led, was still a dangerous enemy.

> "I regret this assault more than any one I have ever ordered."

To make matters worse for the Union war effort, the campaign had also failed in its larger strategic objective of preventing Lee from detaching parts of his army to operate elsewhere. Almost before the shooting stopped at Cold Harbor, Jubal Early left with his Second Corps for the Shenandoah Valley, where Major General David Hunter had replaced Franz Sigel and was again threatening Lee's breadbasket. Early would accomplish his mission, at least in the short term; he drove Hunter out of the valley, and in late June he launched a raid down the Shenandoah Valley that reached the outer fortifications of Washington, D.C., by Independence Day.

Although Grant's dogged persistence had put the Army of the Potomac at the gates of Richmond, the butcher's bill was simply beyond comprehension: From May 4 to June 3, Meade's army and Burnside's Ninth Corps had suffered almost 55,000 killed, wounded, or captured. This number did not include casualties in Georgia, or even in Grant's other offensives in Virginia. The chorus of criticism against Grant reached a crescendo in early June, as the presidential election drew ever nearer. The myth of "Grant the Butcher" truly had its genesis between the Pamunkey and Chicka-hominy Rivers in Tidewater Virginia.[23]

In later years, Horace Porter defended his boss quite specifically against these charges. Porter felt that the officers and men of the Army of the Potomac "were as anxious as their commander to fight the war to a finish, and be allowed to return to their families and their business." The chief critics of Grant's methods he declared to be "stay-at-homes, and especially the men who sympathized with the enemy." Furthermore, Porter made the valid point that "it had been demonstrated by more than three years of campaigning that peace could be secured only by whipping and destroying the enemy."

Whether or not Porter was right in supposing that "if Grant had stopped fighting the cause of the Union would have been lost" is of course impossible to determine, and in any case is irrelevant. In spite of the friction that dogged both armies at Cold Harbor, and in particular the Army of the Potomac, Grant stayed the course, and as Porter points out, "in thirteen months after Lincoln handed him his commission of lieutenant-general, and intrusted to him command of the armies, the war was virtually ended."[24]

In the end, the most important outcome of the Battle of Cold Harbor was Grant's decision on June 6 not to suspend the campaign in light of his heavy casualties and fatigue, but not to continue at-tacking Lee north of the Chickahominy. Instead, he would again try to use maneuver to hold on to the initiative, but in a more auda-cious way than ever. Instead of continuing to slug it out north of the James River, Grant would move his entire force south of the river and target the vital rail and industrial center at Petersburg. Lee would have to follow and defend this critical transportation hub, and in the process Grant could destroy him.

Lee's casualties for the campaign were proportionally as bad as Grant's, and Lee knew without a doubt that where Grant could replace his casualties (indeed, Grant had an entire division of United States Colored Troops, African American soldiers, with the army who had not even seen combat!), Lee could not hope to recoup his losses over the long run. Grant kept this strategic truth in mind, no matter how horrible the cost in blood and treasure.

In terms of leadership, however, the Battle of Cold Harbor, and indeed the entire Overland Campaign, is a wonderful object lesson in the effects of friction on management and organizational effectiveness. The ways in which a leader responds to friction, particularly in the realm of interpersonal relationships and allocation of resources, can have wide-ranging effects. Drastic changes in leadership style, such as Grant's shift back to a more delegating approach, may in fact be counterproductive. Seeking innovative solutions that make use of all available resources, and having the moral courage to face up to and overcome setbacks, may be the only way to mitigate the effects of friction on your organization.

Leadership Lessons from Cold Harbor

- *Don't allow friction to ruin communication between you and your subordinates.* As an organizational leader, the things you say, even in passing, carry much greater weight with those around you. Sherman's insulting remarks about the Army of the Potomac, read by Charles Dana, went uncorrected by either Grant or anyone on his staff. Grant could have used that small incident to offer a vote of confidence in his subordinate generals, but he chose not to. As a result, Grant and Meade were barely on speaking terms by the time of the Battle of Cold Harbor. The collective weight of Grant's unrealized expectations and Meade's resentment combined to wreck Grant's attempt to destroy Lee's army in front of Richmond.

- *Use care when changing leadership styles in difficult situations.* Before the Battle of Cold Harbor, Grant stepped back from directive leadership and allowed Meade to resume tactical control of the Union army, but he did so at the worst possible time and in the worst possible way. Meade neither fully understood the full implications of this shift nor was prepared to resume command of an army that had changed significantly in composition over the past two weeks. The result was a bloody failure that killed or wounded thousands of Union soldiers. Lee, too, attempted a shift back to the delegating style that had made him so successful in the past, and this shift failed for him as well. Selective adjustments in your leadership style to accommodate particular subordinates or situations may be called for, but wholesale changes in midstream can be disruptive or dangerous.

■ *Acknowledge and plan for degraded performance over time.* By the first week of June 1864, the Army of the Potomac was in many respects a shadow of its former self. This was inevitable given the type of campaign Grant wished to carry out, the terrain involved, and the adversary he faced. Grant's mistake as the campaign wore on was not to adjust his own expectations of what his army could realistically accomplish. Lee had a better understanding of what his army was capable of in June 1864—defensive fighting behind fortifications, with small-scale offensives—and adjusted his mindset accordingly.

■ *Rely on moral courage to make difficult personnel moves.* Failure and friction in your business may mean that someone beneath you has to go. Take the example of Lee in his dealings with Ewell. It had become apparent to Lee by late May that Ewell was not going to work out as a corps commander. It must have been difficult for Lee to remove Ewell, who by the time of Cold Harbor was his most senior active corps commander, but he saw what needed to be done and did it in the most reasonable manner possible. Ewell certainly disagreed with Lee's judgment, but again, this is why you are paid the big bucks.

■ *Stay the course.* In the end, who in your organization will stay focused on the task at hand if you do not? If you remain convinced—truly convinced—that your plan is the right one, do not let short-term setbacks derail your plan. This dogged persistence, combined with a clear understanding both of the means at his disposal and of the ultimate outcome, made Grant a great general. Cold Harbor was a tragic defeat, but in true Grant fashion, the general used this setback as a springboard to the next, and ultimately decisive, phase of the war.

CHAPTER 9

To the James and Beyond

Transformational Leadership

"I begin to see it. You will succeed. God bless you all."

—ABRAHAM LINCOLN TO ULYSSES S. GRANT, JUNE 15, 1864[1]

"Live in the world you inhabit. Look upon things as they are. Take them as you find them. Make the best of them. Turn them to your advantage."

—ROBERT E. LEE TO CUSTIS LEE, MARCH 25, 1852[2]

The James River at Weyanoke Point, Virginia, is almost half a mile wide, with deep, treacherous currents and a four-foot tide that makes navigation difficult even today. Grant chose this as the crossing point for his army on its march to Petersburg. The end of a direct line from Cold Harbor to the James, Weyanoke was also far enough downstream from Richmond to allow Grant to steal a march on Lee, at least for a few precious hours.

At this inhospitable place, engineers of the Army of the Potomac constructed the longest pontoon bridge ever built, taking only seven hours to do so. Working simultaneously from both sides of the river, 450 engineers emplaced 101 pontoon boats and the planking that lay over them, enabling the passage of the entire army; all of its artillery, wagons, and ambulances; and much of its herd of beef cattle. Troops began crossing literally as the last planks were laid in place at around 11 p.m. on June 14. The Union navy anchored several schooners upstream of the bridge to provide stability in the fast currents, and sunk ships laden with stone further upstream to obstruct Confederate gunboats. The middle of the bridge could be swung open to accommodate river traffic. It was a model of nineteenth-century military engineering; Horace Porter deemed it a "memorable operation" that would "furnish one of the most valuable and instructive studies in logistics."

A number of observers commented on the pageantry of the scene, and on the almost palpable sense that the army was crossing a Rubicon of sorts, initiating a new and decisive phase of the war. Charles Dana, who was still accompanying the army, wired to his boss, Secretary of War Edwin M. Stanton, "All goes on like a miracle." Porter stood with Grant at the river's edge on the morning of June 15. He recorded the scene as "a matchless pageant that could not fail to inspire all beholders with the grandeur of achievement and the majesty of military power."

Ulysses S. Grant, "the man whose genius had conceived and whose skill had executed this masterly movement," stood watching in silence. After a short while, Grant mounted his horse and crossed to the south bank of the James. The Overland Campaign had reached its conclusion. Before the month of June was out, the armies would be locked in a ten-month-long siege at Petersburg, a siege that would lead to the end of the Civil War.[3]

A pontoon bridge as a metaphor for an organization? In the case of the end of the Overland Campaign, the analogy fits nicely, because this bridge showcased the tenacity, daring, and skill of the officers and men of the Army of the Potomac for all to see. The achievement was especially stunning for the West Point–trained generals in both armies, including Lee, many of whom thought it could never be done. Yet there it was. And there was the Army of the Potomac, pushing remorselessly south toward yet another clash with Bobby Lee.

To the extent that it was possible given the conditions of the time, Grant used the Overland Campaign to transform the Army of the Potomac into a force that was capable of winning final victory in

Virginia. This transformation takes nothing away from Meade, his officers, or the hundreds of thousands of men who served in the army from 1862 to 1865. Rather, it is a tribute to all involved that the leader, Grant, combined with the material at hand, Meade and his army, could create such a formidable combination. To get to this end state, Grant applied his methods of strategic and organizational leadership. The end result, which led to Union victory in April 1865, took the form of *transformational leadership*.

You may be an effective leader, but are you a transforming leader? That is, have you made your organization, and your subordinates, better than they were when you took over? By setting challenging expectations, do you motivate others to do more than they had originally thought possible? The U.S. Army identifies transformational leadership along with its other leadership styles, but it is clearly something different. It creates and grows effective junior leaders along the way through example and practice, leaving them capable of greater responsibility.

Transformational leadership takes advantage of experienced subordinates, and so it may not always be appropriate, especially if the organization is inexperienced. But the benefits of this style are worth the risks. It is most appropriate and effective "during periods that call for change or present new opportunities. It also works well when organizations face a crisis, instability, mediocrity, or disenchantment."[4]

For the last decade, leadership theorists have increasingly contrasted transformational leadership, which helps organizations to accomplish tasks more effectively while improving their personnel at the same time, with a more traditional concept, *transactional leadership*. Transactional leaders specify conditions or performance objectives for their subordinates, monitor those subordinates' performance, and dispense either rewards or punishments depending on the outcome. Certain situations or environments may call for transactional leadership, but research in larger civilian and military organizations has shown conclusively that in the long run, transformational leadership produces better results.[5]

According to leadership theorist Bernard Bass, there are four components of transformational leadership:

- *Individualized consideration (IC).* Transformational leaders develop their followers to higher levels of ability and potential by individualized consideration of their subordinates. The leader recognizes the differences in individuals, listens effectively to them, and exercises accordingly different styles of leadership.

- *Intellectual stimulation (IS).* Transformational leaders approach problems by questioning ingrained assumptions and encouraging inventive solutions. This helps the organization to overcome difficult problems and enhances subordinates' abilities to solve current and future problems. In this environment, leaders at all levels approach old situations in new ways.

- *Inspirational motivation (IM).* This is a quality of leadership that motivates followers to extraordinary levels of accomplishment. IM is concerned mainly with an individual leader's behavior that provides meaning to the work of others. IM allows leaders to communicate their expectations clearly, and it encourages subordinates to want to meet those expectations.

- *Charismatic leadership (CL).* This is the end state of transformational leadership, in which followers seek to emulate a leader, assume his or her values, and make personal sacrifices to achieve a shared objective. Leaders exhibit high standards of ethical and moral conduct, and are willing to take prudent risks.[6]

The Overland Campaign supplied new opportunities, crisis, instability, mediocrity, and disenchantment in spades. As it crossed the James River on June 14, the Army of the Potomac was a very different animal from the force that had crossed the Rapidan on May 4. Because it was different, and in a few months' time *better* than its predecessors, the Army of the Potomac went on to victory.

Lee's Army of Northern Virginia was different as well, but not better by any stretch of the imagination, as Grant's campaign had begun to grind it inexorably to pieces. That does not mean that Lee did not exercise transformational leadership, however. In his case, unlike in Grant's, however, transformational leadership did not equal ultimate victory. In the final analysis, Lee's transformational leadership served to stave off Confederate defeat in the east for almost another year.

Ulysses S. Grant as a Transformational Leader

Although it had most of the same key leaders and the same organizations, the Army of the Potomac had grown and developed into the type of army that Grant, and by extension the Union, needed in order to secure ultimate victory. That army would go on to besiege Lee at Petersburg, cutting his supply links with the rest of the Confederacy one by one and, in early April 1865, shattering his defensive lines and driving him toward Appomattox Courthouse and surrender. For the most part, Ulysses S. Grant fit the mold of the transformational leader.

Followership

It may seem strange to begin a recap of Grant's leadership qualities with a discussion of his followership skills, but those skills set the conditions for everything that Grant was able to accomplish in 1864. By listening to his commander in chief, taking his guidance to heart, and keeping him informed of military developments as much as possible, Grant broke the mold of fractious, acrimonious

> Often mistaking furious activity for progress, Grant frequently formulated complex operational and tactical plans, left little time for his subordinates to plan and prepare, and then failed to stick with one course of action if he encountered initial difficulties.

debate that had characterized Lincoln's relationships with previous Union commanders in the eastern theater.

As a direct result of his solid followership skills, Grant earned from Lincoln the freedom to fight Lee as he saw fit, even in the face of great misgivings over Grant's methods as the campaign progressed. Every leader at the organizational level works for someone; good followership sets a good example for those around you. If your subordinates see these habits in you, they will reply in turn with good followership of their own.

Negotiation Skills

In seeking approval for his vision of success against Lee, Grant applied solid negotiation skills. These skills are especially important for strategic leaders, who may often have to deal with other individuals of their own stature. Before he assumed overall command, Grant proposed a very aggressive, nontraditional scheme for defeating Lee, a scheme that ran counter to Lincoln's personal and political strategic imperatives. Grant quickly realized this, and instead of turning this disagreement into a bone of contention, he altered his thinking to conform more closely with Lincoln's. In doing so, his plan as finally approved retained much of the character of his original proposal.

Synchronization and Orchestration

While Grant's multi-pronged plan for defeating Lee and the Confederacy did not win the war in 1864, because it synchronized the overwhelming combat power of the Union armies and navies, it set the conditions for ultimate victory. Grant showed great energy and vision in creating this idea, earning the approval of Lincoln and his subordinates, and bringing them on board for its execution. The failures of many of Grant's subordinates doomed the plan almost from the outset, but that failure takes nothing away from the sophistication of the concept. At the strategic level, Grant the general in chief did an excellent job of bringing all his war-making resources to bear against the Confederacy. As a result of this synchronization, Union forces had the capability to carry out a sustained campaign on a scale never before seen in the war.

At the organizational level, Grant was less adept at synchronization and orchestration. Often mistaking furious activity for progress,

Grant frequently formulated complex operational and tactical plans, left little time for his subordinates to plan and prepare, and then failed to stick with one course of action if he encountered initial difficulties. At the Wilderness, he and Meade allowed their army to become scattered, endangering it at several points. An awkward command arrangement with the Ninth Corps, which left Burnside answering only to Grant, contributed to this problem. At Spotsylvania, Grant's attacks were aggressive and achieved local breakthroughs, but his failure to prepare attacks thoroughly and to follow through with overwhelming force gave Lee, already a master of defensive warfare, the time he needed to reinforce different sectors of his line when necessary.

> "Lee's army is your objective point. Wherever Lee goes, there you will go also."

The move to the North Anna was also poorly executed, again the victim of an excessively complex plan. Cold Harbor was the last straw; Grant's miscommunications with Meade again led to poorly coordinated, and brutally costly, operations. Grant was certainly not the "butcher" of myth and popular memory, and there is no denying the difficulty of coordinating large troop movements given the communications capabilities of the Civil War period, but Grant fell short as a tactician in this area.

Formation and Dissemination of Vision

The defeat of Robert E. Lee as quickly as possible was an idea to which all soldiers in blue could relate. By giving Meade a clear objective point—"Lee's army is your objective point. Wherever Lee goes, there you will go also"—Grant created an idea that had instant appeal to a war-weary army and populace. Through Grant's leadership, and with the help of Sherman's offensive in Georgia, that idea persisted and built momentum through 1864. In his words, decisions, and actions, Grant displayed a commitment to this vision that inspired those around him. The famous May 7 scene in the Wilderness, in which his men cheered him for turning south toward the Confederate army, is a great example of the fruits of Grant's positive vision.

Persistence, the Ability to Distinguish Between *Reverse* and *Defeat*

Without a doubt, this was Grant's most important leadership trait. Renowned Ohio State military historian Mark Grimsley terms Ulysses S. Grant a "coping" leader, one who employs "a style aimed at shaping any outcome toward a desired objective," as opposed to a "controlling leader," who demands success at every stage of an endeavor.[7] The coping leader will almost always perform better in a chaotic combat situation, and may indeed perform better in today's volatile business world.

Grant's calm, self-possessed demeanor on the evening of May 6, when the Union army's position seemed to be collapsing and the specter of previous defeats was beginning to pervade army headquarters, was an excellent example. In spite of grievous losses and tactical defeats in many phases of the Overland Campaign, culminating in the murderous attacks of June 3 at Cold Harbor, by the end of that stretch Grant had the Army of the Potomac in position to move south of the James River, a turn of events that even Robert E. Lee acknowledged would make ultimate Confederate defeat "a mere question of time." Union generals before Grant had suffered reverses, and through indecision and caution had allowed those reverses to mutate into defeats. Grant did not, and he achieved ultimate victory as a result.

Mental Agility, the Encouragement of Subordinate Initiative

Mental agility allowed Grant to distinguish between reverse and defeat, and to continue to try different solutions to that most difficult problem of all: the defeat of Robert E. Lee. This quality also puts the lie to the "Grant the butcher" myth. In reality, Grant relied on a fairly sophisticated combination of maneuver and overwhelming firepower, and this combination frequently allowed him to get a jump on Lee in the chess match that developed between the two. The initial stages of the Rapidan crossing and the marches to the North Anna and Cold Harbor allowed Grant to seize the initiative from Lee and hold it for the entire campaign.

While not all of Grant's generals agreed with his methods during the campaign, two of them—Winfield Scott Hancock and Philip

Sheridan—flourished in the environment that Grant created. "Hancock the Superb" was not at his best during this campaign because of the aftereffects of his Gettysburg wound, but in spite of this he was the most consistent performer of all of Grant's generals. His place at the front of virtually all of the army's movements attests to his stature in Grant's eyes.

Critics have lambasted Grant for his May 8 decision to allow Sheridan to take the army's cavalry corps on an extended raid toward

> "Mental agility allowed Grant to distinguish between reverse and defeat, and to try different solutions."

Richmond, and on balance it *was* a questionable decision; it was injurious to the army's high command and to its performance at Spotsylvania. But the larger outcome here was a positive one. Sheridan killed Jeb Stuart, Lee's self-proclaimed "eyes and ears," and damaged the Confederate cavalry corps seriously. During the course of the campaign, Sheridan also got better at the traditional cavalry roles of scouting and reconnaissance, and at Cold Harbor he played a critical part in retaining Grant's freedom to maneuver. By June 1864, Sheridan had transformed the Army of the Potomac's cavalry corps into something no army's cavalry force had been at any other time during the war: a fast-moving, powerful, destructive battlefield arm of decision. He did this under Grant's tutelage.

Overconfidence

Ironically, in this case one of Grant's signal weaknesses was also a signal strength. Perhaps that is one of the reasons why Grant remains such a fascinating character to Americans. He consistently based his decisions and plans on the assumption that he faced a beaten enemy, one who was unable to strike back. For a variety of reasons, Grant's overconfidence did not lead to his defeat, but it is nonetheless a dangerous leadership attitude.

At the same time, though, confidence can be the difference between reverse and defeat, as discussed earlier. Mark Grimsley sums up this contradiction very nicely in his masterful account of the 1864 Virginia campaign. "The world is as full of obstacles as it is of losses, and to get anywhere in life one must possess grit, drive, determination, persistence," Grimsley writes. "And so we also need the image of Grant: Grant the implacable, Grant the hammerer, Grant the man who, despite everything, keeps moving on."[8]

Lack of Attention to Interpersonal Relationships

This shortcoming was the most damaging to Grant's leadership ability. During the Overland Campaign, it took the form of a misplaced, or at least inadequately thought out, shift to a more directive leadership style. This shift began almost as soon as the campaign kicked off, and it reached its peak during Spotsylvania and the North Anna battles.

Grant's effort to stick with a dysfunctional command relationship caused deep rifts in his high command, rifts that are made all the more frustrating for the modern observer by the fact that Grant *realized* the difficulties that this relationship caused for Meade and his staff, but did little to correct them. Throughout the campaign, Grant perceived the Army of the Potomac's high command as a problem child that needed correction. Implicit comparisons to the Union's western armies, in the person of officers like James Wilson and Philip Sheridan, whom Grant had brought with him from west to east, rankled the highly competent and seasoned Army of the Potomac staff.

In some cases Grant's army *was* a problem child; years of stunning defeats at the hands of Lee had caused an ingrained caution that was almost always damaging. But Grant gave Meade and his corps commanders little or no opportunity to display the grittiness that had won them a victory at Gettysburg. Individualized consideration for subordinates is not coddling; it is simply vital for maximizing the performance of everyone involved.

Robert E. Lee as a Transformational Leader

By mid-1864, most honest observers had come to the realization that Robert E. Lee and his Army of Northern Virginia were the barrier between the young Confederacy and defeat. The Overland Campaign proved beyond a shadow of a doubt that while Lee was certainly not perfect, as many of his generals and postwar apologists complained, he led his army about as well as one could possibly expect.

Followership

Like Grant, Lee was successful as an army commander in large measure because of his followership skills. While Lee did not assume the Confederate general in chief position until early 1865, Jefferson Davis often consulted him on questions of strategy in other theaters of the war. Lee also communicated well with Davis, keeping him informed about the army's operations. As the army's situation grew increasingly desperate during the Overland Campaign, he was brutally honest with Davis about his chances without "crying wolf" to the disadvantage of Confederate forces in other places. Consider Lee's letter to Davis of May 30, as the armies approached Cold Harbor:

> As I informed you by telegraph, my conference with Genl Beauregard resulted in the conclusion on his part, that he cannot spare any troops to reinforce this army. He thinks the enemy in his front superior to him in numbers. Of this I am unable to judge, but suppose of course that with his means of information, his opinion is correct. I think it very important to strengthen this army as much as possible, and it has occurred to me that the presence of the two armies north and south of the James River, may render it possible to spare with safety some of the troops in Richmond or its defenses . . . and even if they be few in numbers, they will add something to our strength. I submit this proposition to your judgment and hope you may be able to find means to increase our numbers without endangering the safety of Richmond. I think it important that troops enough should be retained to man the works at Drewry's & Chaffin's Bluffs and to support the batteries around the city. . . . If this army is unable to resist Grant, the troops

under Genl Beauregard and in the city will be unable to defend it.[9]

Lee's dealings with Davis and with the other Confederate generals were a model of restraint and prudence. As a result, Lee enhanced his standing within the Confederate government.

Understanding of Subordinates and Self

In his treatment of his generals, Robert E. Lee personified the individualized consideration that is a key to transformational leadership. He knew which buttons to push in order to wring the maximum effort from his commanders and his staff. Lee displayed this sound understanding time and time again, whether in tolerating mistakes by his non-West Point graduate officers or in stepping in to exercise directive leadership when necessary.

Unlike Grant, who maintained a fairly stable high command structure for the duration of the campaign (Grant lost John Sedgwick at Spotsylvania, but this was his only really significant leadership casualty), Lee had to carry out several wholesale reorganizations of his corps, division, and brigade structures in the midst of the most brutal conditions of the entire war. To make matters worse, the leaders that Lee lost during the campaign—James Longstreet, Jeb Stuart, and numerous excellent division and brigade commanders—were critical to his highly decentralized, fluid command style. Lee balanced political considerations, the likes and dislikes of his men, and military necessity and got his combinations right *almost every time*, maintaining his army's efficiency in the face of unbelievable strains. Lee was able to do this because he understood his people—their backgrounds, their capabilities, and their shortcomings.

> Lee's dealings with Davis and with the other Confederate generals were a model of restraint and prudence.

When Lee had to place less experienced officers in key situations, he was sufficiently sensitive to their capabilities to offer more focused direction. As the army left the Wilderness, Lee watched closely over Richard H. Anderson, and as a result the First Corps continued to be an effective fighting force. Lee's belief in the delegating style of command did not prohibit him, in Anderson's case, from watching over a subordinate and setting him up for success.

Synchronization and Orchestration

To be fair to Grant, Lee had an easier task in synchronizing the efforts of his forces because they were smaller and fought mostly on the defensive. Nevertheless, Lee was both a success and a failure in this regard at different times. His use of cavalry was superb, giving his army an information edge over his opponents, but he also made several highly questionable decisions during the campaign, decisions that exposed his army to disaster on a number of occasions. The failure to keep Longstreet's First Corps close to the army at the Wilderness almost led to disaster on May 6, and he consistently misunderstood his enemy's intention at Spotsylvania and the North Anna.

Bearing and Demeanor in Difficult Situations (Setting the Example)

For examples of this quality, one need look no further than the Wilderness on May 6 and Spotsylvania on May 10 and 12. On all three occasions, when his army faced defeat, with Union troops piercing Confederate defensive lines, Lee sensed the desperation of the situation and acted in a personal way to restore the troops' aggressiveness and fighting spirit.

The reaction of his men on all three occasions was absolutely electric. Each time, his troops drove their enemies back; in the case of the Wilderness, they went back over to the offensive and came close to winning the battle. On a larger scale, Lee conducted the Overland Campaign under the pressure of multiple enemy armies converging on the Confederate heartland from multiple directions. In spite of this pressure, Lee made solid decisions and did not overreact to danger. His unflappable, impressive bearing in front of his troops inspired adulation that approached worship.

Absolute Moral Courage in the Face of Impending Defeat

The Overland Campaign put to the test Robert E. Lee's lifelong pursuit of absolute self-control and his insistence on that self-control in others. His reaction to Richard S. Ewell's declining effectiveness is a case in point. With his army approaching very desperate circumstances, Lee could not tolerate loss of control and effectiveness in one of his corps commanders. He had a difficult but necessary decision to make in the removal of Ewell, a long-time associate and trusted fellow officer, but he made that decision nonetheless.

Adaptability in the Face of Changing or Unfavorable Circumstances

This was Robert E. Lee's greatest leadership asset. Throughout the Overland Campaign, Lee recovered from his own mistakes, and the mistakes of those around him, and was able to turn failure into success. At the Wilderness, Grant got a twelve-hour jump on Lee in crossing the Rapidan, but Lee and his commanders responded with dash and audacity, fighting the Battle of the Wilderness on their own terms. When Grant almost stole a march on the Confederates en route to Spotsylvania, Lee again responded with aggressive cavalry actions and local attacks that knocked Grant off balance.

> Lee sensed the desperation of the situation and acted in a personal way to restore the troops' aggressiveness and fighting spirit.

The greatest example, however, occurred at the North Anna River, after the Army of the Potomac had moved south from Spotsylvania and crossed an entire corps to the south of the North Anna, threatening Lee's defensive position. Instead of retreating closer to Richmond, Lee capitalized on the abilities of his subordinates (in this case, his chief engineer, M. L. Smith) and created the perfect defensive position. The Inverted V gave Lee the opportunity to regain the initiative in the campaign.

Failure to Surround Himself With an Adequate Staff

For whatever reason, Lee never managed to surround himself with a staff commensurate with the needs of an army commander. The staff officers that he did retain, such as Walter Taylor and Charles Venable, were capable performers, but they were completely overworked. As a result, lapses like A. P. Hill's faulty position in the Wilderness occurred, leaving the army exposed to defeat. At the North Anna, when Lee fell ill, his staff could only keep up with the pace of operations, instead of taking the commander's place.

Inability to Sustain Directive Leadership

While Lee was effective in the moments when he did assume a directive leadership style (at the Wilderness and Spotsylvania, with Anderson after Longstreet's wounding), he was reluctant to maintain that leadership style, even when it became apparent that his high command was no longer capable of functioning as it had in the heyday of Longstreet and Stonewall Jackson. After the armies left the North Anna, Lee resumed his delegating style, and his new lineup of generals could not respond. As a result, Lee missed several golden opportunities to strike back at Grant and regain the initiative in the campaign. Lee's shortcoming in this area highlights the need for all leaders to be adept at both the delegating and directive modes of leadership, and to be sensitive to the implications of shifts between the two.

Lee, Grant, and Organizational Leadership

While neither Lee nor Grant was perfect, as their partisans have tended to claim down through the years, they both exemplified a variety of outstanding leadership skills on the most demanding stage imaginable. Grant's persistence and ability to overcome obstacles marked him as a great leader, while Lee's imagination, self-control in the face of adversity, and knowledge of his subordinates were paramount.

In the final analysis, Robert E. Lee and Ulysses S. Grant were more alike than they were different. Outward appearances aside, they approached problems and challenges with a fundamentally similar approach. They called on skills learned through a lifetime of intellectual and practical preparation, applied those skills through carefully selected subordinates, and drove their organizations forward with indomitable will and persistence. If one could combine the leadership qualities of these two men into one entity, the organization that that person led would simply be unstoppable.

Appomattox

The Adversaries Meet

For all time it will be a good thing, for the whole United States, that of all the Federal generals it fell to Grant to receive the surrender of Lee.

—EDWARD PORTER ALEXANDER[1]

"There is nothing left me but to go and see General Grant, and I would rather die a thousand deaths." It was April 9, 1865, and with that resigned comment, Robert E. Lee mounted Traveller for the longest ride of his life. This day would see the surrender of his Army of Northern Virginia to Ulysses S. Grant and the effective end of the American Civil War.[2]

Lee's surrender to Grant at Appomattox Courthouse, a small town in west-central Virginia, marked the culmination of the week-long flight of Lee's Confederate army from its fortifications at Petersburg. When Grant's Union armies crossed the James River in June 1864, threatening the vital Confederate rail center at Petersburg, Lee had no choice but to follow. The armies settled into a siege that lasted from late June of that year until April 2, 1865, when a massive Union offensive broke the siege and sent Lee's troops reeling westward in an attempt to escape to the south. This train of events brought Robert E. Lee and Ulysses S. Grant, two of history's great leaders, together in the parlor of the home of Wilmer McLean at Appomattox.

On the evening of April 8, Lee and his generals held one final council of war, in which they decided to make a last attempt to break out of the ever-tightening Federal noose around Appomattox. Lee must have known that April 9 would be a fateful day in one way or another, because he dressed in his finest dress uniform, complete with a red silk sash and an ornamental presentation sword given to him by the ladies of Baltimore, Maryland. By mid-morning, it became apparent that the breakout had failed, and that Lee's only remaining options were surrender or total destruction. He chose the former, and after an exchange of written overtures with Grant, he rode from his headquarters to Appomattox Courthouse to find a suitable place to hold the meeting. Lee's aide Charles Marshall and a courier accompanied the general.

Grant spent much of April 8 and 9 dealing with a blinding migraine headache in addition to the problem of tracking down Lee. When he received Lee's dispatch asking for a meeting to discuss the surrender of the Army of Northern Virginia, the headache magically disappeared. Grant scrawled a reply "agreeing to a conference" and handed it to John Rawlins, his chief of staff. "How will that do, Rawlins?" he asked. "I think *that* will do," Rawlins replied, and an aide galloped off with the dispatch. Grant gathered his staff, mounted his horse Cincinnati, and headed for Appomattox Courthouse.[3]

Lee was waiting in the parlor of the McLean house when Grant and his retinue arrived. Everyone present at the meeting who left a written account remarked on the contrast in appearance between the two men. The patrician Lee looked every inch the general in his immaculate dress uniform and sword, but Grant looked, if anything, like a common soldier. His aide Horace Porter recalled that Grant wore a "single-breasted blouse of dark-blue flannel," upon which he had sewn the three-star shoulder straps of a lieutenant general. Grant's trousers were tucked into "an ordinary pair of top-boots," and the entire outfit was spattered with Virginia mud. Instead of a sword, Grant carried a pair of field glasses.[4] He was, as always, all business. The way the two men dressed reflected perfectly their contrasting styles.

After some hasty introductions, the two generals sat and discussed old times, including their shared experiences in Mexico. They had met briefly while serving under Winfield Scott, and they had many acquaintances in common. After a short while, Lee reminded Grant of their purpose, and they got down to business. After agree-

> "How will that do, Rawlins?"

ing to the basic terms of the surrender—that all of Lee's officers and men would formally surrender and agree never again to take up arms against the United States, and that all military equipment would become Federal property—Grant wrote out the document of surrender.

The exchange that then occurred reminded everyone present of the greatness of these two men. Grant stipulated in the surrender paperwork that all officers be allowed to retain their personal side arms, horses, and baggage. Lee was grateful for this indulgence and made a further request. Since Confederate cavalrymen and artillerists were required to purchase their own horses, and since many of them would have farms and families to support, could those men not keep what was, in essence, their personal property? Grant did not alter the surrender document, but he stipulated to his staff that all Confederates who claimed a horse were to be allowed to take it home in order to help with the coming planting season. Lee was visibly relieved. "This will have the best possible effect upon the men. It will be very gratifying, and will do much toward conciliating our people." Grant's magnanimity and Lee's concern for his men touched all of those present.[5]

As staff officers made copies of the surrender documents, Grant introduced Lee to the Union commanders present. In the midst of what could only have been the worst day of his life, Lee retained the iron self-control that had stood him in such good stead, shaking hands and bowing "in a dignified and formal manner." Once the proceedings were complete, Lee raised one additional concern to Grant: His men had had little or no food since leaving Petersburg on April 2. Grant immediately arranged for rations for 25,000 men to be passed through the lines, and the conference was over. Lee shook hands with Grant, bowed to the other Union officers, and walked out onto the porch of the house. As he waited for his orderly to bring his horse, Lee stood and gazed toward his now-surrendered army, and pounded a fist into his other gloved hand, seemingly unaware of anyone or anything else. Traveller's arrival shook him from this reverie, and he mounted to ride away.

Grant had been watching from the porch, and as Lee turned to leave, Grant raised his hat in salute to the Virginian. The others present followed Grant's example. Lee returned the gesture, and that was that. A few minutes later, as word of the surrender made its way to the Union camps, cannon and rifle fire began to break out in celebration. Grant had no wish to add insult to the injury of defeat, and he put an immediate stop to these displays. "The war is over," he told his staff. "The rebels are our countrymen again; and the best sign of rejoicing after the victory will be to abstain from all demonstrations in the field."[6]

Lee and Grant may have projected very different images at the surrender, but their differing clothing styles could not conceal the deeper similarities between the two. In their words and actions at Appomattox, the two generals, who a few hours before had been the greatest of enemies, set an example of courage, charity, and reconciliation. Lee carried himself with dignity and did not allow anger or sadness to prevent him from seeking surrender terms that were best for his soldiers. Grant's repeated generosity was not in keeping with the legend of "Unconditional Surrender Grant," but otherwise reflected his practical outlook on life. The most important task was to end the bloodshed, and Grant did that as quickly as possible by offering surrender terms that were agreeable to his defeated enemy. The era of Reconstruction would have been much less divisive had more Americans, both Northern and Southern, acted as Lee and Grant did. If setting the example is the ultimate expression of leadership, the surrender at Appomattox showed for all time why Robert E. Lee and Ulysses S. Grant are still worthy of study and emulation.

Lee and Grant in Peace

After the Civil War, neither Grant nor Lee left the public eye. Grant surrendered the position of general in chief to his old friend William Tecumseh Sherman and later in life entered politics, following in George Washington's footsteps as a soldier turned president. However, Grant was much more successful on the battlefields of Mississippi, Georgia, and Virginia than he was on the battlefields of Capitol Hill. His administration, which lasted from 1869 to 1877, was marred by scandal, none of which directly implicated him. Many of the old problems that had made the young Grant a failure in the business world came back to haunt him as president. He tended to be far too trusting of men who deserved no such trust, and he relied on old friends to a fault, whether or not they were really suitable for the posts they sought.

In later years, Grant's health failed him. He turned to the literary world to earn enough money to sustain his family after he died and to address the many critics of his generalship, who became numerous and vociferous as the myth of the Confederate "Lost Cause" gained strength. The creators of this myth, led by Confederate general Jubal Early, held that the Union did not defeat the Confederacy in battle. Rather, Confederate leaders were compelled to seek peace when their society was overwhelmed by superior Northern manpower and resources. In this mindset, brute force and a sort of tragic predestination, not Union political or military superiority, doomed the Confederacy. Grant set out to refute this myth. In less than a year, he penned his *Personal Memoirs*, one of the masterpieces of American letters. In it, Grant pulls no punches in defending his generalship, even to the point of labeling Robert E. Lee a mediocre general who gained great fame at his expense. General Ulysses S. Grant died on July 23, 1885, at the age of 63.[7]

Robert E. Lee had only six more years to live after Appomattox, but he spent his remaining days as he had spent all of his adult life, with a passion for service to his native state and nation. After the war, he campaigned tirelessly for reconciliation between North and South. Unlike many other Virginia generals such as Early, who created and furthered the myth of the Lost Cause and remained "unreconstructed" for the rest of their days, Lee tried to put the war behind him and encouraged others to do the same. Many Southern business enterprises attempted to capitalize on his name in order to regain a solid footing, but Lee rebuffed all such requests. In October 1865 he accepted the presidency of Washington College, a small, struggling liberal arts college in Lexington, Virginia.

At Washington College, Lee became as beloved and effective as a college president as he had been as a general. In his new capacity, he influenced a generation of young Virginians to do as he had and put the Civil War behind them. On the evening of September 28, 1870, Lee suffered a stroke, and a few days later he contracted pneumonia. He died peacefully on October 12, unable to speak for the last two weeks of his life. His last real words, "I will give that sum," spoken at a church vestry meeting the afternoon of his stroke in response to the church's need for $55 for the rector's salary, contained no great truisms or military references, but in fact summed up the quiet, unselfish attitude that shaped his leadership style throughout his adult life.[8]

Order of Battle—Union and Confederate Forces in the Overland Campaign

N otes: Order of Battle as of May 4, 1864, with changes during the campaign indicated in parentheses. The Union army ordered divisions numerically, i.e., First, Second, and so on, while the Confederate army referred to divisions by the last name of the division's original commander; for example, Early's Division remained so named even after Early moved up to corps command.

This Order of Battle does not include artillery units. Each Union and Confederate army corps contained an artillery brigade that supported the operations of the corps.

Union Forces

Lieutenant General Ulysses S. Grant, Commanding Union Armies

Army of the Potomac
Major General George G. Meade, Commanding
    Second Army Corps: Major General Winfield S. Hancock
        First Division: Brigadier General Francis C. Barlow
        Second Division: Brigadier General John Gibbon
        Third Division: Major General David B. Birney
        Fourth Division: Brigadier General Gershom Mott (divi-

sion incorporated into Birney's Third Division on May 13; division reconstituted May 18 with one infantry brigade and one artillery brigade under Brigadier General Robert O. Tyler)

Fifth Army Corps: Major General Gouverneur K. Warren
  First Division: Brigadier General Charles Griffin
  Second Division: Brigadier General John C. Robinson (wounded May 8; division disbanded May 9; brigades incorporated into other divisions)
  Third Division: Brigadier General Samuel W. Crawford
  Fourth Division: Brigadier General James S. Wadsworth (mortally wounded May 6; replaced by Brigadier General Lysander Cutler)

Sixth Army Corps: Major General John Sedgwick (killed in action May 9, 1864; replaced by Brigadier General Horatio G. Wright)
  First Division: Brigadier General Horatio G. Wright (promoted May 9; replaced by Brigadier General David A. Russell)
  Second Division: Brigadier General George W. Getty (replaced May 12 by Brigadier General Thomas H. Neill)
  Third Division: Brigadier General James B. Ricketts

Cavalry Corps: Major General Philip H. Sheridan
  First Division: Brigadier General Alfred T. A. Torbert
  Second Division: Brigadier General David McMurtrie Gregg
  Third Division: Brigadier General James H. Wilson

Ninth Army Corps: Major General Ambrose E. Burnside
  First Division: Brigadier General Thomas G. Stephenson (killed in action May 10; replaced by Major General Thomas L. Crittenden)
  Second Division: Brigadier General Robert B. Potter
  Third Division: Brigadier General Orlando B. Willcox
  Fourth Division: Brigadier General Edward Ferrero

Eighteenth Army Corps: Major General William F. Smith (attached to the Army of the Potomac as of May 30)
  First Division: Brigadier General William T. H. Brooks

Second Division: Brigadier General John H. Martindale
Third Division: Brigadier General Charles Devens Jr.

Confederate Forces

General Robert E. Lee, Commanding

Army of Northern Virginia

General Robert E. Lee, Commanding

First Army Corps: Lieutenant General James Longstreet (wounded in action May 6; replaced by Major General Richard H. Anderson)

Kershaw's Division: Brigadier General Joseph B. Kershaw

Field's Division: Major General Charles W. Field

Pickett's Division: Major General George E. Pickett (joined the army on May 21)

Second Army Corps: Lieutenant General Richard S. Ewell (replaced May 29; by Major General Jubal A. Early)

Early's Division: Major General Jubal A. Early (elevated to command of the Second Corps on May 29; replaced by Major General John B. Gordon)

Johnson's Division: Major General Edward Johnson (captured on May 12; brigades placed under the command of Gordon after suffering severe losses at the Mule Shoe)

Rodes's Division: Major General Robert E. Rodes

Ramseur's Division: Major General Stephen D. Ramseur (division created May 27 in the reorganization following Jubal Early's promotion to corps command)

Third Army Corps: Lieutenant General Ambrose P. Hill

Anderson's Division: Major General Richard H. Anderson (elevated to command of the First Corps on May 8; replaced by Brigadier General William Mahone; division formally renamed Mahone's Division during the Cold Harbor phase of the campaign)

Heth's Division: Major General Henry Heth

Wilcox's Division: Major General Cadmus M. Wilcox

Cavalry Corps: Major General James E. B. Stuart (mortally wounded in action May 11; not replaced during the campaign)

Hampton's Division: Major General Wade Hampton

Fitzhugh Lee's Division: Major General Fitzhugh Lee

W. H. F. Lee's Division: Major General William H. F. Lee

Source: Gordon C. Rhea, *The Battle of the Wilderness, The Battles for Spotsylvania Courthouse and the Road to Yellow Tavern, To the North Anna River,* and *Cold Harbor.* (Baton Rouge: Louisiana State University Press).

Suggestions for Further Reading

Like most other Civil War campaigns, the Overland Campaign does not suffer from a lack of coverage in the historical literature. There are a wide variety of sources that will satisfy a variety of tastes and interests, from the armchair general who is interested in the decisions and actions of high-ranking officers, to the fan of historical biography, to the reader seeking an understanding of the human dimension of conflict. And as with other bodies of historical writing, the sources on the Overland Campaign fall into two broad categories. *Secondary sources* are those that were written after the events in question, by those who did not participate. They can be very general, such as an introductory history of the Civil War, or quite specific, covering a particular campaign or battle. *Primary sources* are written by the participants themselves; they include memoirs, diaries, reminiscences, collected letters or dispatches, battle reports, and newspaper articles. In general, it is best to consult secondary sources to gain a broad understanding of an event, and then consult primary sources for greater insight into individual actions, decisions, and thoughts on the events.

Secondary Sources

Anyone who is interested in understanding the American Civil War should begin by reading one of several one-volume histories of the

221

conflict. The best of these is commonly acknowledged to be James M. McPherson's *Battle Cry of Freedom: The Civil War Era*. Recently reprinted in a beautiful illustrated edition, *Battle Cry of Freedom* won the Pulitzer Prize in 1988. McPherson, who teaches history at Princeton University, writes history with the page-turning style of the novelist and moves easily between great events and the intimate details that make history such fascinating reading. The American Civil War multivolume set published by Time-Life Books is also a favorite of mine. Its volumes are written by prominent historians and are lavishly illustrated with period photographs, paintings and woodcuts, and superb maps.

For the reader seeking a concise one-volume history of the Overland Campaign, look no farther than Mark Grimsley's *And Keep Moving On: The Virginia Campaign, May–June 1864*. Grimsley's combination of solid storytelling and trenchant analysis captures the high points of the various historical arguments that surround the campaign, and the author offers excellent discussions of Grant and Lee. Also useful is Noah Andre Trudeau's *Bloody Roads South: The Wilderness to Cold Harbor, May–June 1864*, winner of the Fletcher Pratt History Award in 1989. A writer for National Public Radio and the author of three other Civil War books, Trudeau has a penchant for storytelling as well. Those interested in the 1864 Shenandoah Valley Campaigns or Butler's abortive offensive against Petersburg should consult Richard R. Duncan's *Lee's Endangered Left: The Civil War in Western Virginia, Spring of 1864* and William G. Robertson's *Back Door to Richmond: The Bermuda Hundred Campaign, April–June 1864*, respectively. These books, together with Richard McMurry's *Atlanta 1864: Last Chance for the Confederacy*, will summarize all of the major operations of the spring and summer of 1864.

If you have the time and interest for an in-depth analysis of the Overland Campaign, Gordon C. Rhea has probably written the last words on the campaign for some time to come. His Louisiana State University Press books on the Wilderness, Spotsylvania, North Anna, and Cold Harbor battles have won most of the major awards for Civil War historical writing and showcase traditional military battle history at its best. Like James McPherson, Rhea has a particular talent for telling a complex story in an interesting and understandable way, but be forewarned: These volumes demand a bit of prior reading for greatest benefit. The author's descriptions of battle scenes are quite detailed, often focusing on individual soldiers and regiments. He frequently moves back and forth between small and large units within a single scene, a technique that creates a fascinating narrative but that demands a certain familiarity with the material. Rhea gives a good bit of attention to both Grant and Lee, and his conclusions on their generalship will probably stand the test of time.

There are a number of excellent biographies on the leaders of the Overland Campaign. The fan of biography will find this a good way to examine the campaign from a variety of different perspectives. Emory Thomas's *Robert E. Lee* devotes only one chapter to the campaign, but it is required reading for anyone who is really interested in Lee's life and military career. While somewhat dated, Douglas Southall Freeman's magisterial four-volume *R. E. Lee*, along with the one-volume abridgement, is unparalleled for its exhaustive treatment of Lee, but be forewarned: Freeman's Robert E. Lee is very much the "marble man" of myth and legend. For a variety of perspectives, both laudatory and critical, on Marse Robert, *Lee the Soldier*, a collection of writings edited by Gary W. Gallagher, also belongs on any Civil War bookshelf.

Those interested in Ulysses S. Grant will find a wider variety of biographies. William S. McFeely's 1997 *Grant: A Biography* won the Pulitzer Prize. Brooks S. Simpson covers Grant's early life and Civil War years in *Ulysses S. Grant: Triumph Over Adversity, 1822–1865*, and the latest offering, Jean Smith's *Grant*, covers the general's entire life, including his troubled presidency. British general J. F. C. Fuller penned two incisive accounts of Grant soon after World War II, an event that no doubt shaped his opinions of the general. *Grant and Lee: A Study in Personality and Generalship* and *The Generalship of Ulysses S. Grant* hail the Union general in chief as the first of the Western world's "modern" generals.

There are also a number of good biographies of other participants in the campaign. Freeman Cleaves's 1960 *Meade of Gettysburg* is somewhat dated, but still useful; Ethan Rafuse's *George*

Gordon Meade and the War in the East is also excellent for its treatment of Meade's role in the Overland Campaign. Most of the Union corps commanders have their biographers. David M. Jordan has written on Winfield Scott Hancock and G. K. Warren, while William M. Marvel's *Burnside* offers a very sympathetic, revisionist interpretation of the oft-maligned Ninth Corps commander. Roy Morris Jr.'s *Sheridan: The Life and Wars of General Phil Sheridan* covers Grant's chief horseman.

On the Confederate side, Jeffry D. Wert's 1994 biography of James Longstreet stands as the best work on Lee's controversial First Corps commander. Donald C. Pfanz's exhaustive biography of Richard S. Ewell is an outstanding source on the Army of Northern Virginia's high command. Professor James I. Robertson, Jr., of Virginia Tech wrote the standard biography of A. P. Hill in 1987, while Emory Thomas's *Bold Dragoon: The Life of J. E. B. Stuart* stands as the best biography of the flamboyant Confederate cavalry chief. Unique among books of this type is *Lee's Lieutenants: A Study in Command*, a three-volume collective analysis of the army's brigade, division, and corps commanders. Volume 3 covers the Overland Campaign.

Two volumes of essays in the University of North Carolina Press Civil War Campaigns series cover the Overland Campaign. *The Wilderness Campaign* and *The Spotsylvania Campaign* bring together short works by prominent Civil War historians on various aspects of both battles, including evaluations of commanders, "microhistories" of specific engagements such as the fight for the Mule Shoe at Spotsylvania, and discussions of the impact of the bloody fighting on both the soldiers and the Union and Confederate home fronts.

A recent, very nontraditional interpretation of part of the Overland Campaign comes from Stephen Cushman, a professor of English at the University of Virginia. *Bloody Promenade: Reflections on a Civil War Battle* (1999) traces the author's fascination with the Battle of the Wilderness back to a book he read and studied as a child, and relates this connection to the battle's interpretations in music, literature, and popular culture.

Primary Sources

Excellent memoirs of the Overland Campaign abound, offering the reader a window into the command decisions of both sides as well as the human side of battles and strategy. As mentioned in the body of this book, Ulysses S. Grant's *Personal Memoirs* is acknowledged to be one of the great works of American letters, with a combination of lucid prose and incisive commentary. Any reader seeking a true understanding of Grant's thought processes must begin here.

Two Union army staff officers, Horace Porter and Andrew Humphreys, wrote excellent memoirs that detail the goings-on at Grant's and Meade's headquarters, respectively. Porter's *Campaigning with Grant* helps the reader to understand further why Grant fought as he did, while Humphreys's *The Virginia Campaign of 1864* is written with the cool detachment and precise detail that made Humphreys a solid chief of staff for the Army of the Potomac. Both have been reprinted in good paperback editions. The letters of Theodore Lyman, Meade's aide-de-camp, have been republished as *Grant and Meade: From the Wilderness to Appomattox.*

The finest Confederate officer memoir, and arguably the finest memoir the war produced on either side, is Edward Porter Alexander's *Fighting for the Confederacy*. Alexander served in the eastern theater from First Bull Run to Appomattox, and for much of the war he was the First Corps chief of artillery. Alexander wrote a superb memoir, largely untainted by postwar controversy and mythmaking. James Longstreet's memoir *From Manassas to Appomattox* covers the Battle of the Wilderness from the First Corps commander's perspective. Also useful and interesting, but definitely more opinionated, is Jubal A. Early's *Memoir of the Last Year of the War*, recently reprinted by the University of South Carolina Press. Early was indeed one of the postwar creators of the myth of the Lost Cause, but those activities do not diminish his status as one of Lee's finest fighting generals.

The final frontier for any comprehensive reading on the Overland Campaign is the 128-volume *War of the Rebellion: Official Records of the Union and Confederate Armies*. Compiled by the U.S.

War Department in the 1880s, the *Official Records*, or *OR* as they have come to be known, gather in one place Union and Confederate commanders' after-action reports from the regimental to the army level for virtually every engagement in the war, as well as telegrams and dispatches written during battles and campaigns. The existence of the *OR* makes it possible for the general reader to consult primary, or firsthand, sources on virtually any Civil War subject. The *OR* is available on CD-ROM from a variety of vendors, and it is also available on the World Wide Web in a free, searchable format at *http://www.ehistory.com/uscw/library/or/index.cfm*. Series I, Volume 36, Parts 1 through 3 cover the Overland Campaign.

Leadership Laboratories

Touring the Battlefields of the Overland Campaign

Reading about Civil War battles is certainly an entertaining pastime, but nothing on the printed page can surpass walking the hallowed ground. Americans are lucky that various groups have paid so much attention to the preservation of Civil War battlefields; in spite of encroaching development and urban sprawl, much of our Civil War heritage remains in an almost pristine state. From this perspective, the beauty of the battlefields of the Overland Campaign lies in their accessibility. From the Rapidan to the James River, these amazing places lie, in most cases, within twenty minutes' drive of Interstate 95 between Washington, D.C., and Richmond. Signs on Interstate 95 point out most places of interest, and a little preparation and map study can yield a fascinating day trip or long weekend. For the business leader seeking a unique and profitable team-building experience, the military "staff ride" concept offers some interesting possibilities.

Two books are essential reading for anyone who is preparing to visit the battlefields. An excellent sourcebook for these pursuits is Charles G. Siegel's *No Backward Step: A Guide to Grant's Campaign in Virginia* (Burd Street Press, 2000). This unique volume combines maps, photographs, historical narrative, and driving directions on modern roads in one convenient place.

For the reader interested in Civil War photography, William A.

The first battlefield tourists: Union soldiers and politicians dedicate a monument at the Manassas (Bull Run) battlefield in June 1865 (Library of Congress)

Frassanito has published a unique series of books that compare wartime photographs of battlefields with contemporary views of the same terrain, from the same perspectives. The product puts the reader on the historical ground in a fascinating way. *Grant and Lee, The Virginia Campaign* (Thomas Publications, 1983) covers the Overland Campaign.

Walking (and Driving) the Ground

The logical place to start your tour of the Overland Campaign is Fredericksburg, Virginia. The "Queen City" of Virginia is a historical treasure in its own right, one of the nation's first industrial towns. It was the scene of fighting throughout the war, not just in 1864, and it suffered extensive damage during Union Army occupations. The headquarters of the Fredericksburg/Spotsylvania National Military Park in downtown Fredericksburg will give you an excellent start on understanding the area's Civil War history.

The Wilderness battlefield as it currently exists is an excellent example of both the good and the bad of American battlefield preservation. Virginia State Route 3, known in 1864 as the Orange Turnpike, leaves Fredericksburg and winds through strip malls and fast food outlets, eventually emerging into the farmlands and forests of the Chancellorsville and Wilderness battlefields. A left turn a few miles past the Chancellorsville Visitor Center takes the tourist to Saunders Field, the site of the first clash of the campaign. This area remains very much as it was on May 5, 1864; an excellent set of preserved entrenchments marks the Confederate line here. A National Park Service loop road circles the battlefield, but modern subdivisions sit in the middle of where much of the fighting took place, making a tour of the Wilderness slightly confusing. The battlefield's other prominent spots, the Widow Tapp field (site of the first "Lee to the rear" incident) and the Orange Plank Road/Brock Road intersection, exist very much as they did in 1864.

The Spotsylvania battlefield, a ten-minute drive down the Brock Road (think of how long it took Grant's army!), exists more in its original state. Along the way, you will spot Todd's Tavern, the site of the May 8 cavalry clash and the stormy meeting between Meade and Sheridan. Much of the original topography of the battlefield is in evidence at Spotsylvania. A monument marks the spot of John Sedgwick's death from a sniper's bullet, and an interpreted hiking trail follows the route of Emory Upton's May 10 assault on the Confederate line. The Confederate entrenchments at the famous Mule Shoe salient have been worn down by time and erosion, but their outlines are still in evidence, and a detailed set of historical markers, complemented by Park Service brochures, will guide you through the brutal fighting that took place there.

Proceeding south on either Interstate 95 or U.S. Route 1, the 1864 Telegraph Road, the North Anna Battlefield Park offers perhaps the best surviving example in Virginia of Confederate field fortifications. The center of Lee's famous "inverted V" entrenchments is well preserved and marked by an outstanding series of interpretive markers, all courtesy of the State of Virginia and the Association for the Preservation of Civil War Sites. Unfortunately, a modern industrial facility mars the landscape, but in one particular part of the line the modern observer can stand in the Confederate trenches and peer down to the North Anna River, much as Lee's men did in 1864.

The Cold Harbor National Battlefield preserves only a few acres of the scene of Grant's greatest defeat, but they are enough to give the visitor a sense of what occurred there. Well-preserved trenches dot the landscape, and an interpreted hiking trail guides visitors through the Union and Confederate lines. Local agencies have purchased and marked other sections of the battlefield as well. A National Cemetery lies next to the park boundary and contains a number of Union graves. A recently published National Park Service pamphlet details a driving tour that follows Grant's route from the North Anna to Cold Harbor, with stops at Totopotomoy Creek and Haw's Shop, scene of a cavalry engagement leading up to the main battle.

In all of these places, touring the battlefields from your car is certainly possible, but any time spent outside your vehicle, walking the ground with books and maps in hand, will be time well spent.

Staff Rides for Business Leaders

Military professionals have long recognized the value of staff rides as a vehicle for leadership training. Historians have traced the staff ride concept to the time of Frederick the Great, who took his generals on structured trips across previous battlefields in an effort to learn lessons that would be applicable to future campaigns. The U.S. Army of the late nineteenth and early twentieth centuries featured staff rides as part of the curriculum of the Command and General Staff College. In one particular case, students rode the length of the Shenandoah Valley on horseback, analyzing the battles of Stonewall Jackson by day and camping out by night. In 1983, Army staff colleges began conducting staff rides once again, and they continue to do so today.

By substituting cars for horses and hotels for campsites, your company or staff can conduct a sort of "staff ride" that will enhance productivity and build team esprit de corps. Several profitable businesses now set up and conduct battlefield tours for business groups, but this sort of event is quite easy to set up yourself. Let's take the material of this book, the Overland Campaign, as an example.

Are you just taking over a new organization? Or are you seeking to reinvigorate veteran subordinates? Get out of the office and do a staff ride. Turning your people into Civil War experts is not the expected outcome; indeed, it is beside the point. The true benefits of an event like this do not hinge on historical knowledge:

- It is a memorable time of companionship, allowing everyone to get to know one another in a less stressful setting. If you have never done one of these events before, trust me when I tell you that your people will be talking about it for a long time afterward.

- It provides a chance to get away from the deadlines and pressures of everyday life. The physical exercise and after-hours socializing that occur on these trips are every bit as important as what occurs on the battlefields.

- It gives an opportunity to examine leadership, both good and bad, in the most difficult and stressful area of human endeavor. As we have seen with Lee and Grant in 1864, military leaders face the same challenges and dilemmas as business leaders, albeit in different form. The qualities of a good general and a good manager are not so different.

- It offers a further opportunity to relate these examples to whatever it is that your organization does. Believe it or not, you will see the connections in spades once you give this method a chance.

So, plan now for a long weekend and do a staff ride. If your schedule permits, go during the week, when you can command the attention and attendance of your subordinates without taking away from their time with their families. This is an event that will enhance productivity and efficiency; why not devote "work time" to it? The suggested itinerary that follows covers the Overland Campaign, but you could easily substitute a destination closer to your part of the country. Very few parts of America are far away from some sort of historic site that involves leadership.

A Sample Overland Campaign Staff Ride

Phase One: Preparation

This phase gives participants a base of knowledge about the campaign and its leaders. With the knowledge gained through reading, study, and discussion, your subordinates will be prepared to discuss leadership on the battlefields. The most informative and entertaining, but also most time-consuming, method of preparation is to allow your staff riders to choose a Union or Confederate leader and assume the role of that person on the battlefield. During the preparation phase, you might have each of these role players give the group a short presentation on the selected leader's background, education, and professional experiences. The endnotes for this book, plus Appendix B, "Suggestions for Further Reading," will give you all the tools you need. Failing this, the staff ride leader should assign some background reading on the campaign so that everyone has some basic knowledge of it.

Phase Two: Execution

Now for the fun part! Pack a bag and get out to the battlefields. Military outfits conduct staff rides by breaking battlefields down into "stands," or stops around the field where the group discusses different topics. Whenever possible, these stands should be roughly in chronological order to avoid confusion. At each stand, the leader or leaders who directed the action in that particular area discuss with the group any decisions or actions that they took during the battle. Then, while everyone overlooks the scene of the action, the group can critique leadership in a "laboratory" environment.

Some possible stands for the Wilderness might be:

1. A trip to the top of Clark's Mountain to see what Lee saw before the campaign. The staff of the park visitor center can give you specific directions. Be careful to avoid private property once you get there. On the mountain, you might have the Lee and Grant characters discuss their decisions and plans for beginning the campaign.

2. The Lacy house, "Ellwood," near Saunders Field. It was here that Meade and Warren made their momentous decision to attack Ewell at Saunders Field. Warren, Meade, and Grant would have parts here.

3. Saunders Field. Here, the group will get a nice feel for the battlefield and how it affected both Lee and Grant's thinking on May 4–5. Lee, Ewell, Grant, and Warren can lead this discussion.

4. The Widow Tapp Field. This is a good spot for a transition to General Lee's battle. You can discuss his handling of Ewell and Hill, the critical mistakes Lee and Hill made on the night of May 5–6, the Union attack early on May 6, and the "Lee to the rear" incident. Virtually all generals can speak here.

5. The Brock Road/Plank Road intersection. This stop will wrap up your Wilderness discussion as you view the key piece of terrain on the entire battlefield. You can wrap up with a recreation of Grant's torchlight movement through his army on the night of May 7–8.

The length of each stop and the amount of detail considered will be up to the staff ride leader, based on the group's level of knowledge and the amount of time you have available. A less complicated method of covering these same stands is to have the staff ride leader present the same material in more of a "tour guide" format, asking pointed questions to spur discussion by the group. This method involves much less preparation for everyone except the staff ride leader, who must bear the burden of driving the discussion at every stop. If you have a participant who is particularly interested or knowledgeable about the campaign, and if he or she has the time to prepare, this might be the way to go for your first staff ride. Either method, with the proper preparation, will accomplish the same objective.

Phase Three: Integration
The integration phase allows your group to reflect on and discuss what was learned during the two previous phases. It is best to wait a little while after the field phase, but not so long that everyone forgets what they saw and felt. You might make a final breakfast or dinner gathering the forum for the integration phase, allowing each participant to share what he or she learned from studying and seeing the battlefields firsthand. This is a vital phase, because it helps participants to make the intellectual leap from the Civil War back to your particular business arena, while taking with them lessons from the staff ride that are useful to them.

As you think about ways to increase the productivity and imagination of your subordinates, remember the staff ride concept. It could push your team to the next level of efficiency, from both a team-building and an educational standpoint. Give it a try, and make history come alive for your people.

Notes

Introduction

1. Private Joseph Graham, quoted in Carol Reardon, "A Hard Road to Travel: The Impact of Continuous Operations on the Army of the Potomac and the Army of Northern Virginia in May 1864," Gary W. Gallagher, ed., *The Spotsylvania Campaign* (Chapel Hill: University of North Carolina Press, 1998), p. 170.

2. Brooks D. Simpson, *Ulysses S. Grant: Triumph Over Adversity 1822–1865* (New York: Houghton Mifflin, 2000), 271.

3. United States Army Field Manual 22-100, *Army Leadership*, Chapter 6, "Organizational Leadership," available at http://www.adtdl.army.mil/cgi-bin/atdl.dll/fm/22-100/toc.htm, accessed January 19, 2004.

4. Ibid., 3-15–3-19.

Chapter 1

1. Quoted in Edward Porter Alexander, *Fighting for the Confederacy: The Personal Recollections of General Edward Porter Alexander* (Chapel Hill: University of North Carolina Press, 1989), 91. Alexander, an artillery officer who rose to command of all guns in Lee's First Corps, was the author of arguably the finest war memoir from either side. Alexander saw the entire war in the east, and wrote about it with a trenchant wit and a commendable lack of bias.

2. Novelist Michael Shaara referred to him this way (with a bit,

but only just a bit, of exaggeration) in his novel *The Killer Angels*. (New York: Ballantine, 1993).

3. Emory M. Thomas, *Robert E. Lee: A Biography* (New York: W. W. Norton, 1995), 20.

4. United States Army Field Manual 22-100, *Army Leadership*, Chapter 1, "The Army Leadership Framework."

5. Thomas, *Lee*, 29.

6. Ibid., 55.

7. Ibid., 56–66.

8. Ibid., 47–55. The valedictorian of the class of 1829, Charles Mason, has become one of history's footnotes. His high standing was the pinnacle of his life; after serving at the academy for one year as an instructor, he resigned his commission and settled in Burlington, Iowa.

9. Lee to Joseph G. Totten, June 17, 1845, quoted in Thomas, *Lee,* 111.

10. Major Charles R. Bowery Jr. and Major Brian Hankinson, USMA Occasional Paper #5, *The Daily Correspondence of Robert E. Lee, Superintendent, USMA, 1852–1855* (West Point, N.Y.: Archives and Special Collections Branch, U.S. Military Academy Library, 2003).

11. A business trip that involves a flight into Richmond International Airport will place the traveler in the midst of the Seven Pines Battlefield. The discerning observer can still spot old artillery emplacements on the airport property, and a drive eastward on Williamsburg Road to the Seven Pines National Cemetery will place one on the ground of McClellan's defensive lines. A few miles east and south lie the battlefields of the Seven Days Battles.

12. Thomas, *Lee*, p. 225; Lee to Major Walter H. Stevens, June 4, 1862, in Clifford Dowdey and Louis H. Manarin, eds., *The Wartime Papers of Robert E. Lee* (Boston: Little, Brown, and Co., 1961); reprint (New York: Da Capo Press, 1987), 183.

13. Lee to Davis, June 5, 1862, in Dowdey and Manarin, eds., *Wartime Papers*, 184.

14. Professor Joseph W. Harsh of George Mason University offers the best analysis of this strategy in his award-winning *Confeder-*

ate Tide Rising: Robert E. Lee and the Making of Confederate Strategy, 1861–62 (Kent, Ohio: Kent State University Press, 1998).

15. Lee to Davis, June 10, 1862, in Dowdey and Manarin, eds., *Wartime Papers*, 188.

16. Lee to Davis, August 14, 1862, in Dowdey and Manarin, eds., *Wartime Papers*, 254; Steven W. Woodworth, *Davis and Lee at War* (Lawrence: University Press of Kansas, 1995). Woodworth's book is the best analysis of the political and strategic relationship between the two men.

17. Stephen W. Sears, *George B. McClellan: The Young Napoleon* (New York: Da Capo Press, 1999).

18. Hillel Italie, "Grann Joins Doubleday as Senior Editor," *Miami Herald*, December 3, 2003.

19. John J. Hennessy, *Return to Bull Run: The Campaign and Battle of Second Manassas* (Norman: University of Oklahoma Press, 1999), 93.

20. Russell F. Weigley, *A Great Civil War: A Military and Political History, 1861–1865* (Bloomington: University of Indiana Press, 2000), 225–229; James I. Robertson, Jr., *Stonewall Jackson: The Man, the Soldier, the Legend* (New York: Macmillan, 1997), 714.

Chapter 2

1. Stephen D. Engle, *Struggle for the Heartland: The Campaigns from Fort Henry to Corinth* (Lincoln: University of Nebraska Press, 2001), 155.

2. Gordon C. Rhea, *The Battle of the Wilderness* (Baton Rouge: Louisiana State University Press, 1994).

3. Brooks D. Simpson, *Ulysses S. Grant: Triumph Over Adversity, 1822–1865* (New York: Houghton Mifflin, 2000), 1–15.

4. Ulysses S. Grant, *Personal Memoirs* (reprint, New York: The Modern Library, 1999), 13. (Original year of publication, 1885.) Along with that of Porter Alexander, Grant's is one of the war's very best memoirs. Even though Grant wrote his memoir late in life, in an effort to earn money to recoup his debts while in failing health, *Personal Memoirs* is filled with accurate observations and no-holds-

barred commentary and has a graceful literary style. In this author's humble opinion, it is one of the classics of American literature.

5. Simpson, *Grant*, 11.

6. Grant, *Personal Memoirs*, 16.

7. Simpson, *Grant*, 16–17; Grant, *Personal Memoirs,* 18.

8. Grant, *Personal Memoirs,* 47.

9. Simpson, *Grant*, 41.

10. Ibid., 33.

11. Robert MacFeely, quoted in Ibid., 58.

12. Ibid., 63–78.

13. James M. McPherson, *Battle Cry of Freedom: The Civil War Era* (New York: Oxford University Press, 1988), 296.

14. Grant, quoted in Simpson, *Grant*, 117; Engle, *Struggle for the Heartland*, 51–84.

15. Grant, *Personal Memoirs*, 193.

16. Ibid., 225–231.

17. Ibid., 233.

18. Russell F. Weigley, *A Great Civil War: A Military and Political History, 1861–1865* (Bloomington: University of Indiana Press, 2000), 264–270.

19. Richard M. McMurry, *Atlanta 1864: Last Chance for the Confederacy* (Lincoln: University of Nebraska Press, 2000), 1–3; Wiley Sword, *Mountains Touched with Fire: Chattanooga Besieged, 1863* (New York: St. Martin's Press, 1995), 355–359.

Chapter 3

1. Simpson, *Ulysses S. Grant*, p. 273.

2. Douglas Southall Freeman, *Lee's Lieutenants: A Study in Command*, Vol. III, *Gettysburg to Appomattox* (New York: Charles Scribner's Sons, 1944), 315–372. Although this classic work of Civil War history is now somewhat dated, it remains the starting point for any reader interested in Lee and his generals. More than any other single post-Civil War writer, Freeman was responsible for the "marble man" perception of Lee's life and career. The reader equipped with a healthy dose of skepticism will gain a great deal from Freeman's magnum opus.

3. Edward Porter Alexander, *Fighting for the Confederacy: The Personal Recollections of General Edward Porter Alexander* (Chapel Hill: University of North Carolina Press, 1989), 346.

4. Lee to Davis, in *War of the Rebellion: Official Records of the Union and Confederate Armies (OR)* 19:2, 643, available at http://www.ehistory.com/uscw/library/or/index.cfm.

5. Horace Porter, *Campaigning with Grant* (New York, 1897; reprint, Lincoln: University of Nebraska Press, 2000), 47.

6. Gordon C. Rhea, *The Battle of the Wilderness* (Baton Rouge: Louisiana State University Press, 1994), 27.

7. J. Tracy Power, *Lee's Miserables: Life in the Army of Northern Virginia from the Wilderness to Appomattox* (Chapel Hill: University of North Carolina Press, 1998), 10.

8. Mark Grimsley, *And Keep Moving On: The Virginia Campaign, May–June 1864* (Lincoln: University of Nebraska Press, 2002). The University of Nebraska Press's series of short books on major Civil War campaigns is an excellent starting point for more in-depth reading on the war. Richard McMurry's *Atlanta 1864* (see Chapter 2) is also a part of this series.

9. Ibid., 3.

10. Rhea, *Battle of the Wilderness*, 33.

11. Ethan S. Rafuse, *George Gordon Meade and the War in the East* (Abilene, TX: Grady McWhiney Foundation Press, 2003), 114–115. Rafuse's book is the first biography of Meade to appear in over forty years and is an excellent short account of Meade's tenure in command of the Army of the Potomac.

12. Brooks D. Simpson, *Ulysses S. Grant: Triumph Over Adversity 1822–1865* (New York: Houghton Mifflin, 2000), 266–281.

13. Rafuse, *Meade*, 115.

14. Ibid., 120.

15. Rhea, *Battle of the Wilderness*, 37–41.

16. Ibid., 58.

Chapter 4

1. Gordon C. Rhea, *The Battle of the Wilderness* (Baton Rouge: Louisiana State University Press, 1994), 77–78.

2. Grant dispatch, quoted in Horace Porter, *Campaigning with Grant* (New York, 1897; reprint, Lincoln: University of Nebraska Press, 2000), 48.

3. Brooks D. Simpson, *Ulysses S. Grant: Triumph Over Adversity 1822–1865* (New York: Houghton Mifflin, 2000), 291–292.

4. Edward Porter Alexander, *Fighting for the Confederacy: The Personal Recollections of General Edward Porter Alexander* (Chapel Hill: University of North Carolina Press, 1989), 349.

5. R. Steven Jones, *The Right Hand of Command: Use & Disuse of Personal Staffs in the Civil War* (Mechanicsburg, Pa.: Stackpole Books, 2000), 58.

6. United States Army Field Manual 22-100, *Army Leadership*, 1-5–1-6, available at http://www.adtdl.army.mil/cgi-bin/atdl.dll/fm/22-100/toc.htm, accessed January 19, 2004.

7. Mark Grimsley, *And Keep Moving On: The Virginia Campaign, May–June 1864* (Lincoln: University of Nebraska Press, 2002), 39.

8. Rhea, *The Battle of the Wilderness*, 141.

9. Ibid., 150–152.

10. Ibid., 101.

11. Porter, *Campaigning with Grant*, 59, 63.

12. David M. Jordan, *Winfield Scott Hancock: A Soldier's Life* (Bloomington: Indiana University Press, 1988), 115–119.

13. Porter, *Campaigning with Grant*, 53.

14. William T. Pogue, *Gunner with Stonewall: Reminiscences of William Thomas Pogue* (reprint, Lincoln, NE: University of Nebraska Press, 1998), 88–89 (Originally published in Wilmington, NC, 1903); Robert K. Krick, " 'Lee to the Rear,' the Texans Cried," in Gary W. Gallagher, ed., *The Wilderness Campaign* (Chapel Hill: University of North Carolina Press, 1997), 161.

15. Peter S. Carmichael, "Escaping the Shadow of Gettysburg: Richard S. Ewell and Ambrose Powell Hill at the Wilderness," in Gallagher, ed., *The Wilderness Campaign*, 152.

16. Pogue, *Gunner with Stonewall*, 89; Jordan, *Winfield Scott Hancock*, 119.

17. Lee to James A. Seddon, May 6, 1864, in Clifford Dowdey

and Louis H. Manarin, eds., *The Wartime Papers of Robert E. Lee*, 722; Krick, "'Lee to the Rear,'" 168.

18. Krick, "'Lee to the Rear,'" 181.

19. Pogue, *Gunner with Stonewall*, 90; Krick, "'Lee to the Rear,'" 185.

20. Porter, *Campaigning with Grant*, 69–70.

21. Ibid., 72–73.

22. Ibid., 78–79.

23. Charles H. Weygant, *History of the One Hundred and Twenty- Fourth Regiment, N.Y.S.V.* (Newburgh, N.Y., 1887; reprint, Interlaken, N.Y.: Heart of the Lakes Publishing, 1995), 304.

Chapter 5

1. *War of the Rebellion: Official Records of the Union and Confederate Armies (OR)*, Vol. 36, Pt. 1, 4, available at http://www .chistory.com/uscw/library/or/index.cfm.

2. United States Army Field Manual 22-100, *Army Leadership*, 3-15, available at http://www.adtdl.army.mil/cgi-bin/atdl.dll/fm/22-100/toc.htm.

3. FM 22-100, *Army Leadership*, 3-16.

4. Ulysses S. Grant, *Personal Memoirs* (reprint, New York: The Modern Library, 1999), 423.

5. Horace Porter, *Campaigning with Grant* (New York, 1897; reprint, Lincoln: University of Nebraska Press, 2000), 84. Gordon C. Rhea offers an excellent analysis of this disagreement in *The Battles for Spotsylvania Courthouse and the Road to Yellow Tavern, May 7–12, 1864* (Baton Rouge: Louisiana State University Press, 1997), 65–68.

6. Ethan S. Rafuse, *George Gordon Meade and the War in the East* (Grady McWhiney Foundation Press, 2003), 125; Porter, *Campaigning with Grant*, 84.

7. Rhea, *Spotsylvania Courthouse*, 68–69.

8. Lee to Stuart, May 7, 1864, in Clifford Dowdey and Louis H. Manarin, eds., *The Wartime Papers of Robert E. Lee* (Boston: Little, Brown, and Co., 1961), 723.

9. Douglas Southall Freeman, *Lee's Lieutenants: A Study in Command*, v. 3, (New York: Charles Scribner's Sons, 1944), 374.

10. Gary W. Gallagher, "I Have to Make the Best of What I Have," in Gary W. Gallagher, ed., *The Spotsylvania Campaign* (Chapel Hill, NC: University of North Carolina Press, 1998), 12, 20; Lee to Richard S. Ewell, May 8, 1864, in Dowdey and Manarin, eds., *Wartime Papers,* 725.

11. Rhea, *Spotsylvania Courthouse*, 187.

12. Porter, *Campaigning with Grant*, 96–97; *OR*, Vol. 36, pt. 2, 611.

13. Rhea, *Spotsylvania Courthouse*, 187.

14. Brooks D. Simpson, *Ulysses S. Grant: Triumph Over Adversity 1822–1865* (New York: Houghton Mifflin, 2000), 307–308.

15. Rhea, *Spotsylvania Courthouse*, 187–188.

16. Terry L. Jones, ed., *The Civil War Memoirs of Captain William J. Seymour* (Baton Rouge: Louisiana State University Press, 1991), 125; Rhea, *Spotsylvania Courthouse*, 255, 279.

17. Jones, ed., *Memoirs of Captain Seymour*, 125; Donald C. Pfanz, *Richard S. Ewell: A Soldier's Life* (Chapel Hill: University of North Carolina Press, 1998), 388–389; William D. Matter, *If It Takes All Summer: The Battle of Spotsylvania* (Chapel Hill: University of North Carolina Press, 1988). Appendix C details the story of the oak tree. The stump is on display in the Smithsonian's National Museum of American History. The original spot of the tree is clearly marked to this day on the Spotsylvania battlefield.

18. William Marvel, *Burnside* (Chapel Hill: University of North Carolina Press, 1991), is the best available biography.

Chapter 6

1. United States Army Field Manual 22-100, *Army Leadership*, 7-1.

2. FM-22-100, *Army Leadership*, p. 7–3.

3. *War of the Rebellion: Official Records of the Union and Confederate Armies (OR),* Vol. 33, Pt. 1, 394–395, available at http://www.ehistory.com/uscw/library/or/index.cfm.

4. The best example of this strategic imperative in action is found in Lincoln's instructions to George Meade when he gave him command of the Army of the Potomac just before Gettysburg. Lincoln mandated that Meade eject Lee from Northern soil, but at the same time that Meade "keep in view the important fact that the Army of the Potomac is the covering army of Washington." *OR,* Vol. 27, Pt. 1, 61.

5. *OR,* Vol. 33, Pt. 1, 394–395.

6. Brooks D. Simpson, *Ulysses S. Grant: Triumph Over Adversity 1822–1865* (New York: Houghton Mifflin, 2000), 273.

7. FM 22-100, *Army Leadership,* 7-3 to 7-6.

8. Ulysses S. Grant, *Personal Memoirs* (reprint, New York: The Modern Library, 1999), 618–619.

9. Ibid., 376.

10. Because the Shenandoah River actually flows northward through the Shenandoah Valley, northward travel there is generally referred to as "down the Valley" because the traveler is moving downriver.

11. Mark Grimsley, *And Keep Moving On: The Virginia Campaign, May–June 1864* (Lincoln: University of Nebraska Press, 2002), 96, 105–109. The site of the Battle of New Market is superbly preserved by the State of Virginia and the Virginia Military Institute, and its position beside Interstate 81 makes it an excellent stopping-off point during a trip through the area.

12. Horace Porter, *Campaigning with Grant* (New York, 1897; reprint, Lincoln: University of Nebraska Press, 2000), 120.

13. FM 22-100, *Army Leadership,* 7-11.

14. Simpson, *Ulysses S. Grant,* 278–281.

15. FM-22-100, *Army Leadership,* 7–10.

16. FM 22-100, *Army Leadership,* 7-11.

17. Ibid., 7-17.

Chapter 7

1. Lee to Davis, May 18, 1864, quoted in Gordon C. Rhea, *To the North Anna River: May 13–25, 1864* (Baton Rouge, LA: Louisiana State University Press, 2000), 162.

2. United States Army Field Manual 22-100, *Army Leadership*, 6-3, available at http://www.adtdl.army.mil/cgi-bin/atdl.dll/fm/22-100/toc.htm.

3. Carol Reardon, "A Hard Road to Travel," in Gary W. Gallagher, ed., *The Spotsylvania Campaign* (Chapel Hill, NC: University of North Carolina Press, 1998), 194.

4. Lee, quoted in Noah Andre Trudeau, *The Last Citadel: Petersburg, Virginia June 1864–April 1865* (Baton Rouge: Louisiana State University Press, 1991), 24.

5. Horace Porter, *Campaigning with Grant* (New York, 1897; reprint, Lincoln: University of Nebraska Press, 2000), 131; David M. Jordan, *Winfield Scott Hancock: A Soldier's Life* (Bloomington: Indiana University Press, 1988), 133.

6. Ibid., 134.

7. Rhea, *To the North Anna*, 212–254.

8. Walter Taylor to Bettie Saunders, May 23, 1864, in R. Lockwood Tower, ed., *Lee's Adjutant: The Wartime Letters of Colonel Walter Herron Taylor, 1862–1865* (Columbia, SC: University of South Carolina Press, 1995), 160.

9. Ibid.; Lee to Jefferson Davis, May 23, 1864, in Clifford Dowdey and Louis H. Manarin, eds., *The Wartime Papers of Robert E. Lee* (Boston: Little, Brown, and Co., 1961; reprint Da Capo Press), 747.

10. Ulysses S. Grant, *Personal Memoirs* (reprint, New York: The Modern Library, 1999), 443; Porter, *Campaigning with Grant*, 141.

11. *War of the Rebellion: Official Records of the Union and Confederate Armies (OR)*, Vol. 36, Pt. 3, 814–815, available at http://www.ehistory.com/uscw/library/or/index.cfm.

12. Rhea, *To the North Anna River*, 289–320, 326.

13. Edward Porter Alexander, *Fighting for the Confederacy: The Personal Recollections of General Edward Porter Alexander* (Chapel Hill: University of North Carolina Press, 1989), 389.

14. Rhea, *To the North Anna River*, 320–323.

15. Taylor to Saunders, May 30, 1864, in Tower, ed., *Lee's Adjutant*, 164; Rhea, *To the North Anna River*, 344.

16. Ibid., 346.

Chapter 8

1. Walter Taylor to Bettie Saunders, June 9, 1864, in R. Lockwood Tower, ed., *Lee's Adjutant: The Wartime Letters of Colonel Walter Herron Taylor, 1862–1865* (Columbia, SC: University of South Carolina Press, 1995), 167.

2. Carl von Clausewitz, *On War*, ed. and trans. by Michael Howard and Peter Paret (Princeton: Princeton University Press, 1984), Book I, Chap. 7, 119–121.

3. Mark Grimsley, *And Keep Moving On: The Virginia Campaign, May–June 1864* (Lincoln: University of Nebraska Press, 2002), 233.

4. Gordon C. Rhea, *Cold Harbor: Grant and Lee, May 26–June 3, 1864* (Baton Rouge: Louisiana State University Press, 2002), 11.

5. Ethan S. Rafuse, *George Gordon Meade and the War in the East* (Grady McWhiney Foundation Press, 2003), 131.

6. Rhea, *Cold Harbor*, 10; Horace Porter, *Campaigning with Grant* (New York, 1897; reprint, Lincoln: University of Nebraska Press, 2000), 215.

7. Rhea, *Cold Harbor*, 25.

8. http://onlineethics.org/essays/shuttle/telecon.html, accessed 2/23/04.

9. Grimsley, *And Keep Moving On,* 189–192.

10. Richard M. McMurry, *Atlanta 1864: Last Chance for the Confederacy* (Lincoln: University of Nebraska Press, 2000), 54–65.

11. Chapter 6 of Grimsley, *And Keep Moving On,* 161–195, and Carol Reardon's essay "A Hard Road to Travel," in Gary W. Gallagher, ed., *The Spotsylvania Campaign* (Chapel Hill, NC: University of North Carolina Press, 1998), are excellent discussions of the physical and psychological stresses of the Overland Campaign.

12. *War of the Rebellion: Official Records of the Union and Confederate Armies (OR)*, Vol. 36, Pt. 3, 206–207, available at http://www.ehistory.com/uscw/library/or/index.cfm.

13. Grimsley, *And Keep Moving On,* 196–202.

14. Donald C. Pfanz, *Richard S. Ewell: A Soldier's Life* (Chapel Hill: University of North Carolina Press, 1998), 395–398.

15. Gary W. Gallagher, "I Have to Make the Best of What I Have," in Gallagher, ed., *The Spotsylvania Campaign*, 17–18.

16. Allan quoted in Gallagher, ed., *The Spotsylvania Campaign*, 18.

17. Pfanz, *Richard S. Ewell*, 396–399.

18. Grimsley, *And Keep Moving On*, 208–209.

19. Rhea, *Cold Harbor*, 318–364.

20. Brooks D. Simpson, *Ulysses S. Grant: Triumph Over Adversity 1822–1865* (New York: Houghton Mifflin, 2000), 328–329; Grimsley, *And Keep Moving On*, 220–221.

21. Union soldier quoted in Grimsley, *And Keep Moving On*, 214; Porter, *Campaigning with Grant*, 179; Simpson, *Grant*, 331.

22. Simpson, *Grant*, 332.

23. Grimsley, *And Keep Moving On*, 224.

24. Porter, *Campaigning with Grant*, 180–181.

Chapter 9

1. Horace Porter, *Campaigning with Grant* (New York, 1897; reprint, Lincoln: University of Nebraska Press, 2000), 47, 199.

2. Robert E. Lee to Custis Lee, March 28, 1852, quoted in Emory M. Thomas, *Robert E. Lee: A Biography* (New York: W. W. Norton, 1995), 414.

3. Noah Andre Trudeau, *The Last Citadel: Petersburg, Virginia, June 1864–April 1865* (Baton Rouge: Louisiana State University Press, 1991), 23–25; Porter, *Campaigning with Grant*, 200.

4. United States Army Field Manual 22-100, *Army Leadership*, 3-16, 3-17, available at http://www.adtdl.army.mil/cgi-bin/atdl.dll/fm/22-100/toc.htm.

5. Bernard M. Bass, *Transformational Leadership: Industrial, Military and Educational Impact* (Mahwah, NJ: Lawrence Erlbaum Associates, 1998), 2–4.

6. Ibid., 5–6.

7. Mark Grimsley, *And Keep Moving On: The Virginia Campaign, May–June 1864* (Lincoln: University of Nebraska Press, 2002), 229.

8. Ibid., p. 239.

9. Robert E. Lee to Jefferson Davis, May 30, 1864, in Clifford Dowdey and Louis H. Manarin, eds., *The Wartime Papers of Robert E. Lee* (Boston: Little, Brown, and Co., 1961; reprint Da Capo Press, 1987), 757.

Afterword

1. Edward Porter Alexander, *Fighting for the Confederacy: The Personal Recollections of General Edward Porter Alexander* (Chapel Hill: University of North Carolina Press, 1989), 540.

2. Emory M. Thomas, *Robert E. Lee: A Biography* (New York: W. W. Norton, 1995), 362.

3. Brooks D. Simpson, *Ulysses S. Grant: Triumph Over Adversity 1822–1865* (New York: Houghton Mifflin, 2000), 432–433.

4. Horace Porter, *Campaigning with Grant* (New York, 1897; reprint, Lincoln: University of Nebraska Press, 2000), 473.

5. Ibid., 479–480.

6. Ibid., 486.

7. Jean Edward Smith, *Grant* (New York: Simon and Schuster, 2001), 622–627.

8. Thomas, *Robert E. Lee*, 411–415.

Index

About the Author

Major Charles Ryland Bowery, Jr., is a United States Army officer. He is a native of New Kent County, Virginia, a suburb of Richmond on the outskirts of the Army of Northern Virginia's first battlefields. Charles was a 1992 Distinguished Military Graduate of the College of William and Mary with a B.A. in history. He has served in various command and staff positions as an army aviation officer, both in the United States and abroad. He is trained and qualified in the army's AH-64 Apache Attack Helicopter.

Bowery's lifelong interest in the Civil War—he has three Confederate army ancestors—led him to pursue a position as a military history instructor at West Point. After earning an M.A. in history from North Carolina State University in 2001, he served as a history instructor at West Point for two years. While at West Point, he published book reviews and encyclopedia articles on the Civil War and military history, and co-edited the official Academy correspondence of Superintendent Robert E. Lee. In January 2004, *Gettysburg Magazine* published his article entitled "Encounter at the Triangular Field: The 124th New York and the First Texas at Gettysburg, July 2, 1863."

Charles currently resides in Bad Windsheim, Germany, where he serves with the First Infantry Division. His wife, Mary Ann, is an army lawyer with the Judge Advocate General's Corps. Charles and Mary Ann spend their free time touring Europe with their Great Dane, Frederick.